Studies in Choice and Welfare

More information about this series at http://www.springer.com/series/6869

Steve Bickerstaff

Election Systems and Gerrymandering Worldwide

Springer

Steve Bickerstaff
University of Texas Law School
The University of Texas at Austin
Austin, TX, USA

Some portions of this book previously appeared in Chap. 9, *Redistricting from a Practitioner's Viewpoint,* by Steve Bickerstaff in the American Bar Association book **International Election Remedies (2017).**

ISSN 1614-0311 ISSN 2197-8530 (electronic)
Studies in Choice and Welfare
ISBN 978-3-030-30836-0 ISBN 978-3-030-30837-7 (eBook)
https://doi.org/10.1007/978-3-030-30837-7

This Springer imprint is published by the registered company Springer Nature Switzerland AG.
The registered company address is: Gewerbestrasse 11, 6330 Cham, Switzerland

This book is dedicated to my wife, Charlotte Carter. Her patience was phenomenal. I am retired so I had to research and write this book primarily from home. Charlotte withstood my grouchy impertinence and made my work environment comfortable and forgiving. Thank you—it could not have been easy.

Acknowledgement

I also wish to acknowledge the invaluable assistance of Sherry McCall and Becky Vragel.

Contents

About the Author

Steve Bickerstaff is 73 and now retired. He is an attorney who initially was with the State of Texas as Parliamentarian of the State Senate, Director of the State Office of Constitutional Research, and Assistant Attorney General. In 1981 he left the state's employ and founded the private law firm of Bickerstaff, Heath and Smiley. The firm grew to 50 attorneys. Steve left the law firm over a decade ago, but it continues to bear his name (Bickerstaff, Heath, Delgado, Acosta).

Among Steve's most prominent achievements as a private attorney were: a judgment for the largest monetary recovery ever awarded against the State of Texas ($204 million in an environmental suit); a multi-year, multi-forum fight to make telecommunications competitive in Texas and other states; a judgment holding the state financially responsible for convicted felons housed in county jails; 42 years representing public entities and officials in redistricting; and the fostering of an independent citizen commission to draw electoral districts in Austin, Texas.

During much of this time, Steve was also an adjunct professor at the University of Texas Law School teaching constitutional law and voting rights. He also taught as a Fulbright scholar in Germany, was a Rockefeller Scholar in Residence at the Villa Serbelloni in Bellagio, Italy, was part of a Carter Commission study of elections in China, and lectured at 16 different universities in Europe, the U.K. and Scandinavia.

Steve was on the governing board of several non-profits, including The Trustees for Alaska, the Board of Visitors for McDonald Astronomical Observatory, and West Texas Public Radio. He remains on the National Council of the National Parks Conservation Association.

Steve is the author or co-author of nine books and 26 law review articles. Virtually all of this writing is on legal issues, such as voting rights and telecommunications regulation.

Chapter 1
Introduction

The origin of this book lies in my belief that there is a dearth of readable works relating, comparing, and analyzing the use and gerrymandering of electoral districts in different election systems worldwide. Moreover, I resent the attitudes I found among many political scientists that gerrymandering to advantage or disadvantage certain candidates or political parties is a problem unique to the United States, and that systems with proportional representation largely escape this problem. As this book demonstrates the drawing of election districts or allocation of seats to states, provinces, administrative units, or multi-member districts, or the failure to do so, for the benefit of specific political officials or interests in the national legislature is common throughout the world and is a form of gerrymandering.

I expected that some of the relatively new democracies would be having a difficult time wrestling with the inherently nuanced political tasks of reallocating seats in the national legislature and fairly redrawing electoral districts. Surprisingly, I also found that some of the fairest allocation schemes were among the newest democracies, while many of the long-established democracies have come to accept and even to institutionalize bias that favors certain political groups, politicians, or interests.

Another reason for writing this book is to help fill the shameful gap in knowledge that exists for most persons, especially Americans, concerning election systems worldwide. Political scientists tend to pidgin-hole election systems into only a few categories without understanding, or at least acknowledging that virtually every country's election system is unique.

Many Americans believe that the U.S. provided a model democratic election system that other nations largely envied and some emulated, but, if so, this model, along with those of the United Kingdom, France, and Germany, was merely a starting point from which many variations emerged. Sometimes a country found that the U.S. model poorly fit its needs and must be modified. In other instances, countries looked at U.S. democracy and concluded that it could be improved. For example, the Electoral College is a singularly unpopular element of the U.S. system; other countries have chosen various proportional representation systems rather than

S. Bickerstaff, *Election Systems and Gerrymandering Worldwide*, Studies in Choice and Welfare, https://doi.org/10.1007/978-3-030-30837-7_1

the plurality election system found in the U.S.; and the concept of equal suffrage (i.e. one person, one vote) that is pervasive in the U.S. has encountered mixed acceptance worldwide. It is wrong for Americans to think at this point that their country's election system is necessarily the preferred democratic structure. Instead, Americans should appreciate the diversity among representative democracies worldwide and the many lessons that we can learn by observing different election systems. This diversity is beautiful.

The most important reason for writing this book, however, is to help understand one of the great failings of representative democracy. The concept of a government controlled by the people it governs through their elected representatives is attractive. Most of the people in the world have come to assume that representative democracy is the preferred form of government. With only a few exceptions, such as North Korea, Saudi Arabia, and China, representative democracy is the claimed objective of nations worldwide. Representative democracy, however, is failing to meet its promises. Gerrymandering of electoral districts is a significant reason for this failure. Any pretense of representative democracy becomes a sham if politicians are allowed to gerrymander and manipulate electoral districts in their self-interest contrary to the public's will.

In recent months there has been an outcry in the United States against gerrymandering. These opponents of the practice charge:

Voters should choose their politicians rather than allowing politicians to choose their voters.

This aphorism is a general truth, but an over simplification of the complex processes and competing interests that affect the allocation of seats in a national legislature and the redrawing of election districts.

Both the timely and fair reallocation of national legislative seats and redrawing of electoral districts to reflect population changes and shifts are critical for maintaining equal voting power for a nation's inhabitants. A failure to perform either process in a fair, transparent, and lawful manner can deny people an equal opportunity to affect the policies of their government and raises questions as to whether the nation is truly a representative democracy. Nevertheless, many of the oldest and most established "democracies" in the world have abused these processes. Too often political scientists in Western countries fail to recognize the achievements of the non-English speaking world, overlook flaws in the longer established Western democracies, and espouse a Westminster or European Model for democracies without clearly understanding or acknowledging the weaknesses of those models or that other models exist.

It is also important for voters to recognize that the presence of gerrymanders is partly their own fault. We have forgotten the meaning of representative democracy and allowed ourselves to accept gerrymanders as inevitable. We even applaud as though at a sporting match when a gerrymander is for "our side." Gerrymanders are indeed inevitable so long as voters refuse to acknowledge that they merely substitute self-interest for democracy and refuse to take the steps necessary to minimize or to prevent them. I hope that a candid look at current systems and recommendations in the conclusion will help in understanding what is working and not working worldwide to preserve and advance representative democracy.

This book achieves its purposes through thirteen chapters, a Conclusion, Appendices, and several Case Studies. Each chapter includes examples to illustrate a point in my text or which I think readers will find interesting. In addition I have given examples of how some nations have structured their election systems. I selected these examples to show the diversity that exists in the world and how the simple categorization of countries or scan of their laws tells very little about what is happening. Many of the footnotes are designed to furnish the reader with additional cxamples.

Chapter 2 discusses the history, purposes, and characteristics of a gerrymander. Chapter 3 describes how electoral districts are used in virtually every nation and have certain advantages and disadvantages. Chapter 4 explains the difference in how we measure an individual's equality in voting power worldwide, and how most nations reject the rigid "one person, one vote" standard found in the U.S.

Chapter 5 discusses how nations use different bases for measuring equality among electoral districts and how in some nations this amounts to a form of gerrymandering. Chapter 6 explains the differences in how the members of the upper chamber are selected and empowered in nations with Bicameral Legislatures.[1]

Chapter 7 describes the proportional representation system in the few nations that exclusively use such a system nationwide and how such a nationwide system has recently been abandoned in two larger countries. Chapter 8 explains how the timing of redistricting or reallocation of seats can operate as a gerrymander. Chapter 9 explains how gerrymandering occurs after seats are allocated to states, provinces, special multi-member districts, or administrative units. Chapter 10 considers gerrymandering in mixed systems.

Chapter 11 describes how various nations protect minority access to the political process. Chapter 12 provides the so-called "neutral criteria" in redistricting that are supposed to govern the shaping of electoral districts and explains how they can be manipulated for political reasons to produce almost any result. Chapter 13 discusses the use of redistricting commissions instead of the legislature for redistricting and reallocating seats and provides the essential aspects of a truly "independent" commission. Chapter 14 considers the role of the courts.

The Conclusion provides my observations about election systems worldwide, including how to recognize a gerrymander and how some of the common claims regarding proportional representation election systems and boundary or redistricting commissions have been misleading. The Conclusion also provides my recommendations for preventing gerrymanders.

At the end of the text of the book, I have included several appendices. Appendix A provides the applicable standards for redistricting issued by several international organizations. Appendix B contains lists of nations using various election systems and practices. Appendix C provides case studies of several nations as a sample of the

[1]Lists of nations having bicameral or unicameral legislatures are provided in Appendix B.

diversity that exists in democratic systems worldwide. I choose these particular countries for my case studies for various reasons: I selected Germany and France because they are internationally important and because their election practices need to be documented in English; The Islamic Republic of Iran and Turkey because they are often misunderstood in America; and Indonesia, Uruguay, and Lesotho to illustrate how each nation's election system is unique and has its own story. Appendix C also contains two short items on the United States, including a case study of a redistricting of congressional districts in Texas that used gerrymanders in a "masterly" fashion to replace eight Democratic incumbents and to strengthen the Republican majority in Congress.

The Bibliography directs the reader to various sources. In view of the unique nature of this book (i.e. looking at the realities rather than the official versions of what was happening in a nation) I was compelled to rely on many websites rather than on published books or articles. I found that such websites often reflected a more current and candid view of the nations.[2] I have also included an Index at the end of this book.

I caution, however, that neither this book nor the general websites shown in the Bibliography should be the sole source of information on any particular country. These websites are invaluable as a starting point, but I found the summary information on these websites sometimes conflicted or was too incomplete, outdated, or shallow to be reliable. For example, it is insufficient to say that a nation has a proportional representation (PR) or mixed election system without indicating whether the PR component of the system is nationwide, by fixed districts (e.g. states), or by special multi-member districts or constituencies, and whether the nation's election system is open/closed, permits independent candidates, has a threshold that is so high that it curtails the benefits of a PR system, or has recently reallocated seats in its national legislature or redrawn its electoral districts.

All of these nations have an agency responsible for elections and, surprisingly, these agencies often maintain a version of their website in English. Anyone looking at a particular country should access that country's relevant website. Unfortunately, the quality of these agency websites varies, or at least in the English-language version. Sometimes they present only a rosy picture of a nation's election system and avoid presenting any information that might allow any meaningful analysis. Nevertheless, they are valuable sources. It is important to use multiple sources as

[2]I was especially aided by the reports of the OSCE/ODHIR (Organization for Security and Co-operation for Europe/ Office for Democratic Institutions and Human Rights) assessing specific countries and elections. Its reports cover 57 (mostly European) countries—Afghanistan, Albania, Andorra, Armenia, Austria, Azerbaijan, Belarus, Belgium, Bosnia and Herzegovina, Bulgaria, Canada, Croatia, Cyprus, Czech Republic, Denmark, Estonia, Finland, France, Georgia, Germany, Greece, Hungary, Iceland, Ireland, Italy, Kazakhstan, Kyrgyzstan, Latvia, Liechtenstein, Lithuania, Luxembourg, Malta, Moldova, Monaco, Mongolia, Montenegro, Netherlands, Norway, Poland, Portugal, Romania, Russia, San Marino, Serbia, Slovakia, Slovenia, Spain, Sweden, Switzerland, Tajikistan, the former Yugoslav Republic of Macedonia, Tunisia, Turkey, Turkmenistan, Ukraine, United Kingdom, United States of America, and Uzbekistan.

verification of the current election system in a country as some are constantly changing.

Few scholarly articles exist that offer critical assessments in English of events or circumstances in some countries. Digging for specific information on redistricting or the allocation of seats in a country is especially difficult because these processes, or lack thereof, often escape attention and are seldom the subject of books, articles or websites—even among major democracies or the websites that pride themselves on reporting on election practices in nations worldwide. Therefore I often was left to examine the electoral districts myself to measure voting equality. Sometimes I found it necessary to separately locate information about the boundaries and number of representatives for individual electoral districts and, where available, the census population or number of electors (eligible voters) within each district. From this information I calculated the number of persons or electors per representative in fixed or multi-member districts and looked for anomalies. Similarly, I used such data to spot single-member districts and seat allocations that varied significantly from the ideal either in population or shape. Where possible I tried to determine the most recent allocation of seats and redistricting for the nations.

It is necessary to clarify the scope of this book and the terminology used in it. My focus is on elections to the national legislature of a country. Rather than identifying each nation's national legislative body by its unique name, I often used the term "national legislature" in reference to that body in all countries. Although my focus is on national legislative bodies, most of the observations about districts and gerrymandering are equally applicable to the gerrymandering of electoral districts for election to a state, provincial, or other local government legislative body. This footnote briefly describes the different types of election systems found worldwide and the initials by which they are generally recognized in the literature and within this book.[3]

In the United States the process of redrawing the boundaries of electoral districts is known as "redistricting." Internationally, academics generally describe the fixing of electoral district boundaries as adjusting those boundaries, and the process as "demarking" or "delimitating" instead of "redistricting." Since I have been involved

[3]PR—proportional representation, voting with each political party entitled to representation according to its share of the vote; FPTP—first-past-the-post, plurality voting with a single winner; TRS—two round system, plurality or majority voting with two rounds of voting to provide a single winner; MMP—mixed member proportional, a mix of FPTP and PR elections with limits on a party's share of seats, but no fixed number of seats in the national legislature; P—parallel system (also called Mixed Member Majoritarian [MMM]), with a mix of FPTP and PR elections and a fixed number of seats; STV—single transferable vote, with ranked or preferential voting designed to achieve proportional representation; AV—alternative vote (also called instant run-off voting) with ranked or preferential voting among multiple candidate designed to achieve a single winner; Blk—block voting (also called multiple non-transferable vote), for electing several representatives of the same party from a single multimember electoral district; SMD—single-member district; MMD—Multi-member district. A more extensive description of these election systems is available in the text of this book.

in “redistricting” electoral districts in the United States for over 40 years, I will stick with the American terminology.

The process of assigning the number of seats for a state in the lower chamber (House of Representatives) of the U.S. national legislature (Congress) is called “apportionment.” A similar process exists in almost every country, with seats in the national legislature assigned to the nation’s states, provinces, administrative units, or predetermined multi-member districts. Most countries regard this process of reassigning the number of seats in a national legislature among these jurisdictions as “redistribution” or “reallocation”. In some systems with a PR component this reallocation among party lists and fixed or special multi-member districts occurs again after the election and is the result of a complicated process that often is unique to the nation. I most often use the words allocation or reallocation in this book except when referring specifically to the apportionment process in the United States.

Nations differ as to whether voting equality should be defined in terms of “total population,” “citizen population” or “electors (registered voters).” I acknowledge that all of these measures are legitimate. Therefore, I refer to equality in terms of “persons or voters” rather than picking one measure or the other as the proper basis for allocating seats in a national legislature or drawing boundaries of an electoral district. However, a nation’s choice among these, and other, options may have a significant impact on the voting power and degree of representation of certain racial or ethnic groups. Therefore, I discuss the effects of these various options in Chap. 5 of this book.

I do not spend much time rehashing the law of redistricting in the U.S. because I expect that most readers of this book are already generally familiar with U.S. practices and are more interested in practices worldwide. Moreover, there are numerous books, articles, and websites on redistricting in the United States. Nevertheless, I often use election cases and practices from the United States to illustrate an issue in the text because my 40 years of experience with redistricting has made me intimately familiar with the best and worst aspects of elections in this country. My mention of United States law or practices is not meant to suggest that election practices in this country are superior. In fact, some are demonstrably inferior to what can be found elsewhere. My references to U.S. law are primarily to little known aspects of that law, and as a means of illustrating election practices in the U.S. as compared to those in other countries.

There are at least 192 nations that call themselves democracies. There are 195 sovereign nations according to the U.N., but another eleven nations are partial members or observer states of the U.N. or de facto sovereign countries.[4] One source lists 240 countries worldwide, but this includes areas that are “part of” another nation, such as Scotland. Some of the areas that are commonly considered “nations”

---

[4]See, www.un.org/undpa/en/members; *Overseas Territories, Dependent Areas, and Disputed Territories*, **One World Online** at www.nationsonline.org and www.worldonline (The Nations Online Project). *How Many Countries Are There in the World in 2018?* **Political Geography Now** (January 11, 2018).

are actually self-governing territories or protectorates of other nations.[5] Different sources vary in their count of countries because they use different definitions of what constitutes an independent nation as opposed to a "self-governing" territory.

Not all of the nations that claim to be democracies are considered by other nations or international organizations to be democracies. Many of these are controlled by a single party or group and do not conduct elections at all or any free and fair elections. For example, according to The African Election Database, in sub-Saharan Africa alone there are 25 countries that conduct elections that are not free and fair, but there are also 18 countries in the region that are considered electoral democracies with governments elected through generally legitimate, free, and fair elections.[6]

A similar scenario can be found on almost every continent, with the number of "true" representative democracies and "restricted" democracies highly subjective and constantly in flux as local circumstances change.

Even the United States has been criticized as not being a "true" representative democracy because two of its last three presidents have won election while losing the popular vote as a result of the Electoral College and its congressional districts are racked with bizarre gerrymanders that distort the popular vote. At the same time, the Islamic Republic of Iran is generally denied status as a democracy even though it conducts elections and the outcome of those elections affects the country and the world.[7] My research suggests that Iran has been unfairly characterized as a "terrorist state" by Western governments and media.

More than 190 nations and self-governing territories have at least one chamber of the national legislature where most of the members are directly elected by the qualified voters of the country and where the equality of voting power is an announced objective. Each of these nations, however, is a little different in its use of electoral districts and its redistricting or reallocation processes. Also, the election systems are constantly changing. For example, while this book was being written the electoral circumstances changed in at least England, Lebanon, France, Italy, Fiji, and the Russian Federation. I have tried to address all changes through 2018.

In many nations the reality is far different from the legal, sometimes constitutional, requirements that have often been the basis for prior studies. Even some of the

---

[5]These include nations such as the United States (e.g. Puerto Rico, the American Virgin Islands, Guam, Samoa, and the Northern Mariana Islands), Great Britain (e.g. the Falkland Islands, Jamaica, Bermuda, the British Virgin Islands, the Cayman Islands, Saint Helena, Jersey, the Pitcairn Islands, Monserrat, the Turks and Cacaos Islands, and Gibraltar), France (e.g. New Caledonia [there are also many overseas départements of France as discussed in Chap. 12]), Tanzania (e.g. Zanzibar), Kingdom of the Netherlands (e.g. Aruba, Curacao, and Sint Maarten), Denmark (e.g. the Faroe Islands, Greenland), New Zealand (e.g. the Cook Islands, Niue, and Tokelau) and China (Hong Kong, Macao, and Taiwan [disputed]). *See, Overseas Territories, Dependent Areas, and Disputed Territories,* **One World Online** @t www.nationsonline.org and www.worldonline (The Nations Online Project).

[6]www.eisa.org.za; and http://africanelections.tripod.com

[7]*See,* Appendix C, A Case Study of Iran. Most political scientists consider Iran a theocracy. Iran considers itself a democracy. Religion (Islam) is a critical element of Iranian government structure, but so are elections. Election outcomes affect both domestic and foreign policies.

oldest and most established democracies have accepted some element of bias in their election systems or have, for various reasons, avoided or postponed compliance with their own laws regarding the frequency and standards for redistricting or reallocation of seats among districts. I have tried to record some of these transgressions.

There are, however, means for minimizing the effect of political self-interest on the manner in which we elect our representatives. At a time when the institution of representative democracy is threatened for being inefficient at best or a sham at worst, it is critical that we not take democracy for granted. We need to understand what is working well and what is failing.

Finally, I write as a practitioner, not a political scientist. Many of the opinions and observations expressed in this book are my own based on my experience aiding governments in redistricting, litigating dozens of redistricting lawsuits, working frankly with innumerable politicians and their staffs, and examining or cross-examining political scientists as "expert witnesses" in dozens of cases on the effects of specific redistricting plans. I think that this experience affords me a valuable tool for ferreting out and understanding the realities of gerrymandering. I realize, of course, that political scientists do not necessarily agree that practitioners have much to offer.[8]

[8]*See. Political Scientists and Electoral Reforms in Europe and Canada: What They Know, What They Do* by Camille Bedock, Damian Bol, and Thomas Erhard, 16 **Election Law Journal** 445 (2017), published online (September 1, 2017). Actually the symposium was called "What Do Political Scientists Know About Electoral Reform **That Practitioners Do Not** (Emphasis added)?".

Chapter 2
The Many Disguises of Gerrymandering

Democracy is a form of government under the control of the people it governs. A representative democracy is one in which the people express their will and act through their elected representatives.

There are many ways to manipulate the election process or rules to favor or disfavor certain groups, individuals, or political parties in a representative democracy.[1] This book focuses on only one—the gerrymander.

A gerrymander is a manipulation of electoral districts such that an incumbent or a political party (usually the dominant one) attempts to use the reallocation of seats or redrawing of electoral district boundaries, or the failure to do so, for their own advantage. Essentially a gerrymander occurs when self-interest is substituted for the public's interest.

The processes of reallocating seats in the national legislature and redistricting (i.e. redrawing electoral districts) are critical to representative democracy. They are the means of assuring that each member of the national legislature represents a roughly equal number of persons or voters and that each person or voter has an equal opportunity to affect the policies of his or her government through his or her representatives despite the inevitable changes and shifts of population that occur over time in every electoral district. This equality of opportunity is the essence of representative democracy. Gerrymandering is a means of

---

[1] *See, CODE OF GOOD PRACTICE IN ELECTORAL MATTERS: GUIDELINES AND EXPLANATORY REPORT, European Commission for Democracy Through Law (2002); ELECTORAL LAWS AND THEIR POLITICAL CONSEQUENCES by Bernard Grofman and Arend Lijphart in the Agathon series on representation (2003); ESTABLISHING THE RULES OF THE GAME: Election Laws in Democracies by Louis Massicotte, André Blais and Antoine Yoshinaka, Univ. of Toronto Press (2004); INTERNATIONAL ELECTION PRINCIPLES by Jack Young, ed., American Bar Assoc. (2015); INTERNATIONAL ELECTION REMEDIES by Jack Young, ed., American Bar Assoc. (2017).*

S. Bickerstaff, *Election Systems and Gerrymandering Worldwide*, Studies in Choice and Welfare, https://doi.org/10.1007/978-3-030-30837-7_2

denying this equality of opportunity and is, therefore, a threat to representative democracy.

Often the word gerrymander conjures up the image of a weirdly shaped electoral district, but, as I discuss later, a gerrymander can be bizarre in shape or compact and aesthetically attractive. The overriding issues are the purpose and intended effect of a redistricting or reallocation plan.

It is fair to ask why I consider the discriminatory reallocation of seats and malapportionment, or the failure to timely reallocate seats or redistrict as forms of gerrymander. Many politicians and some political scientists see these offenses as distinct from gerrymandering. They aren't! They are decisions that affect electoral districts, are harmful to the public, and are intended to serve a political party's or politician's self-interest. Even if elections in a particular malapportioned nation are not seen by some political scientists as causing outcomes that are "biased" toward a particular political party, the malapportionment, or failure to reallocate or redistrict, may have been intended to do so. Gerrymanders sometimes fail. Moreover, a gerrymander is not always about a party's success; it may be designed to maintain the status quo and to reelect incumbents, sometimes from many different parties.

All redistricting or reallocation of seats in a national legislature has political consequences. It is impossible to avoid or even diminish this effect, but it is crucial to the survival of representative democracy that we limit the act of purposefully drawing any electoral district or allocating any seats in a legislative body, or failing to act timely to advantage or to disadvantage a political party, group or individual rather than to meet neutral criteria that benefit the public.

2.1 The Origin of the Word "Gerrymander"

The practice of designing electoral districts for political advantage dates back to the earliest use of districts for elections. This practice was given a name (as Gerrymander) in the Boston Gazette (USA) on March 26, 1812 when the word was first used to describe a redrawing of Massachusetts state senate election districts by the Massachusetts Legislature during the term of Governor Elbridge Gerry. One of the districts was claimed to resemble the shape of a mythological salamander. The word "gerrymander" is a combination of the governor's last name and the word salamander.

This original (now infamous) 1812 gerrymander cartoon depicts the Essex South state senatorial district for the legislature of The Commonwealth of Massachusetts

The 1812 "Gerry-mander" was drawn to benefit Governor Gerry's Democratic-Republican Party. The precise purpose presents an enigma. If the district was drawn so that Gerry's party could win it, the gerrymander failed. The opposing Federalist Party candidate won this district by over 15%. However, if the district was created to pack Federalist voters and drain them from the other senatorial districts, it was a success. The overall redistricting successfully reelected a Democratic-Republican majority in the Massachusetts's state senate.[2]

2.2 Why Gerrymander Electoral Districts

Gerrymandering is usually about power. One group or party dominates governmental decision-making and wants to retain it by maintaining or enhancing its percentage of representatives in the national legislature. Gerrymandering is one means by which it may do so by controlling the allocation of seats or the shape of electoral districts to assure that the persons who have the best chance of winning are those who support the group or party in power.

Gerrymandering is also about political survival—especially for individual politicians. A decision about how many seats to allocate to a fixed or multi-member district, how to shape a particular electoral district, choosing a proportional

[2] *See, Seeking to End Gerrymandering's Enduring Legacy* by Carl Hulse, **New York Times** at A17 (January 26, 2016).

representation system to protect party leaders, or whether to make any changes at all may be perceived by a politician as crucial to his or her ability for winning reelection. Few politicians are willing to forego the opportunity to affect these decisions.

Gerrymandering is also often about a clash of ideas. An incumbent or party in power feels that their ideas are best for the country and that gerrymandering is justified to assure that they remain in office or power to further those ideas. This is contrary to democracy. In a representative democracy, the ultimate judge of the merits of an idea is its acceptance or rejection by the voters through their elected representatives. Any effort to stifle, direct, or manipulate that voting through gerrymandering to bolster an idea or policy is not justified. Personal beliefs about what idea is "best" never justify a gerrymander.

Any definition of gerrymandering is almost meaningless, however, when faced with the difficulties of proving the purpose behind district boundaries or reallocation decisions. As discussed in Chap. 12, almost any district configuration or allocation can be justified by ostensibly neutral factors or criteria even if the real purpose is political. This fact does not make gerrymandering satisfactory, or in the public interest. Instead, it emphasizes the importance of making certain that those persons entrusted with the authority to allocate seats or redraw electoral districts are qualified and free from self-serving or political motives.

2.3 Gerrymandering Is Possible in Every Type of Election System

We usually think of gerrymandering in terms of the process of shaping single-member electoral districts, but it is also a characteristic of PR and mixed election systems.

The failure to timely redistrict or reallocate seats in the national legislature in a fair manner or as populations change is possible in every election system, and is particularly beneficial to incumbents and to the political party or parties in power. Since mixed systems have a single-member district component, the issue of gerrymandering the shape of single-member or multi-member districts is similar to that of majoritarian or plurality election systems that are all single-member. However, gerrymandering also occurs for district or regional proportional representation and mixed systems in the allocation of seats among fixed districts (states, provinces, administrative units or multi-member electoral districts), or the failure to reallocate those seats when demographics change.

2.4 The Reasons for Gerrymandering

Gerrymandering occurs for several reasons:

2.4.1 Partisan Gerrymander

The theory behind the partisan gerrymander is to manipulate the processes of drawing electoral district boundaries or allocating national legislative seats in a plan such that, taken as a whole, the plan gives the dominant party or group the best chance of winning enough seats to continue to control the legislative process and to help party incumbents to win reelection without harming the party's overall objectives. This is achieved through the shaping of electoral districts or allocating of seats in such a way that the probable votes for an opposing candidate or party are wasted.

A political party wants to achieve a result that satisfies its members and guarantees the best chance for electing its candidates and thereby controlling the national legislature. This usually means avoiding any reallocation of seats if possible unless the reallocation furthers or protects the party's interests and shaping electoral districts to increase the chances of its candidates.

It is easier to achieve these results if the requirement for reallocating seats or for numerical equality among the districts is lax. Therefore, it is not surprising that the law of most nations allows considerable disparity in the number of persons or voters among the districts, or why the national legislature in many nations disregards even these legal limits.

The U.S. strict population standard and enforcement of that standard by the courts leave no room for such disparities, but they have resulted in many bizarre and strange looking congressional districts. State legislatures and political parties have used technology to identify "friendly" and "unfriendly" areas and to gerrymander districts so that they meet the strict population standard and still include or exclude areas as needed to achieve their political objectives. The result is districts in the U.S. that are irregular and even bizarre in appearance.

The U.S. has many oddly shaped districts. An example of a bizarre U.S. district caused by partisan and racial gerrymandering can be found in one of the most famous of America's gerrymanders. In 1992, congressional district 12 in North Carolina stretched awkwardly across that state to pack Black voters (assumed by the Republican Legislature to be primarily Democrats) into the district, while leaving the surrounding districts to be dominated by white Republicans The top map shows the districts as enacted by the North Carolina Legislature including the infamous District 12 (yellow) into which a significant proportion of the state's Black voters were packed (Fig. 2.1).

Such shapes continue today as shown in Illinois's congressional districts as they existed until 2013. The boundaries were gerrymandered in a bipartisan deal to protect incumbents in both parties. The oddly shaped District 17 was unofficially nicknamed "the rabbit on a skateboard" for its weird shape. The districts were redrawn in 2013, but continue to be somewhat oddly shaped (Fig. 2.2):

Such weirdly shaped districts are common among congressional districts throughout the United States. In assessing the shape of these districts, however, remember that these districts were also drawn to comply with the requirement that all

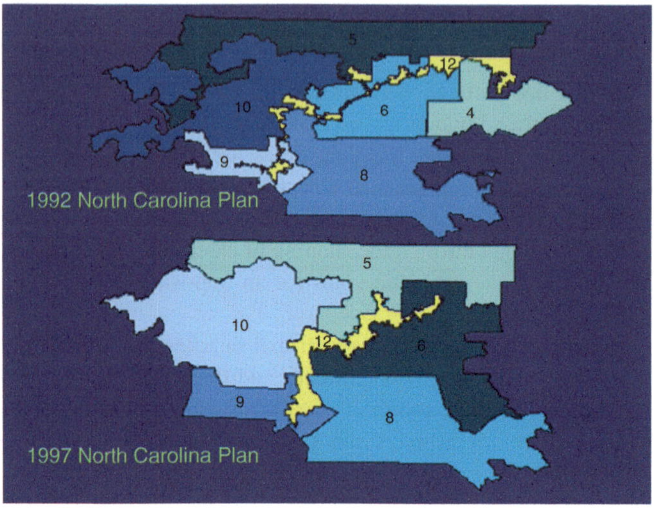

Fig. 2.1 The 1992 North Carolina Congressional Districts. The map is courtesy of Bickerstaff, Heath, Delgado, Acosta LLP @ www.bickerstaff.com

of the districts be essentially equal in population. Thus they reflect an attempt to achieve a particular political result while also achieving absolute equality in the number of persons in each district.

Partisan gerrymandering may be used as an offensive weapon. Appendix C, Case Study of the 2003 Congressional Redistricting in Texas describes a Republican plan that replaced eight of ten targeted Democratic incumbents. In nations with PR elections, political parties may unite in support of a plan that fails to allocate the requisite number of seats to fixed or multi-member districts largely controlled by an opposing political party, or fail to reallocate seats when needed to equalize voting power.

2.4.2 Incumbent Protection

A gerrymander for an incumbent usually means maintaining the status quo as nearly as possible. In an election system with at least some PR elections it means avoiding any reallocation of seats that could affect the reelection of incumbents. In a system using single-member districts it means avoiding the reallocation of seats, if possible, and creating electoral district boundaries shaped for the benefit of incumbents seeking reelection.[3]

A single-member district will usually resemble or remain unchanged from the boundary of the district in which the incumbent was elected in the past. The

[3]It is rare to gerrymander a district for someone who is not an incumbent.

Fig. 2.2 Illinois Congressional Districts in 2003–2013 and in 2013. The maps are courtesy of the Illinois Board of Elections

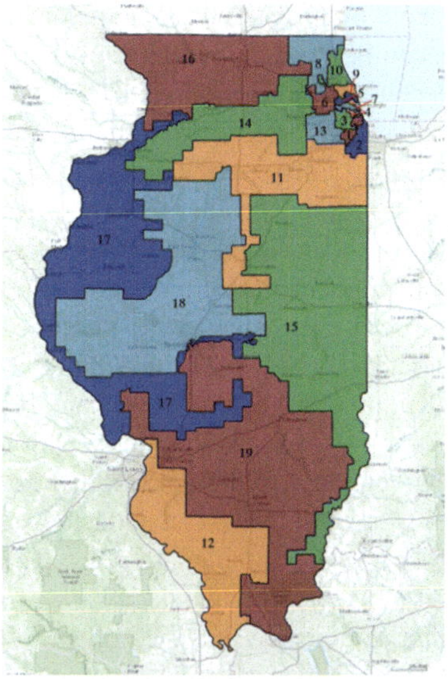

Illinois Congressional Districts 2003-2013

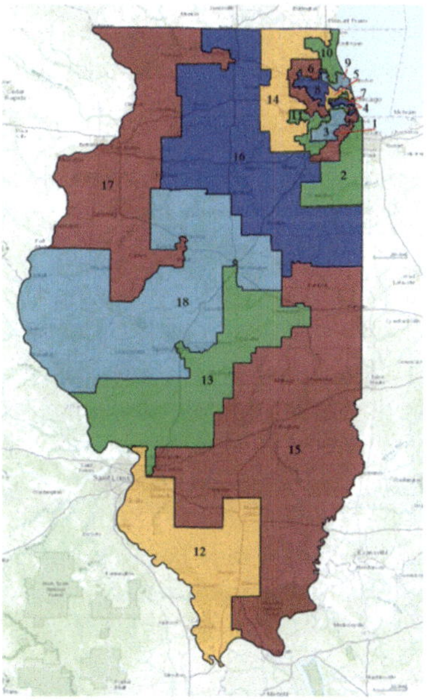

Illinois Congressional Districts 2013-current

boundary may be changed to make the incumbent's reelection more likely by the removal from the old district of areas in which most of the voters were expected to oppose the incumbent's reelection or the addition of areas in which the voters are expected to support the incumbent. Each incumbent is usually eager to find "friendly" voters to help his or her reelection, but often incumbents from the same party have their eyes on the same areas or voters. The intra-party fight over these voters can become desperate, especially if the incumbents believe that their reelection depends on the outcome of the dispute.

In a nation with lax requirements for equality in population or voters, resolving this intra-party dispute is easier. It is common to see an incumbent's single-member district intentionally underpopulated or unchanged, especially if the incumbent is a member of the political party controlling the redistricting.

An Incumbent Protection Gerrymander can receive the support of several political parties, even competing parties. In the United States the Republican and Democratic Parties sometimes unite behind a carefully negotiated redistricting plan that protects incumbents from both parties. So-called "bi-partisan commissions" that were once hailed in the U.S. as a reform of state redistricting have instead become vehicles for the development of "incumbent protection" plans that end up violating "neutral criteria" mandated by state law in order to satisfy incumbents from both parties. For example, after the 2010 census six of the ten plans adopted by such commissions were invalidated.[4]

Some nations accept incumbent protection as an unofficial, but acceptable, criterion for shaping districts or allocating seats. For example, even though not listed in law as one of the guidelines for delimiting constituencies, the protection of incumbents is generally recognized in Germany as an unwritten guideline because it provides "continuity." As explained by one academic observer in Germany,

> As for redistricting boundaries within a state: Districts of an incumbent who has represented the district over the last twenty or so years (and who has worked his or her way to the upper echelons within parliament) are hard to touch. Losing a village from the district? Adjoining a new community? Most incumbents hate such an idea. If they are big shots, they occasionally succeed to prevent any changes until they retire.[5]

Many nations find merit in this idea, although few[6] formally acknowledge incumbent protection in their law or among its guidelines for redistricting.[7]

Not all members of a national legislature start out with an intention to gerrymander the electoral district in which they were elected, or any other district. The idea of "gerrymandering" is abhorrent to them. Nevertheless, as the redistricting or reallocation processes proceed, these members often find that if they remain passive, they soon become victims. Some other members may have fewer scruples about gerrymandering or may have become desperate about their chances for reelection unless they find more "friendly voters," a place to which they can jettison some

---

[4]*Independent Redistricting Commissions for American Cities* by Steve Bickerstaff, 13 **Election Law Journal** 110 (2015).

[5]This statement appears in an e-mail sent to the author by a professor in Germany. I have chosen not to reveal the professor.

[6]Zimbabwe includes "continuity with previous district boundaries" as a criterion for redistricting.

[7]Even U.S. courts have acknowledged the legitimate interest of a state in protecting incumbents with seniority in Congress, but have refused to allow such an interest to justify any deviation from absolute population. *See,* White v. Weiser, 412 U.S. 783 (1973).

"unfriendly" ones, or have an underpopulated district. Any change to satisfy one member affects other districts and soon the changes ripple through any proffered plan. A passive member can find that his or her current district has been deprived of its "friendly" voters or has become the dumping ground for "unfriendly" ones to help another member. The passive member's abhorrence of gerrymandering becomes a regrettable fight for survival. I have often seen members who at first profess that they "do not care" about the makeup of their districts become aggressive defenders of their current district's boundaries.

Redistricting may be divisive, even between members of the same political party. With this political infighting, it is easy to understand why maintaining the status quo has often become the easiest option for national legislatures. The same rationale applies to any possible reallocation of seats. Maintaining the status quo is made easier if the decision remains within the discretion of the national legislature and any legal requirements for periodic redistricting or reallocation are lax, absent, or ignored. Maintaining the status quo to prevent the defeat of incumbents is gerrymandering.

2.4.3 Racial, Ethnic, or Religious Discrimination

A gerrymander can be used to discriminate against a racial, ethnic, or religious group. Such a Racial, Ethnic, or Religous Gerrymander is unlawful in the U.S. under the Constitution and Sect. 2.2 of the Voting Rights Act if the minority group is large enough, politically cohesive, and has historically seen its candidates lose because of the voting of a polarized majority.[8]

2.4.4 Incidental

A gerrymander may not be the result of a Machiavellian conspiracy to affect an election outcome. I have seen candidates try to control the area in their district by gerrymandering a district's boundary to exclude a possible opponent's residence, to include the residence of a family member or important person, to include a prestigious institution, such as a university or medical facility, or to include or exclude areas for seemingly trivial or undisclosed reasons. However, virtually all of such mundane requests have the ultimate objective of creating some political benefit for

[8] *See*, Thornberg v. Gingles, *478 U.S. 30 (1986)*. Ironically, some of the most bizarre congressional districts in the U.S. are ones drawn in an effort to overcome this historical discrimination by creating districts with enough minority voters to assure that they can elect the person of their choice. Unfortunately, the shaping of these remedial districts causes the nearby districts to be mostly white and Republican. Some state legislatures have used the Voting Rights Act as an excuse to pack minority voters in as few districts as possible to reduce their overall political significance.

the incumbent, such as an opportunity for less competition, a less expensive campaign, greater prestige, or larger campaign contributions.

These reasons overlap. For example, a political party that is in power is likely to want to protect its incumbents and therefore is interested in preventing any changes in the allocation of seats or shapes of single-member or multi-member districts that could adversely affect them.

These options for gerrymandering must face the political realities of the legislative body. Sometimes the result desired by the dominant party cannot be achieved. For incumbents, sometimes it can be achieved only with the cooperation of other incumbents, even members of an opposing party. It is common in such circumstances for the incumbents from two or more parties to negotiate an agreed course of action that protects the parties' incumbents.

So also, a gerrymander that advantages a party or incumbent may have the effect of disadvantaging a racial, ethnic, or religious minority. As long as one result (partisan gerrymandering) is legal and the other (racial gerrymandering) is not, the observer and a court have difficulty determining the true purpose of the gerrymander.

2.5 The Essential Tools of Gerrymandering

Gerrymandering begins with the same data that is necessary for any redistricting or reallocation of seats—accurate maps of the affected areas and counts of the number of persons or electors in an area. This data should be available for the smallest geographical areas possible.[9]

Technology now plays a major role in redistricting. Computers with GIS software can calculate data and display proffered redistricting plans in seconds that only three decades ago took hours of work and reams of paper to construct. Special software exists specifically for redistricting and is being used at every level of government in the United States.[10] This technology makes redistricting easier, faster, and more accurate for persons charged with the task, but it also has the same benefits for those persons wanting to gerrymander districts.

An additional bit of information is needed for gerrymandering. Gerrymandering generally works only if the housing pattern in an area is politically segregated so that most persons living in an identified geographical area, such as possibly a whole state or fixed district, dependably vote for the same candidates or political party. A politically homogeneous area is less susceptible, although not immune, to gerrymandering. Therefore, reliable information about how persons have voted in the past and judgment about how they will likely vote in the future is essential.

[9]In the United States, the census provides the number, age, race, etc. for persons in very small geographic areas (census blocks) that may have fewer than 50 total persons.

[10]The basic system is the Geographical Information System (GIS), but much more sophisticated software is now available, including past election results, economic data, etc.

Election patterns are often volatile. Therefore, it is crucial to select the right election or elections to serve as a benchmark for determining an area's voting tendency. By using several elections to give a range of results it is possible to know the high and low of past support in an area for specific candidates or parties. Choosing the right past elections for comparison is key. Again, computers are available to analyze complex statistics and prior election results.

Often, however, the conclusion of "friendly" and "unfriendly" areas for purposes of gerrymandering is not a result of any detailed or technical analysis, but is the result of a politician's practical experience, such as an incumbent's "feeling" that, "they love me there."

The final need is for the mechanical means necessary to achieve the objectives. Such means may be as basic as maps, pencils, official demographic data, and hand calculators, or as sophisticated as computers and specialized software. The adoption of a gerrymander is far more dependent on politics than technology, or as famously voiced about the constituencies in the United Kingdom, "a constituency is created, not found."

2.6 Gerrymandering the Allocation of Seats

The only legitimate basis for allocating seats in a nation's national legislature among its fixed or multi-member districts is equality in the relative number of persons or electors per representative in each such district. There are several acceptable formulas for determining how best to handle special circumstances, such as islands, or how to round a "remainder," but the basic rule is that if a district has sufficient population or electors to warrant a representative, its voters are entitled to elect that representative.[11]

Some nations have discriminated among fixed or multi-member districts by allocating them greater or fewer representatives than the number to which they are entitled based solely on the district's number of persons or electors or refraining from any reallocation at all. This causes the number of persons or electors per representative to vary among the districts. Such discrimination is never appropriate. The effect, and possibly the purpose, of giving a district too few representatives is to lessen the voting power of the residents of that district in the national legislature and to increase the relative voting power of residents in another district.

The reason for this discrimination may lie in official policy, such as the allocation of a minimum number of seats to each fixed or multi-member district,[12] incumbent

[11]This statement assumes that the primary objective is equal treatment of voters. This statement changes if the primary objective is equal treatment of parties. Some existing formulas for the geographical dispersion of seats in a PR system (especially in the PR component of some mixed systems) place a higher priority on assuring that each party receives its share of seats than on whether each vote carries the same weight.

[12]*See*, Chap. 9.

protection, preservation of the voting integrity of remote regions, or in an effort to advantage or disadvantage certain groups, political parties, or individuals, including certain racial, ethnic, or religious groups that are disproportionately located in the affected fixed or multi-member districts. Sometimes many purposes overlap.

The allocation of seats is important to both individual candidates and political parties in all systems because the more seats allocated to a friendly fixed or multi-member district, the greater a party or an individual candidate's chances of winning. This effect is even greater when the number of seats in a particular fixed or multi-member district is to be reduced through a proposed reallocation of one or more seats to another district.

This reallocation may create a situation in which the number of incumbents in one or more fixed or special multi-member districts exceeds the number of seats remaining in that district—meaning that at least one incumbent must step aside or lose.[13] Thus, the incumbents in this district have a personal, sometime desperate, interest in seeing that the proposed reallocation does not occur. There is no incumbent in the other fixed district with an equivalent personal interest since the seats of these incumbents are theoretically unaffected; therefore it is not surprising that the proposed reallocation is often stymied, especially if it requires approval by the national legislature, as has occurred in Germany.

The reallocation of seats is also important to the affected fixed districts themselves, especially if they face the prospect of losing a vote or voice in the national legislature. These local government or party officials can be decisive in the legislative conflict over whether to reallocate seats.

2.7 Gerrymandering Single-Member or Multi-Member Districts

Even in shaping electoral districts, it is wrong to think of gerrymanders as necessarily strange or bizarre in appearance. Some of the most bizarre are benign in purpose. For example, a district that follows a city boundary may be irregular in appearance, but beneficial in its purpose. On the other hand, some of the most regular in shape hide a malign purpose. Later in this book I discuss a congressional redistricting in Texas that produced esthetically attractive districts, with the purpose of essentially fencing Black and Republican voters together in a single overpopulated district in order to advantage the reelection efforts of white Democratic incumbents in the surrounding districts.[14]

[13]In nations using single-member electoral districts within a fixed district, a reallocation of seats among fixed districts which reduces the number of seats in a fixed district may result in one or more incumbents not seeking reelection or two, or more, incumbents seeking reelection in a single district, which is called "pairing."

[14]*See,* Bush v. Martin, 224 F Supp. 499 (S.D. Tex. 1963), *aff'd per curium, 376 U.S. 222 (1964),* discussed in Chap. 9.

2.8 A Gerrymander Is not Always Successful

It is wrong to believe that a gerrymander is necessarily successful in achieving its ultimate goal. History is filled with examples of unsuccessful gerrymanders—beginning with the apparently failed attempt to elect a Republican-Democrat to the Essex South state senatorial district in 1812 and continuing through the victory of Emmanuel Macron's supporters in France in 2017.

2.9 The Tactics of Gerrymandering

In nations that allocate seats to fixed or multi-member districts, the tactic for the party in power is simple—delay reallocation or minimize the number of seats allocated to unfriendly districts and maximize the number allocated to friendly ones.

The three classic tactics of gerrymandering single-member or multi-member districts are known as "cracking," "packing," and maintaining the status quo.

2.9.1 Cracking (Sometimes Called Fracturing)

Cracking occurs when voters that historically vote dependably for opposition candidates or political parties are intentionally split among two or more districts in such a way that these voters are expected to be a minority submerged in a majority that is likely to vote for a competing candidate or political party. An example is in the Russian Federation, where it appears that in the recent districting politically problematic urban areas are split and combined with pro-government areas so that the urban vote is diluted and Putin's Russia United Party can win.[15] Opposition votes are essentially wasted because the candidates supported by a majority of pro-government voters always win.

Cracking the opposition means, however, that the voters intended to be in the majority are also spread among the districts to create as many districts as needed in which the candidates or party favored by the government will win. It also requires reliable information about how persons have voted in the past and judgment about how they will likely vote in the future. If the "friendly" voters are spread too thin, an unexpected voting pattern that benefits the opposing candidates may cause the pro-government candidates to lose in some districts where they anticipated winning.

Thus, it behooves the gerrymander drawer, who is usually pro-government, to search for the right balance—systematically spreading the voters among the districts so that the candidates or party favored by the government will win in as many districts as needed to control the national legislature without unnecessarily creating

[15] *See*, Chap. 7.

the possibility of losing if the voting pattern changes. This strategy is made easier, with more room for error, if the districts are allowed to be unequal in the number of persons or voters per representative in the national legislature, and it is possible to systematically or selectively underpopulate the districts targeted for victory. Such purposeful overpopulation or underpopulation can be intended to advantage or disadvantage an individual candidate, or, if systematic, can advantage or disadvantage a political party or group. The objective from a party's perspective is the total plan, not any single district.

2.9.2 *Packing*

The second method of wasting the votes for opposing candidates or political parties is known as packing.[16] As the name suggests, this method is aimed at placing as many of the opposing candidate's or party's voters in as few districts as possible.[17] A pro-government candidate will have little or no chance of winning in these districts because the voters are overwhelmingly likely to vote for the opposition, but the effect of packing the opposition's voters in only a few districts is to allow the pro-government candidates to more easily dominate in the remaining districts and to win control of the legislative body. See the hypothetical at the end of this Chapter.

2.9.3 *Malapportionment*

The simplest and most effective tactic for achieving an electoral advantage in nations with lax voting equality standards is through malapportionment by overpopulating any single-member district likely to vote for the opposition, or allocating fewer seats than appropriate to a potentially unfriendly fixed or multi-member district. An example of this latter tactic can be seen in those nations that avoid reallocating seats to a growing area that may have a disproportionate percentage of voters likely to vote for an opposing party. This particular tactic is unavailable in the United States

---

[16]*See, Values and Validations: Proper Criteria for Comparing Standards for Packing Gerrymanders by Robin E. Best, Shawn J. Donahue, Jonathan Krasno, Daniel B. Magleby, and Michael D. McDonald, Election Law Journal (2017), published online (March 12,018) @ https://doi.org/10.1089/elj.2017.0471;* and *Toward a Talismanic Redistricting Tool: A Computational Method for Identifying Extreme Redistricting Plans by Wendy K. Tam Cho and Yan Y. Liu,* **Election Law Journal** *(2016), published online (Dec 12,016) @ https://doi.org/10.1089/elj.2016.0384*

[17]*Considering the Prospects for Establishing a Packing Gerrymander Standard* by Robin Boyd, Shawn Donahue, Daniel Magleby, and Michael McDonald, **Election Law Journal** (2016), published online @ https://doi.org (September 26, 2017). The various tests examined in the article were wasted votes, comparing wins, equal vote weight, and seat-dominated symmetry.

because of court enforcement of rigid requirements for population equality among congressional districts in a state.

2.9.4 Maintaining the Status Quo

The most common tactic of gerrymandering is to literarily do nothing. If a party's incumbents prevailed in the latest election, why change the allocation of seats or redistrict even though required by law? The effect is to leave a significant inequality among voters in the districts and to benefit incumbent politicians. This tactic is evident in the oldest democracies, such as France and the United Kingdom, and the newest.

These tactics of cracking or packing the opposition's voters or allowing a person's vote to be more or less important than the vote of another person can be identified worldwide. They often are manifested in elections that are biased for one party or another and a result in which the winner of the most votes nationwide does not necessarily win the most seats in the national legislature. In other circumstances the partisan bias is not obvious, but the gerrymandering is designed to benefit particular incumbents by making it easier to win reelection.

2.10 Conclusion

The easiest way for a political party in most democracies to achieve a political advantage over other parties in elections to the national legislature is to control the processes by which members of that body are elected. Gerrymandering electoral districts is an important means of achieving such an advantage.

It is common to think that gerrymandering and malapportionment are distinct wrongs. Thus is incorrect. Controlling the population or the number of voters in a district for political advantage is gerrymandering.

In a PR system this control allows fewer seats to be allocated to fixed or multi-member districts likely to favor opposition candidates, or the systematic overpopulation of the electoral districts likely to be won by the opposition. Both techniques are forms of gerrymandering. In this scenario, the party drawing the redistricting or reallocation plan wins more seats because the opposition's votes are wasted and the voter's will is denied.

Often leaving the status quo is a tactic used to benefit the party in power or all incumbents. It is amazing to me that a party not in power would find it convenient to support maintaining the status quo, but this is explainable if doing so benefits the party's incumbents or if the party is more comfortable with a "known" role than with the uncertainties of change. A party's leaders are the particular beneficiaries of a "status quo" policy.

A search for gerrymanders on the basis that they are always strangely shaped is wrong. Sometimes they are oddly shaped; sometimes not. Some of the least effective gerrymanders have the most bizarre shape. Some of the most effective gerrymanders are uniform and aesthetically attractive in their appearance. Districts that are bizarre in appearance can become benign, nonpolitical, or even beneficial to a societal objective when explained by competent evidence. In some instances in the United States the most bizarre district boundaries are created for ostensibly positive reasons.[18] However, even those districts can become vehicles for political gain.

The practice of gerrymandering is generally reviled by voters. Therefore, it is popular for opposition candidates to promise to end it if elected. Few, if any, actually try to do so. I generally support Democratic candidates, but I cannot enthusiastically endorse the Party's latest outcry about Republican gerrymandering and campaign to "end this travesty" because I think the Party's objective is not so much to end gerrymandering as to replace gerrymanders favorable to Republicans with ones favorable to Democrats. We can do better.

Gerrymandering electoral districts is contrary to the principles of representative democracy and is a threat to its survival.

[18]See, e.g., the congressional districts created in Harris County (Houston) in 1991 [Chap. 9] ostensibly to benefit minority voters.

Chapter 3
The World's Use of Electoral Districts

An electoral district is a geographically-defined area from which voting members of the national legislature are elected, usually by the resident voters of that electoral district. Virtually every nation uses electoral districts as part of its election system. Chapter 7 discusses those few nations that elect all members of the national legislature nationwide.

Electoral districts can be an invaluable part of representative democracy, intended to assure fairness, voter equality, accountability, and geographical and political diversity in a legislative body. They also, however, can be a means for voter discrimination and entrenchment of the status quo through gerrymandering.

3.1 The Use of Fixed or Special Multi-Member Districts

All democracies, except those in Chap. 7, disperse or allocate at least some of the seats in the national legislature among the country's fixed administrative districts, such as states, provinces, other administrative units, or special multi-member districts. Even in countries that rely only on PR elections those elections usually occur in fixed or special multi-member districts to which seats in the national legislature are allocated.[1] In mixed systems, there are districts for the direct elections, such as single-member districts, but in many nations the PR component also incorporates special multi-member districts.

In most countries these fixed districts are administrative units or governments such as states, provinces, or other administrative units. I refer to these units as "fixed districts."

A few countries, however, have defined a separate set of special multi-member electoral districts within the country. These "special multi-member districts" are

[1]See, Chaps. 9 and 10.

S. Bickerstaff, *Election Systems and Gerrymandering Worldwide*, Studies in Choice and Welfare, https://doi.org/10.1007/978-3-030-30837-7_3

used for PR elections. Each such multi-member district usually has many governmental units in it, but has little or no governmental power itself. It is used only as a part of the election system. As a result, I use the term "special multi-member districts" to encompass these units.

This allocation of seats is common for both upper and lower chambers in nations with bicameral national legislatures and in unicameral national legislatures. In the remainder of this book, however, I deal almost exclusively with districts as they are used in unicameral legislatures or the lower chamber of a bicameral legislature.

The boundaries of these fixed or special multi-member districts seldom change. In some countries, these districts have remained unchanged since the nation was created or became a democracy and may even be specified in the nation's constitution. It is possible to argue that even these states, provinces, administrative units, and special multi-member districts whose boundaries now are largely stable were originally drawn with some political goals in mind. Whatever those goals may have been, however, are far beyond the scope of this book.

It is a mistake, however, to assume that these fixed districts never change. In some countries the number of units has increased, decreased or otherwise changed their boundaries over time as the nation has expanded or the units have been consolidated or divided. For example, the United States originally consisted of 13 states, but now consists of 50 states as a result of the nation's expansion and the division of some states. Other nations, such as India, U.K., Japan, and France have seen similar changes. Turkey's major cities, such as Istanbul and Ankara, have been split into two or three multi-member electoral districts as the population has grown. The same is true in many of the largest cities in nations like Iran.

3.2 Electing from Within Fixed or Multi-Member Districts

The manner of electing representatives within these fixed and special multi-member districts varies among nations.

Some nations elect their representatives at-large in the fixed districts.[2] In other instances, the fixed or special multi-member district functions as a multi-member electoral district.

In some nations, this fixed district is sub-divided into individual districts. In most of these nations, such as France, India, United Kingdom, and the United States (House of Representatives), each of these individual districts elects a single representative to the national legislature using a First Past the Post (FPTP), Two Round System (TRS), or other plurality/majoritarian election scheme.

In a few nations, however, these individual districts are at least partially multi-member, and use a PR, Bloc voting, or other system. A few countries, such as Iran,

[2]The United States Senate is an example. In the U.S. each state has two Senators elected by FPTP in staggered terms statewide.

have both SMDs and MMDs and a unique TRS system. These various systems are discussed further in Chaps. 9 and 10.

In other fixed districts, all of the seats allocated to the fixed district are elected by PR within the fixed district.

The special multi-member districts are found primarily in nations that have PR elections or are used for the PR component of mixed systems.[3]

3.3 The Advantages and Disadvantages of Using of Electoral Districts

All of the geography within each state, province, or administrative unit in the nation is usually included within some single-member district (SMD) or multi-member district (MMD) so that all qualified electors have a vote for at least one voting member or a political party in the national legislature.[4]

Using an election system with at least a component of districts has certain advantages. It allows voters in a constituency to hold a specific representative or group of representatives accountable—voting them out of office if a sufficient number of voters in the district are displeased. Therefore, each representative of a district has reason, whether a matter of loyalty or political survival, to act on behalf of his or her constituency rather than some more abstract interest such as national or political party needs. SMDs provide the most direct link between representative and constituents. This linkage is less in a MMD and lessens further as the number of representatives elected from a district increases and the role of the political party becomes paramount. On a policy plane, election from districts assures representation of more geographical areas in a country and, consequently, greater geographic diversity in the national legislature.

Election from districts also has its disadvantages. Sometimes the interests of a constituency are clearly counter to the interests of the nation or the member's political party. On these occasions, a district member's conscience may be conflicted and his or her vote in the national legislature may be uncertain. Also, if a nation attempts some equality in voting power for its inhabitants, it must provide for the redrawing of the electoral districts at a regular interval or adjust the number of representatives in multimember districts to reflect changes in the relative population or number of voters within each district.

Critics of SMDs also claim that such districts easily lead to gerrymandering and the creation of "electoral fiefdoms" in which a politician can win election and reelection at will. A nation's use of single-member electoral districts is often criticized as resulting in a less politically diverse national legislature than PR

[3]*See,* Chaps. 9 and 10.

[4]An exception exists in the United States, where residents of the District of Columbia (National Capitol) do not have a voting member of Congress.

elections. Support for this conclusion may be found in many countries, but particularly in the latest parliamentary elections in the Russian Federation.

3.4 Conclusion

For purposes of this book, I have divided the discussion of gerrymandering in the current use of electoral districts into: (1) Those countries that elect all members of the national legislature from the nation as a whole (Chap. 7); (2) Those countries which allocate seats to fixed districts, with the fixed district often sub-divided into single-member or multi-member districts (Chap. 9); (3) Those countries which allocate seats to fixed districts or special multi-member districts, with PR elections held at-large in the district (Chap. 9); and (4) Those countries which have a mixed system that combines single-member districts with a proportional representation component (Chap. 10).

Since my focus is on how electoral districts can be gerrymandered, my division is slightly different from the usual political science categorization into:

- Plurality/majoritarian systems in which the candidate or parties with the most votes are considered the winners, such as first past the post (FPTP), party bloc vote (BV), alternative vote (AV), and two-round (TRS) electoral systems.
- Proportional representation (PR) systems in which parties receive approximately the same share of the seats as they receive of the votes cast in the election.
- Mixed systems in which plurality/majoritarian and proportional representation systems are combined in an attempt to have the best aspects of each system.

In reality, both types of classification are useful in understanding the variety of election systems in the world.

A basic tension exists in all election systems between the ability of voters to choose a specific candidate to hold accountable for the locale and the need for a political party to maintain discipline within the party by assuring that the elected candidates are committed to the party's national vision. Each nation has balanced these conflicting interests in choosing its electoral system and modifying it. Districts are a vital tool for achieving that balance.

Chapter 4
Unequal Voting Power

The Code of Good Practice states that "seats (in the national parliament) must be evenly distributed between constituencies."[1] This principle, sometimes popularized as "one person, one vote" is perhaps the most widely acknowledged principle throughout representative democratic societies—i.e. that each person or voter should have an equal opportunity through his or her representative to determine national policy. This equality is measured by the relative number of persons or voters per representative.

It is, however, a principle that has many different manifestations, and often seems more a matter of rhetoric than a reality of representative democracy. In some nations, this requirement has been loosened ostensibly to leave greater room for factors such as natural features, historical boundaries, and recognizing communities of interest and local government lines.[2] These, as discussed in Chap. 12, are considered to be neutral factors and, if embodied in the law, are in the public interest. In some countries the courts have expressly disavowed the U.S. standard of voter parity in favor of community as the most effective means of guaranteeing representative democracy.[3]

In many countries, however, the exigencies of governance and politics simply have overcome this principle of equal voting power for all. Unequal voting power can be a result of gerrymandering:

1. When "unfriendly" fixed or special multi-member districts are allocated fewer seats than justified by population or number of electors to cause the opposition party to "waste" votes;
2. When "friendly" fixed or special multi-member districts are allocated more seats than justified;

[1]Appendix A.

[2]*See*, Chap. 12.

[3]*See,* McGinty v W Australia, 186 CLR 140 (1996); and Reference re Prov. Electoral Boundaries (Sask) [1991] 2 S.C.R. 158, 183 (Can.). Excerpts from these cases appear in Chap. 14.

S. Bickerstaff, *Election Systems and Gerrymandering Worldwide*, Studies in Choice and Welfare, https://doi.org/10.1007/978-3-030-30837-7_4

3. When single-member (SMD) or multi-member (MMD) districts are drawn to "waste" an opposition party's votes by overpopulating districts in which the opposition is likely to win;
4. When SMDs or MMDs are drawn to enhance the dominant party's votes by underpopulating districts in which it is likely to win;
5. When SMDs or MMDs are drawn to help incumbents win reelection by underpopulating the district in which the incumbent will seek reelection; or
6. When the seats are not timely reallocated or the electoral districts not timely redrawn so that the dominant party or incumbents are advantaged by keeping the status quo.

Each of these circumstances represents a deliberate act to advantage or disadvantage a party or individual by manipulating voting power through malapportionment. Therefore, if an imbalance in voting power exists, it justly raises a concern that it exists because of self-interest and is the result of gerrymandering.

My research indicates that gerrymandering is a major, possibly the primary cause of significant malapportionment and voter inequality.

4.1 Different Measures of Equality

Measuring the comparative level of voter equality among nations is difficult because there is no uniform standard. Nations commonly speak of the relative equality of persons or electors among electoral districts in terms of a percentage, such as 10%. This can, however, be very misleading because the use of a percentage without further explanation can have many different meanings.

For example, it is common to describe the standard for state legislatures and local governments in the United States as 10%.[4] This percentage, however, is calculated by adding the numerical sum by which the most and least populous districts vary from this ideal. For example, if the total population of a jurisdiction is 10,000,000 and there are 10 single-member districts (SMDs), the ideal SMD size is 1,000,000 persons. If the most populous SMD is +7% from the ideal (i.e., 1,070,000 persons per representative), then a 10% deviation occurs only if the least populous SMD is −3% (i.e., 970,000) below the ideal. In this example, the total difference, or "total maximum deviation" between the two SMDs in the jurisdiction is 100,000 persons or 10% of the ideal.[5] This measure gives the maximum difference between the value of votes in the jurisdiction.

By contrast, most nations define the number of persons per representative by a percentage above or below the "norm," "quota," or "average" for the measured constituencies. This calculation tells an observer only about that single district, not

[4]The "de minimis" or essentially no deviation standard in the U.S. applies only to congressional districts within a state.

[5]This measure is used in a few nations, including the United States and Japan.

about the plan as a whole. If one such district is 20% above the average number of persons or voters per representative within a jurisdiction, it is possible to achieve this measure of deviation only if this overpopulated district is offset by another district that is (or several districts that total) 20% below the average.[6] Under this measure, a nation may claim that a particular district is only 20% above the average number of persons or voters per representative, but this means that a vote in the district is 50% less valuable than a vote in a district that is 20% below the average.

For example, using the preceding example of a 10 district/1 million population electoral area, a district with population that is 20% above the average has 1,200,000 persons. Necessarily there must also be an off-setting district or districts in the jurisdiction that total 20% below the average (200,000 persons). If there are two off-setting ±20% districts, the total maximum deviation between these two districts is 400,000 persons per representative, or 40% of the ideal. This difference of 400,000 persons is 50% of the least populous district, meaning that, assuming an equal percentage of voters to persons in the two districts, a vote in this district is more valuable than one in the more populous district. This is because there are fewer persons or voters per representative in his or her district than in the other (i.e., one out of 800,000 v. one out of 1,200,000) even though they have an equivalent vote in the national legislature.

It also should be noted that although "norm," "average, and "quota" are often used interchangeably among international standards, they have very different meanings. A quota in this context means the "proportional share" of persons or electors in a jurisdiction that a seat represents. It is easily calculated, and is essentially the same as "ideal." It does not imply that any districts are at the ideal. The same is true of "average." On the other hand, use of the word "norm" or normal suggests that although the particular district's deviation from ideal is great, the other districts are at or near the ideal. This is very misleading. All of the districts could be significantly above or below the ideal.

4.2 Calculating Voter Equality

Any calculation of voter equality in a nation begins with a determination of the quota or ideal number of persons or electors per representative in the national legislature. This determination involves the simple division of the number of persons or electors in the country by the number of representatives in the national legislature.

This calculation can be repeated for each fixed district (SMD) by dividing the district's population or number of electors by the number of seats allocated to the fixed district to determine the quota or ideal number of persons or electors in each SMD within the fixed district. For multi-member districts (MMDs) the process is

[6]For example, in a jurisdiction that has one district that is 20% above the ideal, there necessarily must be districts totaling a negative percentage of 20%, such as four districts each of minus 5%.

similar. The number of persons or electors in each MMD, such as the fixed district as a whole if it is being used as a single MMD, is divided by the number of seats allocated to the multi-member district. These calculations indicate the ideal number of persons or electors per representative for each single-member or multi-member district.

These simple calculations allow a comparison of the value of a vote (i.e. the person or voter per representative), in any SMD or MMD with the national ideal, the fixed district's ideal, and voters elsewhere in the fixed district, special MMD, or nation. They also allow a comparison of the relative voting power of persons or electors in one fixed or multi-member district with those in another district.

If the objective is to calculate the deviation as a percentage from the ideal, then subtract the number of people or electors per representative in the district from the ideal for the nation, if the objective is a comparison with voters nationwide, or the ideal for the fixed district, if the objective is a comparison within a fixed district, and divide the result by the appropriate ideal.[7] This calculation will provide the percentage of deviation in persons or electors per representative for a district from the ideal in the country or fixed district.

If the objective is to calculate the total maximum deviation among districts within a nation[8] or a particular fixed district, add the largest deviation above the ideal to the largest deviation below the appropriate ideal while disregarding the plus or minus signs (e.g. −20% added to +20% = 40%). This also can be obtained by determining the difference in the actual number of persons or electors between the two districts and dividing that number by the respective number of persons or electors in the ideal district. The significance of the difference to persons or voters in the two districts (or any two districts), divide the actual number of persons or electors in one of the districts by the difference in actual number of persons or electors between the two districts.[9]

Both areas elect a single representative to the national legislature. This means that in this example of ±20% a person's vote in the overpopulated district has only 2/3 of the weight as a person's vote in the underpopulated dtrict. A similar calculation can be made by comparing the number of persons or voters per seat among different multi-member districts.

Many other calculations are possible. One of these is to determine how many and by how much deviation is normal. This calculation may disclose that most of the districts are significantly above or below the ideal or average.

---

[7]For example, if the ideal is 50,000 and the district has 40,000 persons or electors, the result is −10,000. If this result is divided by the ideal (50,000), the deviation is −20% from the ideal.

[8]Although the U.S. requires essentially absolute equality in population among congressional districts within a state, there is no such requirement of equality among districts nationwide. However, both calculations are important.

[9]E.g. if the difference is 400 persons or voters, and the number of persons or electors in the smaller of the two districts is 800 persons or electors then the difference is 50% of the smaller district. For the larger district with 1200 persons, the difference is 33.3% of the number of persons or electors in the district.

Making these calculations is important for identifying gerrymanders. Any significant deviation from the ideal or average should be explained and justified by neutral criteria.[10] If not, the odds are that politics is determining the boundaries of districts or the allocation of seats.

4.3 Limits on Deviation Set by Law Vary by Nation

The Code of Good Practice states that "The permissible departure from the norm should not be more than 10%, and certainly should not exceed 15% except in special circumstances (protection of a concentrated minority, sparsely populated administrative entity)."[11] In other words, the Code of Good Practice accepts the principle of equality in voting power, but rejects the total maximum deviation standard for measuring equality.

The maximum deviation allowed by laws in different countries varies from 3% above or below the quota in Macedonia to 25% above or below the quota in Germany (for existing districts), and Canada.[12] The most common allowable legal deviation is 10% above or below the population quota. In many countries, however, the actual deviation among districts nationwide is higher than the limit set by law.

Most often this degree of allowable deviation is given without explanation. It is usually interpreted to mean the percentage from the "average" or "quota" within the nation or a state or province, not as the difference between the highest deviations as occurs if using the total maximum deviation method.

Many nations do not prescribe any objective or maximum deviation.[13] Some mandate "as equal as possible," but effectively leave the actual deviation to be determined by the national legislature or commission with authority to redraw districts or reallocate seats.

The following chart shows the variable legal limit on deviation in a few of the major nations using SMDs (Table 4.1)[14]:

---

[10] *See,* Chap. 12.

[11] Appendix B. Use of the word "norm" is unfortunate and misleading.

[12] These nations include: Albania (±5%), Armenia (±15%), Australia (±15% at creation), Belarus (±10%), Canada (±25%), Croatia (±5%), Germany (±25%), Hungary (±20%), Italy (±20%), Lithuania (±25%), Macedonia (±3%), New Zealand (±5%), Papua New Guinea (±20%), Singapore (±30%), Ukraine (±10%), United Kingdom (±5% with exceptions; pending), United States (court imposed de Minimis), Yemen (±5%), and Zimbabwe (±20%). Most of these measurements are explicitly or implicitly from the quota.

[13] These nations include: Bahamas, Bangladesh, Barbados, Botswana, Bulgaria, Cameroon, Czech Republic, Dominica, Dominican Republic, France, Hungary, Iceland, India, Indonesia, Ireland, Italy, Japan, Jamaica, Kenya, Republic of Korea (South Korea), Lesotho, Malaysia, Mauritius, Mexico, Namibia, Nepal, Nigeria, Pakistan, Palestinian Territories, Panama, Poland, Russian Federation, Saint Lucia, Saint Vincent and the Grenadines, Sweden, Tanzania, Turkey, and Uruguay.

[14] These limits are lifted primarily from *Toward Developing International Standards, Appendix C,* **ACE** (2004). This invaluable compilation of election practices for 87 countries was headed by Lisa

Table 4.1 Example deviation limits

Country	Limit under law	Notes
France	None	20% from quota—court imposed
Germany	15–25%	From quota. If 25%, a district must be redrawn
United Kingdom	Variable	Uniform limit of 5% postponed
United States	0–1%	Total maximum deviation within each state
Japan	None	Court has said 2–1 using total maximum deviation
India	None	
Australia	10%	From quota
Indonesia	None	
Russian Federation	None	
Canada	25%	From quota

Some countries have a limit on the number of persons or electors among PR electoral districts. An example is Croatia at 5%, which elects an equal number of representatives from each domestic multi-member district, but has never changed the MMD boundaries.[15]

4.4 The Challenge of Limits Becoming the Norm

Unfortunately, in many nations this maximum of allowable deviation is more of an accepted and common result rather than an exception. Germany's direct election constituencies are an example. The Bundestag regularly redraws districts that deviate from the Land quota by at least 25%, but leaves the deviation unchanged in the others. The inequality in these districts is left unaddressed until they too reach, or approach the 25% limit. This is gerrymandering!

The Conseil Constitionnel in France[16] is one of several authorities[17] in Europe to recognize the problem that in its country, electoral districts tend to be drawn at the legal limits. The Conseil explained:

Handley, but is incomplete and was based in part on inaccurate surveys. The information contained in this chart is accurate for these countries.

[15] See, THE CONSTITUTIONAL COURT OF THE REPUBLIC OF CROATIA No. U-X-6472/2010 Zagreb (December 8, 2010)

[16] Decision no. 2008-573 DC, Conseil Constitutional (January 8, 2009). *See* Chap. 14.

[17] *See,* **e.g.,** THE CONSTITUTIONAL COURT OF THE REPUBLIC OF CROATIA No. U-X-6472/2010 Zagreb (December 8, 2010) and THE CONSTITUTIONAL COURT OF THE REPUBLIC OF LITHUANIA, ON THE COMPLIANCE OF ARTICLE 9, PARAGRAPH 1 OF THE REPUBLIC OF LITHUANIA LAW ON THE ELECTION OF THE REPUBLIC OF LITHUANIA (CONVENTION OF 6 NOVEMBER 2012) TO THE CONSTITUTION OF THE REPUBLIC OF LITHUANIA, No. KT27-N16 (October 20, 2015).

> [T]he principle of equal electoral law will be violated or, in the interests of favorable election results, abusive by setting boundaries for constituencies. **Therefore, the application of this maximum population deviation is possible only in exceptional cases, with proper justification.**[18] (Emphasis added).

A nation's limit on deviation should not be an invitation for gerrymandering at or slightly beneath this limit. A legislator's wish that his or her district be left unchanged simply because it is below the allowed extreme is a gerrymandering of district boundaries to benefit the self-interest of the incumbent and denial of the voters' right to be treated fairly. Any significant[19] deviation from equality should be justified by criteria that bear the public's imprimatur. Each voter is entitled to be treated equally.

4.5 Inequality in a PR System

Gerrymandering through an inequality in an individual's voting power may also occur in proportional election systems when fixed or multi-member districts are not allocated seats based solely on their population or voters. An example—two districts have an equal number of persons or qualified voters, but one is allocated five seats in the national legislature while the other has eight seats. Both may fall within the allowable deviation from the quota as prescribed by a nation's law, but, in terms of representation in the national legislature, the effect is that a person's vote in one province has less than 65% of the weight of a person's vote in the second province.

In a nation with a population of 20 million and a national legislature with 200 seats, each member ideally represents 100,000 persons. If two fixed or multi-member districts each has a population of one million, but one is allocated five seats in the national legislature (each theoretically representing 200,000 persons) while another has ten seats (each theoretically representing 100,000 persons), it means that a voter in the latter district has twice as much ability to affect national policy as one in the first district.

[18]Decision no. 2008-573 DC, Conseil Constitutional at paras 21 and 26 (January 8, 2009); *See* Decision No. 2008-24 ELEC of May 29, 2008, Observations of the Conseil Constitutionnel on the parliamentary elections of 10 and 17 June 2007.

[19]I acknowledge that some minor deviations from the ideal occur because the legislature or commission finds it easier to draw districts in an allowable range than it is to try to meet an ideal. This is scant justification for any significant deviation.

4.6 The Need for Requiring Periodic Redistricting and Reallocation

The issue of timely redistricting or reallocation is discussed in Chap. 8, but it is important at this point to realize that the presence in a nation of a limit on the allowable deviation from the average, which is discussed above, is different from a requirement to periodically redraw all districts in an effort to achieve equal voting power consistent with the applicable criteria.

It is different in at least two ways. The first is that the limit on the degree of deviation may be applicable in most countries only when the districts are redrawn. Over time a district's deviation may change, but there is no mandate to redistrict. The second difference is that in those nations, such as Germany, where there is a mandate to redraw a district if it exceeds a certain level of malapportionment, which in Germany is 25% from the quota, the particular district may be the only one purposefully redrawn, leaving the other districts unchanged[20] even if their deviation from the average or ideal is significant but less than the maximum limit. The maximum allowable deviation becomes the usual deviation.

Both a limit on acceptable deviation for when districts are redrawn and, where possible (i.e., in nations using an ongoing count or registration of persons or electors), a limit on existing malapportionment are appropriate. Whatever the limit on deviation, there must be a mandate after a clearly stated period of time to review and to redraw as necessary all districts to make them as equal "as possible" in persons or electors per representative. To provide otherwise is to invite gerrymandering. A similar requirement for the same number of persons or voters per seat in a PR system is necessary for voter equality.

4.7 Nations Fail to Comply with Their Own Requirements for Equality

Even among those nations that acknowledge the desirability of equal voting power and by law have set a numerical limit for deviations from equality, many have not lived up to those standards. The nation's legislature or commission has found justifications in geography, history, communities of interest, historical boundaries, or expediency for not strictly adhering to the deviation limit set by law when redrawing a particular district. Almost any outcome can be rationalized, but few can really be explained when the whole plan is examined for consistency in application of a particular justification. Such an examination may reveal that the

[20]Of course, it is impossible to redraw only one district. A change in the boundaries of one district necessarily affects the boundaries of one or more other districts.

proffered rationale for the underpopulation or overpopulation of one district is belied by the inconsistent treatment of other similarly situated districts.

Other nations have given little or no justification for allowing the inequalities to persist. In many nations, this avoidance of prescribed deviation limits has its origin mostly in politics. It is made possible because: (1) there are few enforceable legal requirements that the districts must be redrawn or seats reallocated within a definite period; (2) courts are hesitant to compel timely redistricting in accordance with the nation's legal limits; and (3) the political reluctance to redistrict or to reallocate electoral seats in most nations is not effectively offset by a public outcry against voter inequality.

4.8 Is Voter Equality Important?

Virtually all guidelines for democratic government claim population or voter equality as essential. It is wrong, however, to assume that this guideline enjoys unquestioning worldwide support.

The relatively rigid standards set by courts in the U.S. for congressional districts are often criticized as being unjustified and the cause for widespread gerrymandering of electoral districts in this country. For many observers, there are good reasons for recognizing other criteria, such as geography, local government boundaries, etc. as considerations that serve a valid public interest and should be allowed to offset population or voter equality.

Some critics of the "one person, one vote" doctrine suggest that it is more important that a voter be able to identify with a local community than that each person's vote has absolutely equal weight and that equal suffrage may be best achieved through boundary assignment based on specific redistricting criteria. Courts in Canada and Australia have expressly rejected the rigid American standard in favor of "effective representation".[21]

In 1964, the U.S. Supreme Court considered this argument and concluded, "legislators represent people, not trees or acres" and "legislators are elected by voters, not farms or cities or economic interests."[22] The Court was reacting to the decades in which state legislatures, sometimes contrary to a state's own constitution, had found some rationale for not redistricting at all or for not equalizing persons or voters among its electoral districts.

I have always thought that the unwillingness of the U.S. Supreme Court to accept neutral factors, such as the recognition of political subdivision boundaries, in the redistricting of congressional districts, was an indication of its basic distrust of state legislatures to draw the districts in good faith and without discriminatory influences.

---

[21] *See,* McGinty v W Australia, 186 CLR 140 (1996); and Reference re Prov. Electoral Boundaries (Sask), 2 S.C.R. 158 (Can.) (1991).

[22] Reynold v. Sims, 377 U.S. 533, 562 (1964).

The emphasis on absolute voter equality for congressional districts[23] limits the discretion of state legislatures and their ability to gerrymander congressional districts behind the cloak furnished by redistricting criteria.

As important as this legal notion of equality in voting power has remained for U.S. redistricting, it is clear that most other countries do not share this view. It is also clear, however, that some national legislatures simply avoid redistricting or reallocation of seats altogether unless there is judicial intervention. Some do so openly, such as India and France. Others achieve a similar result indirectly by delaying release of the census where obligated to redistrict after the census, such as Lesotho, or delaying the effective date of changes and thereby minimizing effects on existing office-holders, such as the U.K.

4.9 A Lax Standard for Voter Equality Encourages Gerrymandering

The presence of a lax limit on equality or the failure to enforce existing limits are invitations for the drawing of districts or allocating of seats for the purpose of advantaging or disadvantaging a political party or candidate—in other words a gerrymander.

This effect can be significant. Assume a scenario in which a jurisdiction with ten million voters is to be divided into 100 single-member electoral districts. The ideal number of voters or quota in each district is 100,000. In this hypothetical, only 40% of the voters in the jurisdiction prefer Party A, while 50% prefer Party B. In an unbiased system it is reasonable to expect that the 100 representatives elected in the jurisdiction would roughly reflect this same 50/40 split,[24] with party A winning a majority of the seats. In this scenario, however, Party B controls the redistricting and, within the hypothetical nation's legally allowable limit of plus or minus 20% deviation from the quota, systematically overpopulates the districts likely to favor Party B and systematically underpopulates the districts likely to favor Party A. Given favorable demographics, Party B could actually win a majority of seats even though only favored by 40% of the voters.

In some circumstances the highest deviations found worldwide are singular events caused by unusual geographical features, such as making an island a single district despite its underpopulation or overpopulation or occur because a state or province is guaranteed a certain number of seats regardless of its population, which

---

[23]The Court has allowed state and local governments greater leeway in drawing their districts. The strict standard applies only to congressional districts within a state. I doubt that the Supreme Court foresaw how technology would allow legislatures the flexibility and means to meet this voter equality requirement, and by gerrymandering to still achieve most of their political goals.

[24]In the hypothetical illustrated at the end of this chapter I added a third party C with 10% of the vote. The presence of this third party is intended to give the hypothetical a European flare, but is not necessary for the result that Party A can win a majority of the seats.

is a regrettable relic of the past and causes some of the most extreme deviations. These are forms of legal manipulation of district boundaries, rather than gerrymandering. They have their basis in law; although they may become gerrymanders when they reflect an intentional bias toward one group of voters. The Constitutional Council of France has struck down that nation's statutory guarantee of two seats for each département because it unfairly favored the rural areas.

In many circumstances, however, this legal maximum for deviation has become a victim of politics with districts at or above the maximum becoming the rule rather than the exception.

4.10 A District's Shape Is Not Necessarily Indicative of Whether It Is Gerrymandered

An example of how the shape of an electoral district is not necessarily an indication of gerrymandering and how a significant deviation in population can be an effective gerrymander is the 1958–1964 congressional redistricting in Texas. Situated in the upper center of the following Texas map is District 5 (yellow). It is compact, contiguous, regular in shape, and encompasses only one county, Dallas County. It seems the perfect non-gerrymandered district.

It was, however, the most populous congressional district in the United States (951,527) in 1964. Next to it was the least populous congressional district in Texas, District 4 (Fig. 4.1).

Why did this configuration exist? Democrats controlled the Texas Legislature, but more and more Texans were voting Republican, especially in Dallas County. The Legislature's redistricting plan solved this political problem in part by making Dallas County a single, overpopulated district.

The Legislature's malign motive for its treatment of Dallas County was shown by comparison to how it had inconsistently split the state's other populous county, Harris (the city of Houston), into two districts. By keeping all of Dallas County in one district, the legislature limited Dallas Republicans to only a single congressman, denied black voters in Dallas County an opportunity to elect a person of their choice to Congress, and kept a white Democrat in office in District 4. It was an effective gerrymander even though the district shape appeared benign.

In 1964 U.S. Courts invalidated Texas' redistricting plan because of its malapportionment and instituted a requirement of population equality among congressional districts in each state.[25]

[25]Bush v. Martin, 224 F Supp. 499 (S.D. Tex. 1963), *aff'd per curium*, 376 U.S. 222 (1964).

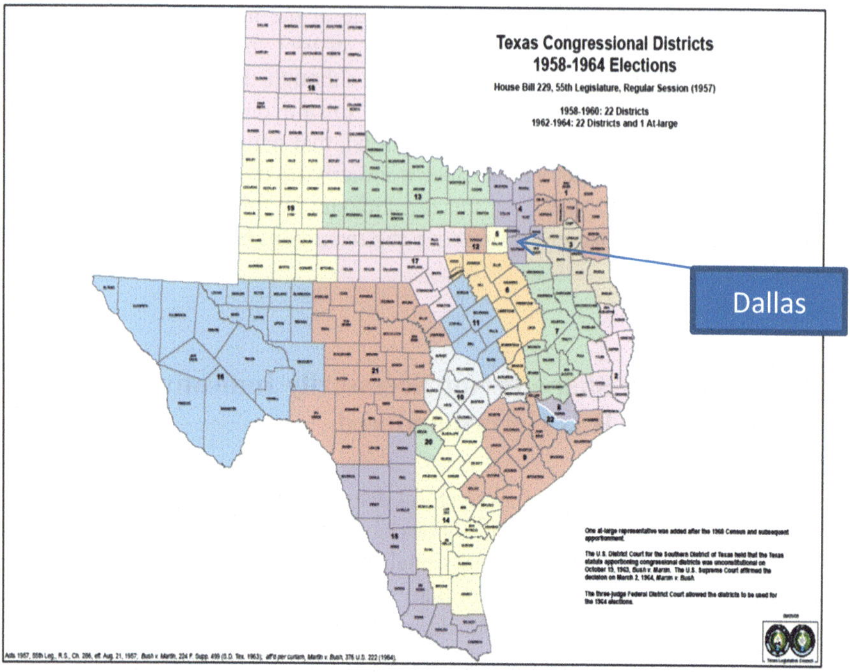

Fig. 4.1 Gerrymandering by overpopulation, Texas in 1956–1964. This map was furnished by the Texas Legislative Council

In many other nations, however, a significant deviation in population or voters among electoral districts is common. Is such a deviation a form of gerrymandering? I believe the answer is "Yes!"[26]

4.11 Conclusion

This chapter points out six major problems that harm representative democracy.

First, the practice of describing electoral districts in terms of their variance from the quota for a jurisdiction allows politicians to hide discrimination for or against a particular individual candidate or group because it tells nothing about the fairness of a redistricting or reallocation plan as a whole. To say that a district is only 10–20% above or below the quota hides the fact that there must be enough districts in the plan with the opposite sign to establish the quota. Also, use of the word "norm" to mean "ideal" is misleading.

[26]Still, gerrymandering of equally populated districts in the United States is always a subject of interest worldwide. Appendix C describes another incident of congressional redistricting from Texas in 2003 that attracted worldwide attention.

Second, the allowable limit on the relative number of persons or electors per representative (the result of allowing deviation among the electoral districts) is far too high in most nations. A limit of 10–20% deviation from the quota for a fixed district may sound inconsequential when considered in isolation, but it may result in a difference of 20–40%, or higher, for voters within the same jurisdiction. For example, if the quota is 100,000 persons or electors with a potential allowable deviation of 20%, it means that one member of the national legislature represents 120,000 persons or electors while another represents only 80,000; yet both have an equal voice and vote in the national legislature. This same analysis applies to the allocation of seats. There are circumstances, such as an island, in which the presence of a significant deviation may be justified by neutral factors, but this should be the exception, not the rule.

Third, some nations don't have standards or even abide by their own laws or rules for the maximum allowable deviation because there is little or no means of enforcement of these laws or guidelines and no public outcry for violating them. These legislative actions seem to clearly be gerrymandering for the benefit of incumbents and the dominant party.

Fourth, nations should have a requirement both for periodic review and redistricting of all districts and a limit on deviation of districts from an ideal or quota. Where possible (i.e. where current data is available) the limit should be applicable for when a district is redrawn and on an ongoing basis when the malapportionment meets a certain level. Germany has the right idea, but needs to add a requirement for periodic redistricting of all districts.

Fifth, a lax requirement for equal voting power among voters encourages gerrymandering because it means that district shapes can be more easily adapted to advantage or disadvantage an individual, group, or political party without attracting attention as appearing bizarre or misshapen. The stricter the requirement for equality among voters, the more likely the gerrymandered districts will reveal themselves with bizarre shapes.

Sixth, the calculation of voter equality should be made on a national basis. The fact that a single-member district varies only slightly from the ideal within a fixed district is not sufficient. The U.S. requirements for voter equality apply only within a state. History may be adequate justification for that country's discrimination, but not as a model for other nations.

Some nations have refused to follow the rigid system of equality found in the U.S. for legitimate reasons such as (1) they are appalled by what many see as the unnecessary and largely meaningless chaos in the U.S. after each decennial census; (2) they reject the U.S. notion of "voter parity" in favor of a more "pragmatic, pluralist, and group-based" concept that leaves room for community interests; and (3) they accept the reasoning that "effective representation is at the heart of the right to vote" not "equality of voting power per se."[27]

---

[27] *See,* McGinty v W Australia, 186 CLR 140 (1986).

I do not suggest that nations should adopt the rigid standards of the U.S., but the level of deviation that is permitted by most nations is far too high, especially if it serves as a standard for all districts instead of only extreme cases. It is above the recommended limits and encourages gerrymandering. A nation's national legislature or courts may find the strict standards of the U.S. to be too extreme, but there is no bona fide reason for ignoring the international guidelines, its own laws, or the welfare of its inhabitants.

4.12 Gerrymandering Hypothetical

The following chart demonstrates the potential effects of gerrymandering. The hypothetical uses the gerrymandering tools of packing, fragmenting, and population variance to allow a party with 40% support to likely control elections in a jurisdiction of one million voters divided into ten single-member districts of unequal population or voters ranging between ±20% (Table 4.2).

Under this hypothetical, Party A, with only 40% of the voters in the jurisdiction, is likely to win as many as seven of the ten districts (Districts 1–7) based on past voting trends. Approximately 350,000 of Party A's voters are spread among these seven districts, giving the Party with an outright majority in three districts (Districts 1–3) and a majority over Party B in four others (Districts 4–7). Of course, predicting future voting trends is never easy or guaranteed.

Party B has 500,000 supporters, equaling ½ of the voters in the jurisdiction, but may win in only two or three districts, with 180,000 of its voters "packed" in two districts (Districts 8 and 9), where it has an outright majority, and the remaining 220,000 "fractured" among the others.

Districts 6 and 10 present interesting cases. District 6 becomes a toss-up if the 15,000 Party C voters join with Party B's voters to support the Party C candidate. In

Table 4.2 Hypothetical gerrymandering

District voters	Party A (400,000)	Party B (500,000)	Party C (100,000)	Total voters (1,000,000)	Deviation (%)
1	45,000	35,000	–	80,000	−20
2	45,000	35,000	–	80,000	−20
3	50,000	40,000	–	90,000	−10
4	50,000	35,000	5000	90,000	−10
5	55,000	40,000	5000	100,000	0
6	50,000	35,000	15,000	100,000	0
7	50,000	45,000	15,000	110,000	+10
8	20,000	90,000	–	110,000	+10
9	20,000	90,000	10,000	120,000	+20
10	10,000	55,000	50,000	120,000	+20
Total	400,000	500,000	100,000	1,000,000	0

District 10, Party A is very unlikely to win, but if its voters join with those of Party C, the Party C candidate will probably win and leave Party B winning only two districts. This possibility offers a bargaining tool for Party A to get Party C cooperation in District 6.

A hypothetical gerrymandering of seats in a PR election can produce a similar result.

Gerrymandering in the real world to produce a designed result is replete with uncertainties that are not evident in this hypothetical, including the quality of candidates, the mood of the voters, etc. The most thoughtful redistricting plan may become a sacrifice to reality.

Chapter 5
Equality in Electors or Persons

Assuming that the relative equality of voting power is a priority, there are several bases for measuring that equality. The Code of Good Practice states that:

> [Voting power] entails a clear and balanced distribution of seats among constituencies on the basis of one of the following allocation criteria: population, number of resident nationals (including minors), number of registered voters, and possibly the number of persons actually voting.[1]

In a homogeneous society, where age, citizenship, voter registration, and voter turnout are uniform among all regions and racial, religious, or ethnic group, these bases should produce roughly the same result. As we know, however, these factors are not always uniform. As a result, the choice of the base upon which to equalize districts can have a significant political effect, and overrepresent or underrepresent certain regions or groups in a national legislature.

The three most commonly used bases for redistricting and reallocation of seats are the number of persons (total population), the number of citizens (including young), or the number of electors (eligible voters or citizens of voting age [CVAP]).[2] In most cases the measures produce similar results, at least at the macro level and particularly if a nation's standard of equality are lax. Pockets exist, however, in which an abnormally large number of noncitizens cluster together. These are common in many countries, but often are insignificant to the overall tasks of redistricting or reallocation. In some nations, however, a base that does not include non-citizens can produce very different outcomes.

---

[1] Appendix A.

[2] It was difficult for me to find reliable data on whether a country uses population or electors for redistricting or reallocation because many countries simply have not engaged in these tasks recently or sources conflicted because they made assumptions without focusing specifically on the issue. As a result, Appendix B offers only a partial list of countries. Also, it should be noted that "citizen population" is a popular base in European Countries.

S. Bickerstaff, *Election Systems and Gerrymandering Worldwide*, Studies in Choice and Welfare, https://doi.org/10.1007/978-3-030-30837-7_5

Districts equal in census population are not necessarily equal in the number of citizens or eligible or actual voters. For example, the current 36 congressional districts in Texas are absolutely equal in persons (698,488, according to the 2010 census),[3] but vary widely in the number of eligible voters, registered voters, and actual voters in prior elections. The Texas Legislative Council reported that in the congressional districts enacted in 2011, one district (District 21) had 542,873 registered voters (requiring citizenship) while another (District 33) had only 261,615. The voter turnout figures for the two districts showed a similar disparity in the 2016 legislative election at 365,284 (District 21) compared to 130,923 (District 33).[4] This disparity is attributed to the make-up of the districts. District 21 is 64% Anglo; while District 33 is 66% Hispanic, with a much larger percentage of noncitizens and persons under 18 years of age.[5]

In some countries, such as Germany, Finland, and many other European countries, the base is "citizen population." Most of these countries also recognize citizenship as something that passes from one generation to another through "blood," not necessarily place of birth. This distinction has at least two effects. First, it removes the ability of some persons to claim citizenship as a birth-right even though born and residing in a country. Second, it means that persons can also claim citizenship and vote even though their family now and possibly for generations has resided outside the country. As a result, some countries have created "constituencies" for this "diaspora" with separate candidates and separate seats in the national legislature.[6] The issue of citizenship is discussed further later in this chapter.

Provinces and territories in at least two nations, Canada and Australia, diverge. Seats are allocated from the national level on the basis of population, but single-member districts in the provinces are drawn on the basis of electors. For the reasons set out below, some fear that states under Republican domination in the U.S. will begin using the number of electors as the basis for redistricting, especially if the census is changed to ask if a person is an American citizen.

The bases for redistricting or reallocating seats among fixed or multi-member districts are:

---

[3]Actually District 33 is one person short of this total at 698,487.

[4]www.tlc.state.tx.us/redist.html. Not all of this disparity is attributable to citizenship or age. Hispanics have a notoriously low rate of voter registration and turnout even among eligible voters.

[5]For example, although the two districts are equal in population, District 33 has only 469,456 in voting age population (VAP), compared to 553,018 in District 21. www.tx.leg. Another district had only 471,352 VAP. *Id.*

[6]*See, New Borders and Anomalies in the Balkans: Croatia's Diaspora Constituency* by Tihana Bartulac-Blanc, **National Endowment for Democracy** (2007) available at www.ned.org. Other nations with separate constituencies for the diaspora include Spain, Greece, Hungary, and several other European countries.

5.1 Using Population

The most popular base worldwide for drawing single-member districts and allocating seats is total population. At least 65 countries claim this base (see Appendix B), but my count is incomplete as I was unable to find the base for every nation.

For most nations, using total population requires that the nation have a recent, dependable census or registration of all inhabitants. Such a census or registration often is unavailable. As a result, some nations that by law are supposed to use total population have used some substitute for drawing electoral districts. For example, in 2009, the Federal Supreme Court in Iraq required the use of food ration cards as the best proxy available to show the population of its 18 governorates serving as multi-member electoral districts. The Court rejected the use of registered voter data because the nation's constitution required equality in persons, not voters. On the other hand Liberia in 2005 suspended the legal requirement of using total population data since the last census occurred in 1984 and was believed to be outdated. The national legislature combined voting precincts to establish electoral districts. In 2008, the country completed a census, and seats in the national legislature were reallocated and constituency boundaries redrawn at that time according to the new census.[7]

5.1.1 The U.S. Experience: Using Census Population

The U.S. is known for using total population as the basis for redistricting. The U.S. Constitution[8] explicitly requires that seats in the U.S. House of Representatives be apportioned among the states according to the number of "persons" within each state as determined by the decennial census.[9] Redistricting and gerrymandering in the U.S. assumes the availability of a reliable, unbiased census.[10]

[7]*See*, Delimiting Electoral Boundaries in Post-Conflict Settings by Lisa Handley at page 191 in **Redistricting in Comparative Perspective** by Lisa Handley & Bernard Grofman, eds., Oxford Univ. Press (2008).

[8]*Article 1, section 2 of the U.S. Constitution.*

[9]The Constitution does not specify, however, what basis should be used by states for drawing the congressional districts, or for drawing the electoral districts for the state legislatures or local governments. States might be able, like provinces and territories in Canada and Australia, to use the number of electors, or, as popularly known in the U.S., citizen voting age population (CVAP) or eligible voters.

[10]State and local governments in the U.S. have overwhelmingly used population as the basis in the past (with minor modifications [e.g. removing the population of prisons in a jurisdiction where its inmates cannot vote) largely because the census data is an enumeration (an actual count of people instead of an estimate) and is considered the most comprehensive, uniform, accurate, and objective information available.

The U.S. Census is conducted every 10 years. It is conducted for one date (April 1 of the last year of a decade [e.g. 2020]) and is intended as a count of every inhabitant of every place, however remote, in the nation on that date. The census not only counts persons, but obtains a wide variety of information about conditions and people. This information is collected, organized, and then released in a series of reports (now largely computer tapes or data dumps) over several years.

The first release of census data in the U.S. comes early in the year (e.g. 2011) following the census and relates demographic data, including race and voting age, for all geographic areas in the country and shows this data down to very small areas generally equivalent to a city block. This detail, combined with computer software designed specifically for redistricting, generally shows which electoral districts are overpopulated or underpopulated compared to the ideal under the new census and allows state legislatures, local government officials, redistricting commissions, and the general public to draw and proffer redistricting plans based on the new population data.[11]

5.2 The Arguments for and Against Using Population

Those in favor of requiring total population to be equalized among electoral districts emphasize that every inhabitant is entitled to equal representation and that non-citizens and the young have legitimate issues too. A favorite analogy is of two institutions, one an orphanage, the other a retirement center. Both seek government funding. Although, in the analogy, they are equal in population, all of the residents of the retirement center are electors, but none of the residents in the orphanage is old enough to qualify as a voter. Should only the retirement center have a right to representation in the contest for government funding? Similarly, areas inhabited primarily by non-citizens or the young have needs, such as health care and housing. Should these areas be entitled to equal representation in the national legislature?

Opponents of using total population as the basis for drawing districts point to several drawbacks. Census data may be inaccurate. In 2010 it was estimated that the U.S. census undercount was about 1.6%, with a higher percentage for certain minorities.[12] Census data also becomes obsolete. Districts drawn on the basis of a periodic census become malapportioned as the population changes or shifts during that period. It may be financially or practically infeasible to do a national census

[11]Therefore, redistricting in the United States generally occurs during the first year of each decade when the results of the decennial census are first released and show that the electoral districts are malapportioned. The U.S. courts have usually required use of data from the last census even later in a decade rather than permit districts to be redrawn based on population estimates or projections that the courts fear could be manipulated for political gain.

[12]*See,* www.census.gov/data

more often than once per decade; therefore, a reliable census may be unavailable later in a decade.[13]

5.3 The Argument for and Against Using Electors, Citizen Population, Eligible Voters, or Citizen Voting Age Population (CVAP)

The claim that electors, eligible voters, or citizen voting age population are more appropriate measures of equality among districts appears on first blush to be sound since only citizens and persons over a certain age are allowed to vote. Many of my colleagues, especially those teaching at universities outside the U.S., advocate this view. Their argument is that it is nonsensical to allow noncitizens and the very young to affect who are representatives in a democracy in which they are ineligible to vote.

Some of the same reasoning supports a base of "citizen population," which includes citizens too young to vote.

The use of eligible voters, citizen population, CVAP, or electors as a basis for redistricting is particularly widespread among European countries. An effect is that in some countries segments of society in a country not only may remain unable to vote but are underrepresented in the allocation of seats in the national legislature. For example, the United Kingdom uses the number of registered voters as its base, thereby leaving out a portion of its adult population. Also, Muslims, particularly from Turkey, have constituted a part of the population of Germany for most of the twentieth century, but many Muslim inhabitants have remained citizens of their country of origin and have declined or been unable to become German citizens.[14] They have a limited ability to affect the allocation of seats in Germany's complex PR election process or government policy.[15] A similar effect exists in several other European countries. Whether it affects election outcomes or governmental policy is beyond the scope of this book.

---

[13]France found a solution to the possibility that a census might show a need to redistrict —abolish the census.

[14]An estimate made in 2015 calculated that there are 4.4 to 4.7 million Muslims in Germany (5.4–5.7% of the population). About 1.7 million are German citizens.

[15]One of the issues of growing significance on which these Muslims might have a view is immigration. *See*, *The Many Sides of Muslim Integration: A German-American Comparison* by Ariane Chebel d'Appollonia, Lily Gardner Feldman, Mathias Rohe, Raida Chbib, Rauf Ceylan, Tara Bahrampour, **AICGS** (2010); *Immigration and Socio-Spatial Segregation—Opportunities and Risks of Ethnic Self-Organisation* by Rauf Ceylan, 46 **German Journal of Urban Studies** (2007).

5.4 Defining Citizenship

In a general sense, there are essentially three ways in which countries define citizenship—by blood (Jus sanguineous), by birth (jus soli), or by naturalization. Countries, however, vary greatly in their specifics about who or how a person can become a citizen. Many countries provide citizenship on preferential terms to individuals with ethnic ties to these countries (so-called lieges sanguinis).

The most common method of obtaining citizenship is by Jus Sanguinis (Latin: right of blood). It is a principle by which citizenship is not determined by place of birth or necessarily residence, but by having one or both parents who are citizens of the nation. Children at birth may automatically become citizens if their parents have citizenship, even if they are born abroad.

Many nations[16] have some form of birthright citizenship, or Jus Soli. In many cases, however, this right is limited by requiring that least one parent must be a citizen or long-term resident of the country. In a slightly different twist, Iran grants citizenship at birth to persons born in Iran of foreign parents if one or both of the parents were themselves born in Iran. The current U.S. President, Donald Trump, has questioned whether the U.S. should keep birthright citizenship because, in his view, the right is being abused by pregnant immigrants.

At a time of greater international mobility and number of refugees, the application of these citizenship principles has become mixed and less susceptible to clear distinction. For example, Germany, long an example of Jus Sanguineous, loosened its policy in 2000, replacing the parent's citizenship requirement with a requirement that children born to a parent who has had a German permanent resident permit for at least 3 years or has lived in Germany for at least 8 years can get German citizenship. On the other hand, the United Kingdom used to grant birthright citizenship, but with an increasingly international population coming to the country, the government removed unconditional citizenship by birth in the British Nationality Act of 1981. Children born in the UK today can get citizenship only if they have at least one parent who is a citizen, a "settled" resident of the country, or a resident of the British territories, or upon the tenth birthday of the child.

Naturalization is the legal act or process by which a non-citizen may acquire citizenship or nationality in a country. It is available in most countries. The specifics vary greatly, including issues such as marriage to a citizen, continuous residence in the country,[17] knowledge of the country and the government, and whether the country permits dual citizenship. Many nations also have a denaturalize process through which it deprives one of its citizens of citizenship.

---

[16]These include Antigua and Barbuda, Argentina, Barbados, Belize, Bolivia, Brazil, Canada, Chile, Cuba, Dominica, Ecuador, El Salvador, Fiji, Grenada, Guatemala, Guyana, Honduras, Jamaica, Mexico, Nicaragua, Panama, Paraguay, Peru, Saint Kitts and Nevis, Saint Lucia, Saint Vincent and the Grenadines, Trinidad and Tobago, United States, Uruguay, and Venezuela. Ireland was the last country in Europe to abolish unrestricted birthright citizenship.

[17]Some countries require lengthy residence. For example, most countries require at least 10 years of continuous residence.

Historically, there are many instances of mass naturalization by law, such as when Greece in 1922 naturalized all the Greek refugees returning from Turkey. A second massive naturalization process occurred when Armenian refugees from Turkey went to Syria, Lebanon or other former Ottoman countries. Reciprocally, Turkey massively naturalized the returning refugees of Turkish descent. In the United States citizenship was extended in mass to citizens of Puerto Rico, the United States Virgin Islands, Guam, and the Northern Mariana Islands. Native-Americans became citizens of the United States under the Indian Citizenship Act of 1924.

5.5 *Evenwel v. Abbott*: Population or Eligible Voters

In 2016 a unanimous United States Supreme Court in *Evenwel v. Abbott*, 578 U.S. ___ (April 4, 2016) upheld the right of Texas to draw its state senate districts using total population numbers from the census, but did not foreclose the use of "eligible voters" (i.e. CVAP) in the future.

Proponents of using population pointed to the history of the usage of total population for redistricting in the U.S. and the initial decision of the members of the Constitutional Convention in 1787 to use total population as the basis for apportioning seats in Congress. Writing for the Court in *Evenwel*, Justice Ginsburg explained:

> As the Framers of the Constitution and the Fourteenth Amendment comprehended, representatives serve all residents, not just those eligible or registered to vote. . . . . Nonvoters have an important stake in many policy debates—children, their parents, even their grandparents, for example, have a stake in a strong public-education system—and in receiving constituent services, such as help navigating public-benefits bureaucracies. By ensuring that each representative is subject to requests and suggestions from the same number of constituents, total population apportionment promotes equitable and effective representation.[18]

The Court's opinion allowed the Texas Legislature to use census population.[19] In *Evenwel* two justices (J.J. Alito and Thomas) concurred with the judgment in opinions indicating that jurisdictions could use total population for redistricting, but also expressly indicated that it was permissible to use eligible voters. The Court left this issue unresolved in an apparent effort to reach a unanimous decision on a short-handed Court.

---

[18]At page18 of the slip opinion.in Evenwel v Abbott.

[19]The Court opinion in *Evenwel* dealt only with state senate districts in one specific state (Texas), where the state's constitution did not expressly require redistricting on the basis of persons (a previous version of the provision as adopted in 1876 invited use of the number of "qualified electors" for drawing the state's senate districts). The Court in Evenwel did not address other instances where the applicable wording is different, such as language requiring the use of population. The opinion does not indicate that as a general matter equalizing eligible voters (i.e. CVAP) instead of persons is forbidden; nor does it approve such usage.

5.6 The Brewing Controversy in the United States Regarding Citizenship

The difference between redistricting on the basis of population or citizen voting age[20] is great in parts of the United States. Recent U.S. censuses have not enumerated the number and specific location of citizens. As a result, the use of "eligible voters" as a basis for drawing districts currently has been possible only by extrapolation of census data and is less precise and reliable than the census enumeration of persons. As a result, courts have rejected the use of "eligible voters" or CVAP on the few occasions when it has been proposed.

This may be changing. A current controversy in the U.S. is over whether the census should be changed in 2020 to ask if each person in a household is a citizen.[21] Several lawsuits are pending, but the issue has reached the Supreme Court and it is expected to rule by late June, 2019.

Critics of this change are concerned that it will cause an inaccurate census and a significant undercount of both noncitizen and citizen immigrants, such as noncitizen parents with citizen children in their household.[22] A recent court decision has questioned whether the citizenship data from the census would be reliable because, even if the question on citizenship is included in the census, privacy concerns would require that the data be reported only for large census areas. For purposes of this book, the primary concern is that the inquiry on citizenship is the precursor for redistricting on the basis of "eligible voters" (CVAP) or electors instead of population.

It is likely that this issue of which base will be used for redistricting will be vigorously litigated in many jurisdictions over the next decade, with the outcome varying according to the wording of applicable state laws or constitutions and the political offices at stake.[23]

---

[20]Since the U.S. has a right of citizenship based on birth, many non-citizen families have one or more citizen children. Thus a potential way of reducing the count of immigrants for redistricting purposes is to count only citizens over 18 years of age – thus the critics of using total population urge using "citizen voting age population" (CVAP) rather than "citizen population."

[21]*See, What to know about the citizenship question the Census Bureau is planning to ask in 2020* by D'Vera Cohn, **Pew Institute** (March 30 2018) @ www.pewresearch.org; *Census deadline looms for public to comment on adding citizenship question* by Deborah Barfield Berry, USA TODAY (Aug. 7, 2018) @ www.usatoday.com. If an inquiry on citizenship is added to the U.S. Census, the uncertainties of extrapolation disappear. The citizen number could become as reliable as the rest of the census. However, asking the "citizen" question in the census could reduce the number of census responses from Hispanic and Asian citizens and increase the undercount of language minorities that are citizens. Moreover, having an enumeration of citizens and non-citizens could undercut enforcement of the Voting Rights Act.

[22]These critics suggest that many Hispanic and Asian persons will avoid answering the census questionnaire altogether because they fear a possibility that the government in the future will use this citizenship data to find and deport them even if they currently have a legal right to remain in the U.S.

[23]This issue is of grave political importance in the U.S. because such a change in the base for redistricting would significantly reduce the number of districts with Democratic majorities, especially at the state and local levels (the U.S. Constitution's use of "persons" for apportioning seats in

The argument for using electors or CVAP in lieu of population has become politicized in the U.S. Many current electoral districts have significant and disproportionate percentages of Hispanic or Asian noncitizen inhabitants and citizens too young to vote. These heavily Hispanic or Asian districts have usually elected Democratic representatives to Congress, state legislatures and local governing boards.

Some Republicans are prepared to push for redistricting on the basis of CVAP numbers to reduce the number of such districts[24] and the number of Democrats elected to state legislatures, local governments, and Congress. Therefore, any decision by state or local governments to equalize citizen population or eligible voters among districts instead of population is seen by some Democrats as a partisan grab by Republicans for political power rather than a rational alternative basis for redistricting.

5.7 Increasing Importance for the Distinction Between Elector and Population

This distinction between total population and citizens, citizen population, electors, or eligible voters for redistricting and allocation of seats will take on increased importance in some countries, given the mass movement of refugees throughout the world. These immigrants are not citizens upon arrival; therefore they cannot vote and in many countries are not included in the basis for redistricting or allocating seats in the national legislature. Since these and other immigrants cluster together in their new nation, these areas can become underrepresented in the national legislature and in the nation's law-making.

5.8 Civil Registry

Several nations have effectively replaced or supplemented their census with a requirement that all residents or citizens must periodically register at a certain age or in order to vote.[25] Civil registration allows a national government to record the

Congress makes it difficult [but not impossible] to conclude that it is legally permissible for a state to use CVAP for drawing U.S. House of Representative districts).

[24]A shift of the base for redistricting from total population to electors or citizen voting age population would cause minority persons (i.e. non-citizen or underage) to be a majority of voters in fewer districts, reduce the number of districts with significant Hispanic and Asian inhabitants and voters, and probably reduce the number of Democrats elected to congressional, state legislative and local government offices.

[25]Among countries deriving the base to be used for the allocation of seats or redistricting from such registries are France, United Kingdom, Germany, Iceland, Namibia, South Africa, Romania, The Netherlands, Sweden, Mexico, Brazil, The Philippines, and Australia. Some countries use the registry to derive eligible voters; others use it to derive total population.

vital events, such as births, marriages, deaths, etc., of its residents. As an incentive some of these nations tie benefits, such as public health care, to this registration. Depending on its nature, registration can be used to support redistricting or reallocation on the basis of population, some sub-set of population, or electors. Usually, however, a national registry is used to provide a base of registered voters.

Using registrants as the base of equalization among electoral districts has the benefits of not requiring a census to know the number of persons or eligible voters and theoretically being updated periodically to allow redistricting more often than possible with a census.

It is acknowledged, however, that any list of registrants is likely to be unreliable. For example, the U.K. Electoral Commission estimated on December 1, 2015 that between 7.6 and 8.3 million eligible people were not correctly registered to vote at their current address across Great Britain.[26] Another source estimates that three million eligible voters are entirely left out of the current registration roll in the UK.[27] Also, registration is often disproportionately deficient in registering specific groups, such as minorities, the young, or urban dwellers, thus resulting in an underrepresentation of these groups in the national legislature.

In addition to requiring enrollment in the civil registry, Australia requires all eligible Australian citizens and British subjects living in Australia to enroll and to vote in federal elections, by-elections and referendums, but the modest fine ($180 Australian dollars maximum) and availability of exemptions mean that some eligible voters do not register or vote. Several other countries mandate that their citizens vote.[28]

The United States does not mandate registration or voting and is unlikely to ever use registered voters as a basis for redistricting.[29]

---

[26]*See, New registration system sees more accurate registers; but further action still needed to encourage electoral registration,* **The Electoral Commission of the United Kingdom** (14 Jul 2016); *Electoral statistics, UK: 2017,* **Office for National Statistics** (2017).

[27]*See,* **PUTTING VOTERS IN THEIR PLACE** by Ron Johnson & Charles Pattie, Oxford Univ. Press (2006).

[28]In at least eleven countries in the world have laws that require mandatory voting. These countries include: Argentina, Australia, Brazil, Democratic Republic of the Congo, Ecuador, Luxembourg, Nauru, North Korea, Peru, Singapore, and Uruguay.

[29]The problem of using registered voters to determine the number and location of electors is great in the United States, where it is very unlikely that redistricting on the basis of registered voters will ever be legally acceptable. The U.S. has no national civil registry of citizens or inhabitants. Registration occurs only as a requirement for voting, is voluntary, and is the responsibility of each individual state. States actually vary in their definition of who is eligible to register (e.g. several states have limitations on the voting rights of convicted felons). The registration process may vary by state or local government—in some jurisdictions it may occur on the day of the election. Moreover, the accuracy of registered voter lists may vary by state and by jurisdictions within a state because it often relies on the vagaries of local officials and may include dead or ineligible persons in some jurisdictions whose names have not yet been purged from the list, while excluding eligible persons who do not register or register late.

5.9 Voters in the Last Election

Several countries[30] have opted for measuring the equality of their electoral districts according to the number of persons who actually voted in the last election. Interestingly the Supreme Court of Croatia used this data to conclude that the PR multi-member districts in the country were malapportioned.[31] This basis is administratively simple, but is subject to many variables, such as turnout, and can easily lead to districts that are badly malapportioned based on population or eligible voters.

At least one nation, Uruguay, has recently discontinued allocating seats on the basis of a fixed district's vote in the recent general election. It now uses population.

Many nations not only allocate seats to fixed or special multi-member districts before an election, but have a formula for reallocating those seats after an election in PR systems or an election in the PR component of a mixed system. This formula is based on the actual vote for a party in a region, fixed district, or special multi-member district. This issue adds a possibility of unequal voting power for individual voters and is discussed further in Chap. 10.

5.10 Expediency

There are several examples in which new or strife ridden nations lacked a reliable census or count of electors to use for drawing electoral districts and used other data temporarily as a rough equivalent. For example, as discussed above, elections in Iraq after the U.S. invasion used food ration cards to identify voters.

5.11 Conclusion

It is wrong to assume that the choice of the base for redistricting is a form of gerrymandering. The decision is complicated and there are legitimate reasons for the choice of using citizens, citizen population, eligible voters, or electors instead of population other than to advantage or disadvantage political parties or elements of society. Nevertheless, use of any base other than a reliable enumeration of all persons has the potential effect of advantaging or disadvantaging certain groups and candidates by underrepresenting certain areas and persons. To this extent, it has many of the effects of gerrymandering.

---

[30] *See, e.g.*, Belarus.

[31] *See*, THE CONSTITUTIONAL COURT OF THE REPUBLIC OF CROATIA No. U-X-6472/2010 Zagreb (December 8, 2010). Further discussion of this case may be found in Chap. 14.

The question of whether to use population or another base for redistricting is largely unimportant today in most countries because these countries cannot get past the initial question of whether to redistrict or reallocate at all and because for most countries the differences of using one base or another would be small, at least on the national level. This question, however, is already important in some countries and will become more important worldwide as a political issue in the future as more and more persons immigrate and become non-citizen residents in their new country. The question is certain to generate disagreement in the United States.

Chapter 6
The Upper Chamber of a Bicameral National Legislature

Although this book deals primarily with unicameral national legislatures and the lower chamber of bicameral legislatures, it would be inappropriate to entirely ignore the upper chamber of bicameral legislatures.[1] At least 48 nations have bicameral national legislatures in which the members of the upper chamber are appointed, including those in which these members are "indirectly elected" by state, provincial, or other local legislative bodies.[2] Another 28 nations have bicameral national legislatures in which at least some in the upper chamber are directly elected.[3] At least 128 have unicameral national legislatures.[4] Appendix B provides a list of

[1]*See, Does Bicameralism Matter?* by Michael Cutrone and Nolan McCarty (Princeton Univ. 2006) later printed by Oxford University as part of **The Oxford Handbook of Political Economy** (2008).

[2]The nations with bicameral national legislatures in which the upper chamber is appointed or "indirectly elected" include: Afghanistan, Austria, Bahamas, Barbados, Belarus, Belize, Bermuda, Bhutan (Monarch appoints 11 members), Bosnia & Herzegovina, Botswana, Cambodia, Cameroon, Canada, The Democratic Republic of the Congo, Republic of the Congo (Brazzaville), Ethiopia, France, Gabon, Germany, Grenada, Indonesia, Ireland, Jamaica, Jordan (appointed by Monarch), Kazakhstan, Lesotho, Malaysia, Myanmar, Morocco (appointed by Monarch), Namibia, Nepal, Netherlands, Pakistan, Rwanda, Russian Federation, Saint Lucia, South Africa, Sudan, Swaziland (appointed by Monarch), Thailand (appointed ½ by lower chamber and ½ by government), Tajikistan, Trinidad and Tobago, Saint Lucia, Uzbekistan, United Kingdom (appointed mostly by Monarch), and Yemen.

[3]These nations include Australia (STV), Belgium (PR), Bolivia (PR), Brazil (3 elected by majority for each of 26 states and Federal District), Chile (PR), Colombia (PR), Czech Republic (TRS), Dominican Republic (FPTP), Haiti (3 elected by majority [TRS] in each of 10 administrative départements), India (STV), Indonesia (SNTV), Italy (P), Japan (P), Kazakhstan (FPTP, with 9 appointed), Liberia [2 elected in FPTP from each of 15 counties for 9 year terms], Mexico (P), Nigeria (FPTP), Palau (In MMDs, there are no political Parties), Paraguay (PR), Philippines (nationwide through majority at-large voting), Poland (FPTP), Romania (PR), Spain (FPTP), Switzerland (FPTP), United States (FPTP), Uruguay (PR nationwide), and Zimbabwe (PR, with addition of eighteen selected by the tribal chiefs and two people with disabilities).

[4]The nations with unicameral national legislatures include: Andorra, Anguilla, Albania, Algeria, Aruba, Azerbaijan, Armenia, Bangladesh, Benin, Botswana, Bulgaria, Burkina Faso, Cameroon,

S. Bickerstaff, *Election Systems and Gerrymandering Worldwide*, Studies in Choice and Welfare, https://doi.org/10.1007/978-3-030-30837-7_6

nations with bicameral and unicameral national legislatures. In most of the nations with bicameral legislatures, only the members of the "lower chamber" are directly elected.

This possibility of a "second house" of a national legislature not based on equal representation of persons or voters is recognized in the Code of Good Practice, which provides that the principle of equal voting power among constituencies "must at least apply to elections to lower houses of parliament."[5] There is, however, considerable variation among bicameral nations in how the members of the upper chamber are selected and how they are empowered.

6.1 Differences in How Members of an Upper Chamber Are Selected

Among nations with a bicameral national legislature, there are apparently three general methods for deciding how members of the upper chamber are selected—by the legislature or council of a local government or province, by some other designated authority (usually the head of state or lower chamber of the national legislature), or by direct election. Many nations combine these methods in selecting their upper chamber.

6.1.1 Appointment by a Local Government (Indirect Election)

The most common method, which appears often in combination with other methods, is appointment by a local government, region, or province.

Cape Verde, Central African Republic, Cook Islands, Costa Rica, Cote d'Ivoire, Cyprus (North), Cyprus, Croatia, Denmark, Djibouti, Dominica, El Salvador, Ecuador, Estonia, Egypt, Eritrea, Equatorial Guinea, Falkland Islands (Maldives), Finland, Fiji, Georgia, Guernsey, Ghana, Greenland, Gambia, Guinea, Guinea-Bissau, Greece, Guatemala, Guyana, Honduras, Hong Kong, Hungary, Iceland, Iran, Iraq, Israel, Jersey, Kenya, Kosovo, Republic of Korea, Kosovo, Kyrgyzstan, Laos, Latvia, Lebanon, Lithuania, Libya, Luxembourg, Macedonia, Macau, Mali, Malta, Malawi, Marshall Islands, Mauritius, Monaco, Mongolia, Montenegro, Monserrat, Micronesia, Republic of Moldova, Mozambique, Nauru, New Zealand, New Caledonia, Nicaragua, Niue, Norway, Papua New Guinea, Palestinian Territories, Panama, Peru, Portugal, San Marino, Saint Helena, St. Kitts and Nevis, St. Vincent and Grenadines, Samoa, Senegal, Serbia, Seychelles, Sierra Leone, Singapore, Slovakia, Slovenia, Sri Lanka, Suriname, Sweden, Taiwan, Tanzania, Togo, Tonga, Tunisia, Turkey, Uganda, Ukraine, Vanuatu, Venezuela, Virgin Islands (British), Virgin Islands (U.S. territory), Wallis and Fortuna, Zambia, and Zanzibar.

[5]Appendix B.

If the members of the upper chamber of a bicameral national legislature are selected by local legislatures or councils,[6] it is often said that they are "indirectly" elected and represent persons within those provinces, administrative units, regions, states, or even tribes in the nation's lawmaking. The nature of these local entities varies greatly based on the history of the country. For example, the Russian Federation has different "federal subjects", including 22 republics, 46 oblasts, nine krais, three federal cities, four autonomous okrugs, and one autonomous oblast, each of which sends two "senators" to the country's upper chamber. I treat those members as appointed because they are not directly elected by the voters and some, such as in Germany, serve at the will of the local government instead of for terms.

Many countries use this indirect election method for determining the members of the upper chamber, but the procedure varies widely. In the Netherlands, for example, the upper chamber (Eerste Kamer) has 75 members selected for a 4-year term by the provincial councils on the basis of proportional representation at the provincial elections. In Germany, the members of the upper house are selected by the state (Lander) legislatures, but have no term and can be replaced with a change in the state government. In France the upper chamber is chosen primarily by local councils. In Namibia the upper chamber is selected by local councils, but is only advisory. The upper chamber in the Russian Federation has 170 members consisting of two representatives for each of its 85 "federal subjects." One representative is selected by the local executive and one by the local legislative body.

6.1.2 Appointment by Nation's Executive or an Outside Authority

There remain at least 24 nations with constitutional monarchies bound to exercise their powers and authorities within the limits prescribed by an established legal framework.[7] The powers actually exercised by the monarch vary by country and are beyond the scope of this book.

In most of these countries, the constitutional monarch appoints at least some members of the upper house. For example, in Bhutan the monarch appoints five of the 25 members of the upper chamber, while in Swaziland (now the Kingdom of

[6]Initially the United States utilized such a scheme by which the legislature of each state was authorized to determine the manner of selecting the state's United States senators. Most state legislatures initially decided to make the selection themselves and generally choose among their own members. Gradually more and more states changed to a system under which the U.S. senators were directly elected by a state's voters. The United States Constitution was amended through the Seventh Amendment in 1911 to require direct election of U.S. senators in all states.

[7]These include Andorra, Bahrain, Belgium, Bhutan, Brunei, Cambodia (elective monarchy), Denmark, Japan, Jordan, Kingdom of Lesotho, Lichtenstein, Luxemburg, Kuwait, Malaysia (elective monarchy), Monaco, Morocco, Netherlands, Norway, Spain, Swaziland (now the Kingdom of Eswatini), Sweden, Thailand, Tonga, and the United Kingdom.

Eswatini) the monarch appoints 20 of the 30 members of the upper chamber and ten members to the lower chamber. Interestingly, the other ten members of the upper chamber in Swaziland are appointed by the lower chamber. In many countries the appointment by the monarch is largely ceremonial, with the country's Prime Minister deciding who to appoint. For example, although some members of the House of Lords in the United Kingdom are appointed by the monarch, it is on advice of the UK Prime Minister.

In addition, there are 16 countries that are independent, but are part of the British Commonwealth and still recognize the UK queen or king as their monarch.[8] The role of the UK monarch as head of the British Commonwealth is largely ceremonial. In these states, the UK monarch does not directly appoint the members of the upper chamber, but the country's Governor General, representing the UK monarch, may make the appointment. For example, members of Canada's Senate are appointed by the Governor General with the advice of the Prime Minister of Canada.

In some nations, the selection of members in an upper chamber is made by some other authority, such as the head of the national government itself.[9] In Myanmar the military appoints approximately 1/3 of the members of the upper chamber; with the remainder elected. The Myanmar military also appoints 1/3 of the members of the lower chamber. In Ireland the appointments are made by the president and the leader of the opposition party.

In a few countries the appointment of members of the upper chamber is left to the members of the lower chamber. In others, the appointment is made by a trade association or other citizen group. In some nations, the seats in the upper chamber are hereditary. The House of Lords in the United Kingdom is an example of a legislative body in which some members hold hereditary titles. Another example is the Kingdom of Lesotho in which the Senate (upper chamber) has 33 members—22 hereditary chiefs and 11 individuals appointed by the King on the advice of the Council of State.

It is common to see a mixed method of selection in an upper chamber, such as combining appointment of some members by the president or monarch and some elected.

[8]These include Antigua and Barbuda, Australia, Bahamas, Barbados, Belize, Canada, Grenada, Jamaica, New Zealand, Papa New Guinea, Saint Kitts and Nevis, Saint Lucia, Saint Vincent and the Grenadines, Solomon Islands, Sudan, and Tuvalu.

[9]These include Belarus, Rwanda, and Ireland.

6.1.3 Election

In some nations, the members of the upper chamber are directly elected by the voters of a state or province.[10] In others the seats in the upper chamber are filled by a national election, such as in Uruguay.

A common characteristic in many bicameral national legislatures is that each state or province is guaranteed one or more seats in the upper chamber regardless of its population or number of voters.[11]

The United States Supreme Court has acknowledged the legitimacy of the requirement of two U.S. senators for each state, but it has specifically banned the states themselves from using this "Senate Model" to create a chamber of any state legislature based on anything but equal representation of voters. The Court described the U.S. Constitution's "Senate Rule" as a unique and necessary compromise that made the union possible—for reasons that were not applicable to a state's recognition of counties or parishes.[12]

The Court distinguished between the status of the states as separate sovereigns at the time the Constitution was ratified, and the status of counties and parishes as entities created by a state, and therefore subject to change. In theory, the Court's reasoning would also apply in nations that have allowed unequal electoral systems recognizing administrative units, states, or provinces that the national legislature creates and can change. However, most of these nations also have a historical justification for this inequality.

Nations vary greatly in their election methods for the upper chamber. Some countries elect nationwide using PR voting, such as Columbia, Uruguay, and Paraguay. Others, such as Poland *and Switzerland, use the FPTP plurality method from single-member constituencies. Bolivia has* four senators elected by a closed PR system for each of its nine administrative départements; Brazil elects three for each of 26 states. The list of differences goes on and on.

---

[10]Nations electing members of the upper chamber from fixed districts include Argentina (Blk Vote), Australia (STV), Bolivia (PR), Brazil (Blk Vote), Cambodia (PR), Philippines (Blk Vote), and the United States (FPTP).

[11]The U.S. Senate is an example. In the U.S. Senate, each of the 50 states has two senators, even though the states vary widely in the number of persons or voters. Wyoming is the least populated, with the state having only 563,626 inhabitants according to the 2010 census. California is the most populated state, with 37,254,956 inhabitants according to that census. Each state elects two senators and has the same number of votes in the U.S. Senate. In other words, there is no pretense of each person or voter within the states being equally represented in the U.S. Senate. In the United States, this is called the "Senate Model." It was part of the political compromise between large and small states that made it possible to adopt a U.S. Constitution and to form a union in 1789.

[12]See, *Lucas v. Forty-Fourth General Assembly of Colorado, 377 U.S. 733 (1964); Reynold v. Sims*, 377 U.S. 533, 562 (1964).

6.2 Differences in How Upper Houses Are Empowered

In most of these bicameral national legislatures, the upper house has only limited law-making powers compared to the popularly-elected lower house. For example, there are two chambers in the Parliament of the United Kingdom. The members of the "House of Commons" are directly elected from districts (constituencies), while the members of the upper "House of Lords" hold their titles by hereditary right or appointment, but have only limited law-making authority. In Namibia the upper chamber is only advisory. The Netherlands' upper chamber can only accept or reject legislation, not amend it.

In a few nations, however, the upper chamber has law-making powers that are comparable to those of the lower chamber, even though the members of the upper chamber are appointed or elected from electoral districts with unequal numbers of persons or voters. The U.S. Senate (elected) and the French Senat (appointed) are examples. Italy's upper chamber has law-making powers comparable to the country's lower chamber and is elected from constituencies ostensibly roughly equal in population.

6.3 Conclusion

The method of choosing members of the upper chamber of a bicameral national legislature and the law-making authority of such chambers deserve more attention than is given in this book. Nevertheless, certain observations can be made.

First, these upper chambers are difficult to categorize as elected or non-elected because many are composed partially of members chosen by election and partially of members who are appointed, particularly by local legislatures or councils or by the head-of-state.

Second, there is no expectation that members of the upper chamber will be selected on a basis of equality among members of the public. In general, these upper chambers appear oriented toward assuring that each of a nation's states, provinces, or administrative units is represented in the national legislature or giving the government an opportunity to control one chamber of that nation's legislature. An effect of representing the local states, councils, or administrative units regardless of population is to bias these upper chambers toward rural interests. There are exceptions, such as those nations that elect members of the upper chamber nationwide. There are exceptions, such as those nations that elect members of the upper chamber nationwide.

Third, the law-making powers of the upper chamber vary greatly among the nations that are bicameral; from being purely advisory to having authority comparable to the usually directly elected lower chamber.

Fourth, the U.S. model of an equal number of senators directly elected from each state regardless of the state's population has been a model that many nations have followed, but with one big difference. In most of these countries, the upper chamber's powers are limited in comparison to the lower chamber. The US model gives the Senate powers that are comparable to the House and thus puts disproportionate power in the hands of voters in smaller, often less populous states.

Fifth, there are electoral districts in some countries that are susceptible to gerrymandering, but these are rare and of little legal consequence given the policy that the upper chamber is not expected to meet voter equality and the large number of nations that rely on appointments to fill seats in the upper chamber.

Chapter 7
Proportional Representation and Electing Nationwide

A handful of democracies conduct only nationwide elections for the unicameral or lower chamber of its national legislature. These include Kazakhstan (PR, some appointed), Kosovo (PR), Kyrgyzstan (PR), Moldova (PR), Monaco (FPTP and PR), the Netherlands (PR), Fiji (PR), Serbia (PR), Slovakia (PR), Namibia (PR), and Israel (PR). Sources differ on whether Rwanda elects a majority of its unicameral national legislature through a PR system or is operating under a post-conflict agreement that divides the seats between Hutus and Tutsis. This list does not include those few countries or territories whose existence is disputed and are not in the United Nations, such as Taiwan, Western Sahara, South Ossetia, Northern Cyprus or Abkhazia.

It would seem natural for small countries to utilize only national elections instead of dividing the country into even smaller electoral districts, but a country's size is only one factor. Many of the smallest countries in the world, such as Luxembourg, Nauru, Liechtenstein, and Lesotho, utilize electoral districts, while, as discussed below, at least two much larger nations, Italy and the Russian Federation, experimented with using a purely nationwide PR system before changing to a mixed system with both FPTP and PR elections.

7.1 Countries Currently Using Only Nationwide PR Elections to Elect National Legislature

The Netherlands is a constitutional monarchy. The national legislature (Staten-General) is bicameral.[1] The lower chamber (Tweede Kamer) has 150 members, directly elected nationwide for a 4-year term. The proportional representation

[1]The upper chamber (Eerste Kamer) of the Netherland national legislature has 75 members chosen (appointed) for a 4-year term by councilors in each of the twelve provinces based on proportional representation in the provincial elections.

S. Bickerstaff, *Election Systems and Gerrymandering Worldwide*, Studies in Choice and Welfare, https://doi.org/10.1007/978-3-030-30837-7_7

threshold is 1/150th of the nationwide vote (one seat), with the residual seats assigned to a party using the highest averages method.

Moldova has a 101-member unicameral parliament that is elected for a 4-year term through proportional representation in a single nationwide constituency. One third of the registered voters must participate in an election for it to be valid. Political parties need to receive 6% of the valid votes to participate in the allocation of seats in the parliament. Out-of-country voters have an opportunity to vote without prior registration. To estimate their number and potential polling station locations, the government created a website for voters to declare their residency abroad.

Slovakia has a unicameral national legislature (Narodná rada Slovenskej Republiky) consisting of 150 members directly elected nationwide for 4-year terms. Serbia has a unicameral national legislature (Narodna skupština Republike Srbije) with 250 members elected nationwide for 4-year terms. Both Slovakia and Serbia have a threshold of 5% of the national vote.

Kazakhstan is bicameral, with the lower chamber (Mazhilis) having 107 seats, with >80% of the seats controlled by one party. The members are elected for 5-year terms. Most (98) are directly elected nationwide, but nine are chosen by the Assembly of Kazakhstani Nation, which is a presidentially appointed advisory body designed to represent the country's ethnic minorities. The threshold for party representation is 7% of the national vote. Kyrgyzstan is unicameral and also has a 7% threshold for a party's membership in its 120 member national legislature, but actually has a "Double Threshold" because it limits parties to a maximum of 65 seats.

Namibia is bicameral.[2] The law-making power rests with the lower chamber, the National Assembly. The National Assembly has 102 members of which 96 are elected by direct popular vote nationwide for a 5-year term, and a maximum of 6 non-voting members are appointed by the president. A single party (SWAPO) has dominated elections since 1989.

Israel has a unicameral national legislature (the Knesset) consisting of 120 members elected nationwide for 4-year terms based on a closed party list, with a threshold of 3.25% (up from 1%) of the national vote.

Monaco is a constitutional monarchy. The Conseil National has 24 members, elected nationwide for a 5-year term. It is unique in having a mixed nationwide system. Sixteen of the members of the national legislature are elected by a winner-take-all plurality system and the other eight by proportional representation. Each voter may cast a ballot with up to 16 candidates' names. If two or more majoritarian candidates tie, the older candidate prevails.[3]

Fiji also presents an unusual case. In 2014 for the first time Fiji elected members of its lower chamber of a bicameral legislature through nationwide open list PR

[2]The upper chamber consists of 26 representatives (2 selected [appointed] by each of 13 regional councils).

[3]By contrast, if two or more candidates tie in an Italian FPTP constituency election the youngest candidate wins.

elections. In the past, the nation's system underwent many changes as a result of at least four coups. The nation has been torn by racial division and strife. In an effort to quell this conflict, its parliament at one time was elected according to race-based communal constituencies, with members elected using multiple voter rolls and multiple ballots to choose 25 members by universal suffrage (the voter and candidate could belong to any race or ethnicity); 23 by indigenous Fijians; 19 by Indo-Fijians; 3 by other "minority" groups; and one by Rotuman Islanders. The current nation-wide PR election system (but including a separate seat for the island of Rotuman) used in 2014 was intended to treat all eligible voters alike as "Fijians." The national threshold for representation under the new system is 5%. The Fiji Senate was abolished in 2013.[4]

Several nations have PR elections at the Fixed or special Multi-Member district level (see Chap. 8), but also have "adjustment" or "leveling" seats based on the party's performance nationwide. These seats are awarded based on the difference between a party's number of seats won in the multi-member districts and the number of seats that the party would have won in a proportional contest held in a single, nationwide constituency. These "adjustment" or "leveling" seats are intended as a compensatory measure to ensure proportional representation of parties at the national level.

Since all of these nations use at least some PR elections, this is an opportunity to discuss the advantages and disadvantages of proportional representation (PR) elections.

7.2 The Advantages and Disadvantages of Proportional Representation

Most of these countries use a wholly proportional representation (PR) system.[5] The system theoretically is very straightforward. An election is held to elect members of the national legislature. The vote is for a party not for an individual.[6] Each party theoretically then is allocated the same proportion of seats in the national legislature

[4]For a discussion of the election system history and changes in Fiji *see, A New Electoral System for Fiji in 2014: Options for Legitimate Representation* by Norm Miller, **Pacific Islands Brief** (No. 3, 2013, Pacific Islands Development Program); *Top 10 things you need to know about Fiji's new electoral system* by Thomas Carnegie, **Pacific Scoop** (August 31, 2014).

[5]For a discussion of proportional representation systems in general *see APPORTIONMENT METHODS AND THEIR APPLICATIONS by Friedrich Pukelsheim, (Springer International Publishing 2014); PROPORTIONAL REPRESENTATION (Second Edition 2018); Seat biases of apportionment methods for proportional representation* by Karsten Schuster, Friedrich Pukelsheim, Mathias Drton, and Norman Draper, 4 **Electoral Studies** 22 (2003); and *How Proportional Representation Elections Work*, **FairVote** @ www.FairVote.com

[6]Some courts have found PR systems or the PR component of a mixed system unconstitutional on the basis that a vote for a party is not a "direct" election. *See,* Chap. 14.

as it receives of the total valid votes in the national election. There are different formulas for how the allocation is made,[7] but the most common is some form of the d'Hondt method.[8]

However, as so often occurs in electoral matters, there are other factors that affect the result. The law of most of these nations establishes a "threshold" of the national vote (up to 10%) that a party must receive of the vote in the national election to be entitled to a seat in the national legislature.[9] The votes attributable to the parties that do not reach the applicable threshold are usually spread as a residual among the parties that meet the threshold and these parties receive additional seats. One result of a threshold in an election is that a proportion of the electorate may cast their votes for parties which are not represented in Parliament. The higher the threshold; the more of the electorate are left in this position. In a recent election in Turkey (with a 10% threshold) reportedly 45% of votes were "wasted" in this fashion. A high threshold defeats the purpose of proportional representation. In some nations the law allows political parties to form coalitions to increase their chances of meeting this threshold;[10] in others not. Some with nationwide PR systems are closed list; some are open list.

Many political scientists praise the PR system as being "fairer" than a majoritarian/plurality system, such as FPTP single-member districts, because it tends to encourage the creation of multiple small parties, which then leads to the inclusion in the national legislature of all significant groups with different ideologies and agenda. A PR system is seen as leading to greater voter participation, better access

[7]There are several variables that affect how votes are allocated for parliamentary seats in a PR system. The two main formulas are the greatest remainder method and the highest averages method, although each type includes several variations in how the conversion takes place. The most common is the highest averages formula that divides the number of votes gathered by a party list in the electoral area (the nation for these countries or in a given district for most countries). The calculation is performed by means of a series of divisors. Variations in this method concern the divisors, for example, the simple 1, 2, 3, 4, etc. progression (d'Hondt formula); the odd-number 1, 3, 5, 7, etc. series (Saint-Lague formula); or its variant 1, 4, 3, 5, 7, etc. series (modified Saint-Lague formula). In each case, the mathematical operation results in an average, a quotient, with seats for party lists distributed successively according to the highest quotient, until all seats are filled.

[8]The d'Hondt method of allocating seats among parties in a PR system is named after Netherland's political scientist, Victor d'Hondt. It uses whole numbers and is generally considered fair. Some critics believe it slightly favors large parties and coalitions over scattered small parties. Most nations with PR elections use this method of allocation, or some variation, at a national or regional level. These nations include Albania, Angola, Argentina, Armenia, Aruba, Austria, Belgium, Bolivia, Brazil, Bulgaria, Burundi, Cambodia, Cape Verde, Chile, Colombia, Croatia, the Czech Republic, Denmark, the Dominican Republic, East Timor, Ecuador, El Salvador, Estonia, Fiji, Finland, Guatemala, Hungary, Iceland, Israel, Japan, Kosovo, Kazakhstan, Kyrgyzstan, Macedonia, Moldova, Monaco, Montenegro, Mozambique, Netherlands, Nicaragua, Northern Ireland, Paraguay, Peru, Poland, Portugal, Romania, San Marino, Serbia, Slovenia, Slovakia, Spain, Switzerland, Turkey, Uruguay, and Venezuela.

[9]There are several nations with PR voting that have no threshold or a threshold that is equivalent to one seat. An example is the Netherlands.

[10]Usually the threshold is raised for party coalitions.

for minorities and women, and avoidance of "regional fiefdoms" created by the dominance of a single party in a district.

After a PR election the national legislature may be composed of members from many parties without any party having a ruling majority—thus resulting in the need to form coalition governments consisting of two or more parties. Critics of the PR election system urge that the creation of multiple small parties usually causes a fragmented party system, extremist parties, internal disputes, and coalition governments that are unstable.

Much has been written about the relative benefits of both PR and plurality/majority electoral systems. I cannot hope to resolve this dispute in this book by advocating for or against either system. Either can generate gerrymanders. These countries with nationwide PR elections are instructive, however, on some of the issues that arise under PR election systems.

7.3 Variations in a PR Election System

7.3.1 Winner Bonus

In an apparent effort to address the issue of instability for a coalition government in a PR election system, several nations modified the system. In Europe, at least four nations (Italy, San Marino, Armenia, and Greece) adopted a "Majority Bonus" that awarded extra seats in the national legislature to the party that won the most votes in a legislative election to assure that the party would have a majority of seats.[11]

This modification of PR voting actually has a long history—first used in Italy by Benito Mussolini in 1924. It reemerged at the national level in Italy in 2006. The Constitutional Court of Italy struck down the bonus in 2013 as violating the Italian Constitution because it was an open-ended entitlement to the party with the most votes regardless of the percentage the party received of the total vote.[12] It reappeared in the latest Italian election system, but with the requirement that to be eligible for the majority bonus, a party had to lead the voting and have at least 40% of the seats in the national legislature.

It appears that Greece, Armenia, and San Marino still use the modification. In Greece, a fixed 1/6th of the seats in the national legislature are reserved as additional seats for the party that wins the most seats in the election. Greeks sometimes call their system "reinforced proportionality." In San Marino, the winning party receives however many additional seats are necessary to give it a 35 seat majority in the

[11]*See, Electoral systems with a Majority Bonus as Unconventional Mixed* Systems by Camille Bedock and Nicolas Sauger, *Project: Electoral systems and their consequences (2014) @ www.researchgate.net*

[12]Judgment No. 17, Italian Constitutional Court (2017). *See, The Italian Constitutional Court Rules on Electoral System* by Giacomo Delledonne and Giovanni Boggero in **the Int'l J. Const. L. Blog** (Feb. 8, 2017) @http://www.iconnectblog.com. *See also*, Chap. 14.

nation's 60 member unicameral national legislature. In Armenia, the size of the national legislature can vary. If no party wins a majority of seats in a general legislative election or no coalition government is formed within a few days after that election, a second round of voting is held matching the two parties with the highest number of seats. The seats won by other parties remain unchanged. The party that wins the second round of voting gets 54% of the total seats in the national legislature, with seats added to the national legislature until this percentage is reached.

At least one nation, Kyrgyzstan, actually limits the size of the majority to a maximum of 65 seats in its 120 seat unicameral national legislature.

7.3.2 Double Simultaneous Vote

Some nations in Latin America, including Argentina,[13] Uruguay, and Honduras,[14] have used a different modification of the PR system. It is called the "double simultaneous vote" system, best known in Latin America as "Ley de Lemas." The mechanism fuses national legislative elections with other elections, such as presidential elections. The parties are "Lemas." Each Lema may have multiple "Sublemas," containing a list of candidates for various offices. Different Sublemas within the same Lema may have different candidates for the same office. Each voter has a single ballot.

The winning party is the one which receives the most votes after the votes won by each of its Sublemas have been added together. Within a Lema (i.e. party), the winning Sublema is the one which, individually, won the most votes. Once the number of votes received by each Lema and Sublema is counted, seats are allocated to each proportionally, typically using a system such as the d'Hondt method.

This complex system is designed to allow persons to support a party, while also increasing the voter's choice of candidates and avoiding a party's selection of candidates in secret.

7.3.3 Block Voting

Several nations use a block voting system in which seats are allocated to the nation's fixed districts or special multi-member districts as in a PR system. Parties put forth a list of candidates in each district to fill all of the seats allocated to the district. The party that wins the most votes in a district fills <u>all</u> of the district's seats.

---

[13]Only some of Argentina's states continue to use the double simultaneous vote system. It is possible that by the time this book is published no Argentinian state will use the system any longer.

[14]Honduras now uses an open list PR system in 18 multi-member constituencies based on the départements ranging in size from 1 to 23 seats.

7.3.4 Choosing a Party's Candidate: Open and Closed Lists

A common issue among all countries using a proportional representation system is the manner of choosing who among a party's candidates is seated in the national legislature. In all nations using a PR election system, each political party prepares a pre-election list ranking at least some candidates in the order in which they will be chosen based on the number of representatives to which the party is entitled according to the party's showing in the nationwide election. This list gives the party officials considerable control over who will represent the party in the national legislature.

A PR system deemphasizes the importance of the individual candidate or office-holder while emphasizing the roles of the party and party leaders, thus prioritizing the goals of a party, but entrenching power within a sometimes obscure cabal of party loyalists, and making it more difficult for voters to hold any specific person accountable. In a twist, the parties in Guyana publish their list of candidates ordered alphabetically. This allows party leaders even more scope to reward party loyalty because seats are only allocated to individuals once the result of the vote is known.

The pressure is great to modify the PR system in a country to allow some opportunity for regional representation and accountability. In response, several of the countries using a PR system allow an exception to the party list in an apparent effort to attract voters. This exception allows voters to express a "preference" for an individual candidate on a party list. Systems allowing a voter's preference for a candidate on a party list are sometimes called "open lists", but the specific rules vary among nations.

For example, among the nations that rely exclusively on PR national elections, the Netherlands allows a party to use different lists in different electoral areas and a person to vote for a party and for a preferred representative from the party list. Theoretically a candidate who receives at least 25% of the electoral quota nationwide is deemed elected regardless of his or her place on the list. However, the effect of this exception has been limited because often the lists are the same in all of the areas or vary only near the bottom among candidates who are celebrities or known locally and are likely to attract voters to a party but are unlikely to serve. In Slovakia, there is a single nationwide list for each party, but also the ability for a voter to indicate a preference for a candidate on the list and an allowance for a candidate who receives a preferential vote equivalent to at least 10% of the party's vote to move up the party list.

In most of the nations with PR election systems that use open party lists,[15] the vote for a candidate as well as a party is optional and, because most voters mark their ballots for parties only rather than candidates, the candidate-choice option often has limited effect. Sweden is an exception. Over 25% of the Swedish voters regularly

[15]Among the countries using some variation of PR with an open list as part of their election structure are Austria, Belgium, Bosnia and Herzegovina, Chile, Columbia, Croatia, Cyprus, Czech Republic, Denmark, Estonia, Ecuador, El Salvador, Finland, Greece, Honduras, Indonesia, Iraq, Iceland, Latvia, Lebanon, Liechtenstein, Luxembourg, Japan, Norway, Poland, San Moreno, Serbia, Slovakia, Slovenia, Spain, Sweden, and Switzerland.

choose a candidate as well as a party, and a number of individuals are elected who would not be if the list were closed.

A "closed list" requires a voter to vote for only the party and does not allow a voter to express a preference for someone on the list.

One effect of such a system is that it gives party leaders an advantage in winning seats in the national legislature.

Israel uses a purely closed list and provides an example of how the manner for selecting candidates on a party's list varies. In some parties, the party leadership determines the list. For example, the candidates of the *Yesh Atid, Shas and Yisrael Beyten*u parties are created in accordance with the desires of the respective leaders of those parties. In some parties, the list is determined by a small group of party elite, such as an "appointment committee" or "nomination committee" while in other parties the party list is established through a party congress or a council, with delegates chosen by the party members. Since 1992 several parties in Israel have adopted party primaries as a means of determining the names and ranking of candidates on the party's list. In 2016 elections, three parties, the *Habayit Hayehudi,* the *Likud,* and *the Labor Party*, used primaries.

Several nations use a closed list PR system.[16] It should be noted, however, that many of these countries use the closed PR system for election to the national legislature from within local fixed or multi-member districts; not nationwide. Thus they retain a geographical element and, presumably, greater accountability in their election structure. In Italy, however, party leaders are allowed to appear on up to ten regional lists, thus almost assuring their election to the national legislature.

In Kosovo, a switch from closed to open lists actually enhanced the presence of more extremist candidates. There are instances in which the use of an open list proved advantageous or disadvantageous for the representation of women.

7.3.5 PR Systems that Require Voting for Individual Candidates

By contrast, Brazil and Finland use PR list systems, but voters must vote for the individual candidates rather than a party: the number of seats received by each party within a jurisdiction is determined by the total number of votes gained by its candidates. The order in which the party's candidates are elected to these seats is determined by the number of individual votes they receive.

While this gives voters much greater freedom over their choice of candidate, it also has some less desirable side effects. Since candidates from within the same party are effectively competing with each other for votes, this form of open list can lead to

[16]Among the nations using a PR or mixed system with a closed list are Albania, Angola, Andorra, Guatemala, Hong Kong, Iceland, Israel, Italy, Macedonia, Montenegro, Portugal, Serbia, South Africa, Spain, Sri Lanka, Turkey, and Uruguay.

internal party conflict and fragmentation. It also means that the attempt of a party to feature a diverse slate of candidates can be ineffective because voters can skip the minority or female candidates and vote only for majority males instead.

7.3.6 Thresholds

The threshold for receiving a seat in the national legislature is important to parties striving to reach the threshold and the larger parties that stand to receive the additional seats if any party fails to meet the threshold. A high threshold (e.g., Turkey [10%], Kazakhstan [7%] and Russian Federation [7% in 2011, but 5% today]) helps the larger parties by increasing the percentage of additional seats that they obtain after the election. This threshold can operate as a barrier to some parties, especially those with primarily a regional base of support. An example is how the high 10% threshold in Turkey functioned for years to keep the pro-Kurdish parties from winning seats in that country's national legislature.[17] When parties are allowed to form coalitions, the threshold is generally higher.

7.4 The Effect of Population Centers

Another characteristic of electing by PR election from a nation as a whole or even a large multi-member district is that it allows population centers, if their inhabitants vote overwhelmingly for parties that have a greater local presence, to disproportionately influence an election outcome and increase the chance that candidates from those areas will defeat rural candidates in races for the national legislature. This effect in turn means that a party may achieve representation by focusing primarily on candidates from and turn-out in these urban areas and may find it unnecessary to try to compete nationwide. The 2011 election in the Russian Federation provides an example.

The experience of Italy and the Russian Federation illustrate some of these aspects of a national PR system.

7.5 Italy

Italy is known for unstable coalition governments. The nation has changed its election system at least five times since WW II. In 2005 the Italian Parliament adopted a nationwide closed PR electoral system, with potentially different lists in

[17]See Appendix C, A Case Study of Turkey.

26 districts. The law also provided for an "unlimited majority bonus" of seats in the national legislature for the party that had won the most seats in the PR election, thus assuring a majority for that party in Parliament. This system was intended to benefit the ruling Democratic Party and to produce a stable national government to tackle the difficult problems, especially economic, confronting the nation, but was unpopular because it caused long party lists with no avenue for voters to show a preference for individuals.[18]

Efforts in Parliament to change the system failed. On December 4, 2013, the Italian Constitutional Court found the election system unconstitutional because, in part, it provided an unlimited majority bonus. The Court also struck down the "closed" nature of the PR election, explaining:

> [B]y not allowing the elector to express any preference for candidates, but only to choose a party list (the election was indirect). . . . [T]he Constitution presupposes the existence of a mandate given directly by the voters. . . . [B]y subtracting from the elector the right to choose the elected one, they would ensure that the vote is neither free nor personal.
>
> . . . .
>
> Ultimately, it is the fact that, without exception, no Member of Parliament elected is supported by the individual votes cast by voters which violates the requirement of representativity enshrined in the Constitution. Due to these voting conditions which require voters to select a list and thereby choose en masse also the numerous candidates included in the list, whom they have not had the opportunity to know and assess and who, by virtue of their position in the list, are automatically destined to become Members of the Chamber of Deputies or Senators, the legislation under examination is not comparable either with other systems in which there are closed lists only for some seats, or with those comprised of geographically smaller electoral constituencies in which the number of candidates to be elected is sufficiently low that it is effectively possible to know them and correspondingly that the efficacy of the choice and freedom in voting are guaranteed (as occurs in single-member constituencies).[19]

Although relying on specific wording in the Italian Constitution for its ruling, the court opinion can be also seen as general criticism of an electoral system that does not allow some means of voting for individuals or at least for voters to express a preference among names on a party list. To the Italian Constitutional Court, this was especially a problem in large jurisdictions like Italy.

After several false starts (a TRS was proposed, but was struck down by the Court in 2017) the Italian Parliament in 2017 adopted a new mixed parallel (P) electoral system for both chambers that had both FPTP (36.8%) and PR (61.2%) components.[20]

---

[18]*See, Tricks and Treats: The 2005 Italian Electoral Law and Its Consequences by* Gianfranco Pasquino, 12 **South European Society and Politics** 79–93 (2009).

[19]The Italian Constitutional Court, (No. 1 of 2014) @ www.cortecostituzionale.it. Many constitutional or supreme courts provide English versions of some of their opinions. This is true of the Italian Constitutional Court.

[20]*See, The Italian Constitutional Court judgement on the 'Italicum' electoral law: another new reform for Italy?* by Roberta Damiani, **The Constitution Unit [UCL]** (July 2018).

The PR component for the upper chamber is based on PR in the regions. The PR component for the lower chamber is based on a party or coalition of parties meeting a national threshold, but seats are distributed among 63 regional districts, each with 3–9 seats, and 2 single member districts.[21]

The "majority bonus" survives in the lower chamber, but only for a winning party with at least 40% of the PR vote. This party is guaranteed 340 seats in the lower chamber. The party lists in the lower chamber are "blocked" at the top to guarantee a seat for party leaders, who can choose to be on as many as ten regional lists. Voters are entitled to one preference in the upper chamber and two (one male and one female) in the lower chamber. Italians abroad elect six members of the upper chamber and 12 members of the lower chamber, which is about 2% of each chamber. The first election under the new system occurred in March, 2018.

7.6 Russian Federation

The national legislature (Federalnoe Sobranie) of the Russian Federation is bicameral. The lower chamber (State Duma [Gosudarstvennaja Duma]) has 450 members elected for 5 year terms (previously 4 year terms). The upper chamber is discussed in Chap. 6.

The country experimented with electing its lower chamber nationwide. In 2008, the country did away with single-member district elections and adopted a nationwide PR system in which all 450 members of the lower chamber of the national legislature were elected using nationwide elections and closed party lists. The threshold was set at 7% of the national vote and the ability of parties to form coalitions was restricted. These changes were adopted ostensibly for the purpose of strengthening Russia's political parties and party system by reducing the number of competing parties. However, critics claimed that the main objective was to eliminate regionally based parties and to increase the dominance of one party nationwide, *United Russia.*[22]

The change did not go smoothly. The regional governors were reluctant to embrace the change because they feared becoming too dependent on *United Russia* and preferred to create their own alliances for the purpose of retaining control over regional assemblies. More importantly, the only parliamentary general election under the new system (2011) went poorly for *United Russia,* which won the election, but with only 49.32% of the vote (down from 64.30% in 2007), taking 238 seats or 52.88% (down from 70%) of the Duma seats.

The outcome in 2011 demonstrated that more than one party could win substantial representation in the national legislature under a nationwide PR election system

[21]These single-member districts are in Valle d' Acosta and Tretino-Alto Ariga.

[22]*See, Putin and the Russian Electoral System; Reforms to Prevent Regime Change by Darrell Slider and Paul Rodrick Gregory,* **Soviet and Post-Soviet Review** *(2012)* reprinted as *Putin Changes September Election Rules To Prop Up His 'United Russia' Party by Patrick Roderick Gregory,* **Forbes** *(Mar 14, 2016; The Electoral System of the Russian Federation,* by Bill Bowring, **The European Parliament** *(2011)* available at www.europarl.europa.eu

by focusing on campaigning primarily in the major cities. This election showed that such a system created the possibility of a second major party to challenge *United Russia*. This was especially true when the party's opposition tended to be in urban, populous areas such as Moscow and St. Petersburg and could do well in parliamentary elections under a nationwide PR system. Protests followed the election, alleging that the *United Russia* party had relied on election fraud to hang onto power.

The change in 2015, with the first election in 2016, to a mixed parallel (P) system of an equal number of single-member districts and proportional representation in a nationwide election (with change to a 5% threshold) is, according to Putin critics, a plan to maintain United Russia's dominance, because that party is better positioned to win district elections. This proved to be the case in 2016 when the party ran candidates in 206 of the 225 single-member districts.

The new mixed system had several characteristics that favored the *United Russia* Party. The single-member constituencies were decided by FPTP elections with only a single round of voting. There were 6–13 candidates in each constituency in 2016, allowing most candidates to win with far less than a majority of the votes. Turnout in the more liberal centers of Moscow and St. Petersburg was a low 28%. *United Russia's* candidates in the single-member constituencies in these cities won with as little as 26% of the vote.[23]

Moreover, the new system created the opportunity for gerrymandering the single member districts in urban areas to dilute the opposition to *United Russia* by "packing" these voters into a few districts[24] or combining opposition areas with those more friendly to *United Russia* in the traditional "cracking" tactic. *United Russia* supporters were spread among the districts giving *United Russia* an edge in the multi-district urban areas, such as Moscow and Saint Petersburg. The shapes of the resulting single-member legislative districts or constituencies in these cities suggest gerrymandering when compared to electoral districts for local elections in those cities.[25]

The population deviation among electoral districts is great, but this is largely caused by the allocation of at least one seat to each federal subject or administrative unit regardless of population. However, there was a pattern in 2016 of *United Russia*

---

[23]Only one of *United Russia's* candidates received over 50% of the vote in the 13 electoral districts in these 2 cities.

[24]The fact that *United Russia* did not even field a candidate in 19 districts is suggestive of this result. However, since most of those seats were won by parties aligned with *United Russia*, the lack of a *United Russia* candidate may have been intended to prevent the parties from splitting the vote. These districts were primarily among Russia's ethnic republics, however, there are districts in Moscow and Saint Petersburg that ssuggest this tactic.. Interestingly, the *United Russia* candidate in Sevastopol (disputed part of Ukraine) won with only 34.5% of the vote.

[25]In 2018 municipal elections several parties other than *United Russia* won the largest percentage of the vote in areas near the center of these cities. An overlay of the boundaries of the 2016 legislative constituencies shows that these non-United Russia areas are carved up and submerged in areas that supported United Russia—a classic example of the gerrymandering tactic of fracturing the opposition's areas of support. United Russia won several legislative constituencies in Moscow or St. Petersburg with as little as 22–35% of the vote.

winning by large margins (up to 75–80% of the vote) in these underpopulated districts. Not surprisingly, the districts in Moscow and Saint Petersburg are among the most populous.

The effect of the change in election systems was very positive for *United Russia*. Out of 206 constituencies in which *United Russia* ran a candidate, they won 203, losing 3 contests to the Communist Party of the Russian Federation. Out of 19 constituencies which did not have a *United Russia* candidate, seven were won by A Just Russia, five by the Liberal Democratic Party of Russia, four by the Communist Party, and one each by an independent candidate (allowed to run in the SMDs), the Civic Platform Party, and the Rodina Party. Most of United Russia's losses or decisions not to run a candidate were in federal subjects or republics in the eastern or southwestern parts of the country. *United Russia* ended up with a super majority of 343 seats (>76% of the 450 seats) in the Duma, plus the reliable support of several other parties, including the Communist Party, Liberal Party, and A Just Russia Party. This was achieved with only 54.3% of the vote nationwide.

These observations about the 2016 election are cursory. A more complete analysis is needed.

It is possible to argue that Putin and *United Russia* have learned from the U.S. how to use gerrymandering to control election outcomes.

7.7 Conclusion

The nationwide PR systems do not use districts; therefore they are not subject to gerrymandering.

Although only a few countries elect all members of its national legislature nationwide, many countries utilize PR voting within fixed districts or nationwide for the PR component within a mixed system. An example of a nationwide PR component in a mixed system is the current Russian Federation. Also, as described in Chap. 11, nationwide elections are sometimes used to fill seats reserved for minority voters and candidates, and for women. These are discussed in Chap. 11.

The small number of nations using a solely nationwide PR system shows the importance of a geographical or district component in almost all election systems. Even some of those nations that elect all members of the national legislature in a nationwide PR election have opened their party lists to permit voters an opportunity to express a preference among candidates on the list. Although this opportunity has proven more theoretical than real in some nations, its mere existence acknowledges a public unwillingness to forego the possibility of voting for preferred candidates and to trust entirely in a party's selection process.

The experiences of Italy and the Russian Federation demonstrate that a solely nationwide PR system is ill-suited for large nations.

The experience in the Russian Federation shows that in a mixed system gerrymandering single-member districts can become a political tool.

Chapter 8
Gerrymandering by Untimely or Malapportioned Redistricting or Reallocation of Seats

A fixed or multi-member district has the advantage of not needing to be periodically redrawn like a single-member district. This advantage, however, does not avoid the task of accommodating demographic changes. As the Code of Good Practice states, "With multi-member constituencies, seats should be redistributed preferably without redefining constituency boundaries, which should, where possible, coincide with administrative boundaries."[1]

Reallocating seats among fixed or multi-member districts is not always easy to achieve. Unless the number of seats in the national legislature increases, each addition of a seat to one fixed or multi-member district requires the elimination of a seat in another fixed or multi-member district. This elimination of a seat not only alters the voting power of constituencies, but may mean that an incumbent, party, state, or province will lose a seat in the national parliament. Therefore, it is not uncommon for this reallocation to become ensnarled in politics and to be delayed or avoided altogether.

This dispersion or allocation of seats among fixed districts can become a vehicle for gerrymandering regardless of whether the ultimate election system is Plurality/ Majoritarian or PR. Periodic reallocation of seats among fixed districts or special multi-member districts is essential for maintaining a national equality of voting power for persons in the face of inevitable population changes and shifts that occur over time. Unfortunately, it sometimes does not occur.

For a good overview of the history of redistricting in certain subject countries *see* **REDISTRICTING IN A COMPARATIVE PERSPECTIVE** by Lisa Handley & Bernard Grofman, eds., Oxford Univ. Press (2008).

---

[1] Appendix B.

S. Bickerstaff, *Election Systems and Gerrymandering Worldwide*, Studies in Choice and Welfare, https://doi.org/10.1007/978-3-030-30837-7_8

8.1 An Inadequacy in the Code of Good Practice

A mandate for periodic review is consistent with the Code of Good Practice, which states, "In order to guarantee equal voting power, the distribution of seats must be reviewed at least every 10 years, preferably outside election periods."[2] Unfortunately, an obligation to review the distribution of seats is not a mandate to make that distribution more equal.[3]

Provision for periodic redistricting or reallocation of seats by law should mean that all districts will be reviewed and adjusted as necessary to reduce the existing inequality among districts nationwide. Perhaps the drafters of the Code believed that review would necessarily bring corrective action. It hasn't.

In most nations there is no reliable and effective mechanism for forcing the legislature to timely approve the needed changes.[4] This is true even if the changes are recommended by a boundary commission or other commission. Often the national legislature has discretion to approve only some or none of the recommendations, or to postpone action.

In the legislature, there are many pressures for avoiding change, such as protecting incumbents from having to seek reelection in a redrawn district or satisfying a state or province that is upset about possibly losing a seat in the national legislature. There are few, if any, for making it. Even if action is taken, it may be piecemeal.

8.2 Legal Requirements for Periodic Redistricting or Reallocation of Seats

Many nations with electoral districts have a time interval, or prescribed circumstance, such as a specified level of malapportionment, which by law should trigger at least the review of the need for reallocation or redistricting.

This mandatory time varies between 3–12 years. The most popular period is 10 years with the law of at least 20 nations prescribing this timeframe.[5] In some nations the law mandates review of the allocation of seats every 5 years, such as Albania, Bahamas, the Czech Republic, Turkey, and Zimbabwe. In others, such as the U.K., the law permits 12 years or longer to pass between the redrawing of constituency boundaries, but allows the Parliament to postpone the review. France

[2]Appendix B. Please note that this guideline provides only for "review" at least every 10 years, not for action.

[3]The Venice Commission should not be blamed for an expectation that if a review showed an imbalance, the national legislature would act to correct it.

[4]*See*, Chap. 14, The Role of the Courts.

[5]These include Botswana, Canada, India, Japan, Kenya Lesotho, Malaysia, Mauritius, Mexico, Nepal, Nigeria, Pakistan, Papua New Guinea, Tanzania, the United States, and Yemen.

had a requirement for periodic redistricting (12 years), but is an example of a nation that has been too busy on other matters to meet its own laws about when reallocation and redistricting should occur. France's ultimate solution—do away with the national census and the statutory requirement for periodic redrawing of districts and reallocation of seats.[6]

There is tension between a requirement for when a review occurs and whether it should occur more often as population changes. In the U.S. the courts have accepted the "fiction" that a decennial census remains valid for 10 years until after the next decennial census. This allows a reprieve from redistricting and makes sense in nations which use periodically determined census population rather than registration to measure equality. However, it provides no check on the inevitable climb in malapportionment that occurs during the interval between censuses.

By providing for periodic redistricting or reallocation of seats, a nation effectively forestalls those processes from occurring earlier even though particular districts may exceed the prescribed limits during the interim period. In some instances this sets the stage for governments to overpopulate single-member districts or to allocate too few representatives to a fixed district even with the knowledge that the area in question is likely to experience disproportionately high population growth over the next period. This is a particularly pernicious form of gerrymandering that worsens the effects of an initial gerrymander.

Some nations, such as Australia, have tried to combat this circumstance, requiring by law that population projections be considered in redistricting. By contrast, U.S. courts have distrusted redistricting on the basis of projected growth[7] or estimated population, insisting instead on the use of decennial census figures even late in a decade.

8.3 Triggers in Lieu of a Period Between Redistricting or Reallocation

In many countries, there is no specific time interval prescribed by law. There is no provision at all for redistricting or redistribution of seats, or these are triggered in the law by other factors, such as prior to each national legislative election, a change in the number of seats apportioned to an area, changes in administrative boundaries, or when a prescribed level of malapportionment is reached. Two examples are useful at this point.

Germany is an example of a nation that has on-going data about the number of voters and reviews it regularly before each new legislature, but distinguishes between the deviation permitted when a district is redrawn (15% from the quota)

[6]It did so in 2002.

[7]Projections of growth are notoriously unreliable. Different experts may disagree about when, where, or even if such growth will happen.

and the deviation that requires a district to be redrawn (25%). This has allowed piecemeal action aimed only at the districts that exceed the maximum deviation rather than a nationwide redistricting or reallocation of seats.

Turkey[8] is an example of a nation in which a reallocation of seats for PR elections occurs prior to each general legislative election (5 years) based on an ongoing count of registered voters. An independent judicial commission allocates the legislative seats among the provinces based on the number of electors. Neither the legislature nor the executive has a role in this reallocation.

8.4 The Guarantee of Seats to a Fixed District

8.4.1 The United States

Most writers who discuss the U.S. Supreme Court's "one person, one vote" principle focus on the requirement that congressional districts must be as equal in population as is "practicable" (i.e. de minimis).[9] It is often overlooked, however, that this requirement for absolute equality among congressional districts applies only to those districts within a state, not among the states.

The number of congressional districts apportioned to each state in the United States is adjusted each decade to reflect changes in population as shown by the decennial census. Since each state is apportioned seats based on its current population and must redraw its congressional districts to reflect any such change, the population of most of the nation's congressional districts fall within a narrow range. According to the 2010 census, the average population of a congressional district is 710,767 persons.

Nevertheless, the U.S. Constitution creates inequality because it guarantees that each state has at least one member in the U.S. House of Representatives. There are seven states that have only a single member of that chamber.[10] The least populous of these is Wyoming, with 563,626 inhabitants according to the 2010 census. The least populous congressional districts, however, are in the state of Rhode Island. With a total population of 1,052,567, the state had enough population in 2010 for two districts, with approximately 526,283 people in each one. By contrast, the most populous congressional district in the U.S. is Montana with 994,416 persons according to the 2010 census. Unfortunately, Montana had more than enough inhabitants in 2011 for one congressional district and too few for two districts. This guarantee that the voters of each state elect at least one member to the

---

[8]*See,* Appendix C, A Case Study of Turkey.

[9]U.S. courts have rejected congressional districting plans with less than a 1% deviation among congressional districts.

[10]These are Wyoming, Montana, South Dakota, North Dakota, New Hampshire, Vermont, and Alaska.

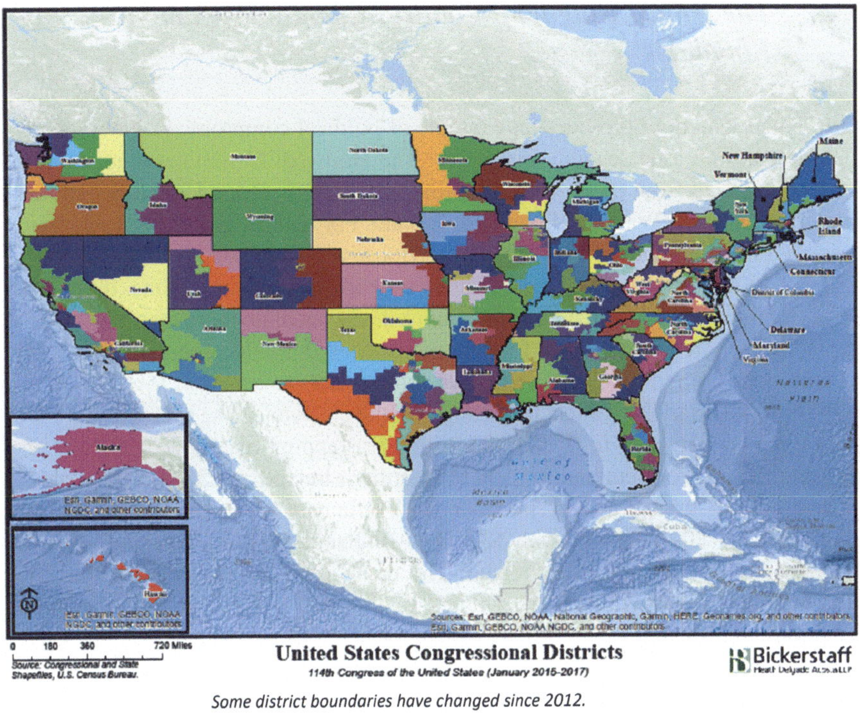

Fig. 8.1 United States 2016 single-member congressional districts. The map is courtesy of Bickerstaff, Heath, Delgado, Acosta LLP

U.S. House of Representatives was part of the compromise between large and small states in the U.S. Constitution in 1787 (Fig. 8.1).

Many other nations operate under similar political compromises that have institutionalized inequality in population or voters among constituencies by guaranteeing a minimum number of seats to states, provinces or other administrative units. This guarantee, which generally has existed in nations for generations, has inevitably benefited rural areas because of the migration of people from rural to urban areas.

The guarantee of seats in a unicameral legislature or the lower chamber of a bicameral legislature to fixed or multi-member districts is very common among nations. The highest number of guaranteed seats appears to be five for each province in Australia and Indonesia. Among the many nations having one or more guaranteed seats are Germany, France, Mexico, Brazil, and Japan. Canada handles the guarantee in a slightly different manner—guaranteeing no fewer than the number each of its ten provinces and three territories had in either 1976 or 1984.

8.4.2 The United Kingdom: Political Compromise among Kingdoms[11]

The United Kingdom provides an example of political compromise among entities that were at one time separate kingdoms. The House of Commons is made up of members elected from constituencies in the four regions of the United Kingdom—England, Scotland, Wales and Northern Ireland. For historical reasons, each region has had a fixed number of members in the House of Commons.[12]

The nation has Boundary Commissions for each of the four regions. In the past, these Commissions have strived to maintain a deviation of no more than 5% from the quota in each region, subject to exceptions caused by local conditions.[13] The commissions are required by law to carry out reviews every eight to 12 years and to re-draw boundaries to reflect the changes in the electorate. The average number of voters in a constituency for the 2010 election was approximately 70,000 voters for England, 66,000 for Scotland, 64,500 for Northern Ireland and 56,000 for Wales.[14]

The current breakdown of members of Parliament representing the different entities of the UK is as follows: 533 from England, 59 from Scotland, 40 from Wales, and 18 from Northern Ireland. The breakdown as proposed for the Sixth Constituency Review is that there will be a total of 600 constituencies in the United Kingdom (and four protected island constituencies in Scotland and England). This total is to be distributed across the four parts of the United Kingdom in accordance with a formula which relates the number of seats in each part to its share of the national electorate. If the Sixth Constituency Review is finally implemented (see below) England will have 501 seats (down from 533), Scotland 53 (down from 59), Wales 29 (down from 40) and Northern Ireland 17 (down from 18).

---

[11]See, **PUTTING VOTERS IN THEIR PLACE** by Ron Johnson & Charles Pattie, Oxford Univ. Press (2006); **FIXING THE BOUNDARIES: DEFINING AND REDEFINING SINGLE-MEMBER ELECTORAL DISTRICTS** by Ian McLean & David Butler, eds., Dartmouth Pub. Co. (1996); *Electoral Distortion Despite Redistricting by Independent Commissions: The British Case, 1950–2005* by Ron Johnston, Charles Puttie, and David Rossiter at page 205 in **Redistricting in Comparative Perspective** by Lisa Handley & Bernard Grofman, eds., Oxford Univ. Press (2008); and **DRAWING A NEW CONSTITUENCY MAP FOR THE UNITED KINGDOM: The Parliamentary Voting System and Constituencies Bill 2010** by Michel Balinski, Ron Johnston, Iain McLean, Peyton Young, and Angela Cummine, a report prepared for the British Academy London (2010); and *National Parliaments: United Kingdom*, **Library of Congress** (accessed July, 2018).

[12]The House of Commons Redistribution of Seats Act 1958 eliminated the previous common electoral quota for the whole United Kingdom and replaced it with four separate quotas. These first quotas were England 69,534, Northern Ireland 67,145, Wales 58,383 and in Scotland 54,741 electors.

[13]Islands create a special case, see Chap. 12. The Parliamentary constituency with the smallest-sized electorate in 2017 was Na h-Eileanan an Iar in Scotland [21,200 electors] and the largest was the Isle of Wight [109,900 electors] in England. Both are islands with a single constituency.

[14]In 2017, the median total parliamentary electorate across constituencies was about 72,200 in England, 56,000 in Wales, 68,300 in Northern Ireland, and 67,200 in Scotland.

8.5 Avoiding the Requirement for Redistricting or Reallocation of Seats

Unfortunately, the mandatory time or circumstance prescribed by law in many nations for redistricting or reallocation is often ignored as political conflicts and gridlock forestall legislative action on the changes. These conflicts and gridlock are usually quarrels over gerrymandering.

One means by which some nations have tried to avoid a political gridlock caused by an attempt to reallocate seats among fixed districts is to add new seats to the national legislature and to award those new seats to those fixed districts that have disproportionately increased in persons or electors. This action provides some short-lived political relief, but is imprecise and soon falters as the fight over the size of the legislature produces its own gridlock. Iran is an example—seats were added to the Tehran district as the population in that area of the country grew faster than in the more rural areas, but caused resentment among those officials who feared that Tehran would come to dominate the national legislature.

A second way to avoid the need to reallocate or redistrict is to change the election system itself and grandfather the current incumbents in office until the next election as part of the transition. An example is Hungary which, along with Albania, has had at least seven different election systems in the past 40 years. One writer has observed that in some of Eastern Europe's new democracies it was easier to change the system of government than to reallocate or redraw electoral districts.[15]

A third way is to limit remedial action to only the worst malapportioned districts instead of correcting any imbalances nationwide. Such action is especially present in nations that have only a trigger tied to a level of malapportionment. The important distinction between requirements for periodic redistricting and triggers for redrawing boundaries of a single district is discussed earlier in Chap. 8. A trigger, such as a certain level of malapportionment in a district, has the advantage if followed of preventing any district from exceeding the limit (usually high) during a period between general redistricting. The lack of a requirement for periodic general redistricting, however, can mean that other districts below the trigger level are left unchanged even if they significantly vary from the ideal number of persons or electors and can result in a significant and uncorrected imbalance among the overwhelming majority of districts. This imbalance can grow over time toward the higher trigger limit.

A fourth approach is to draw most or all of the districts at the highest permissible limit rather than at or near the ideal. Constitutional courts or authorities in countries, such as France and Lithuania, have warned against this effect and cautioned that the

[15]*See, Districting and Redistricting in Eastern Europe: Regulations and Practices* by Marina Popescu and Gabor Toka, at pages 251 and 260 *in REDISTRICTING IN COMPARATIVE PERSPECTIVE, by Lisa Handley & Bernard Grofman, eds., Oxford Univ. Press (2008).*

limits of deviation are for only the extreme or extraordinary circumstances where justified by the public interest.[16]

Another approach is to eliminate a legal requirement for periodic legislative action to redistrict or to reallocate seats. In 2002 the French Parliament repealed the statutory provision for a national census and, along with it, the requirement for periodic redistricting. In a similar move in 2002, Lithuania changed its law. The country's election law initially required that the population of constituencies be within ±10% of the national average. This was amended to allow for a deviation of ±20%. According to the Lithuanian authorities, this amendment was adopted because demographic changes would have resulted in substantial changes to the boundaries of constituencies if the original limit of ±10% had remained in place. According to the OSCE it was deemed more politically acceptable to increase the permissible deviation than to change constituency boundaries.[17] As a result, there was a large disparity in the population size among constituencies. The nation's Constitutional Court intervened[18] and the districts were redrawn to meet a 10% limit.

The sixth and most common way to avoid this responsibility is simply to find an excuse to ignore the legal requirements. Such a rationale was given in 2005 when the then President of France explained that, even though the nation had not redistricted or reallocated seats since 1986 (based on the 1982 census), the national legislature was "just too busy" to bother with the "highly time-consuming and politically fractious process" of redrawing the nation's electoral districts even though the Conseil Constitutional prodded the House of Delegates for action.[19] A much-criticized redistricting and reallocation was finally adopted by the national legislature in 2010 after repeated court intervention.

Other tactics for avoiding the immediate political repercussions of redistricting or reallocating seats include unnecessarily dragging out the review process, delaying or postponing approval of the changes, or approving the changes, but making them effective at some date in the future. The United Kingdom House of Commons is fond of using these tactics, with the result that redrawn constituencies, when implemented, are based on outdated data and are even less equal than when

---

[16]Several of these courts and authorities are quoted in Chap. 14.

[17]*See*, REPUBLIC OF LITHUANIA, PARLIAMENTARY ELECTIONS 2036, Final Report, at page 4, **OSCE/ODIHR** (October 9, 2016).

[18]*See*, Chap. 14.

[19]The quotations in this paragraph are from *Redistricting in France under Changing Electoral Rules by Michel Balinski* at pages 173 and 185 in **Redistricting in Comparative Perspective** by Lisa Handley & Bernard Grofman, eds., *Oxford Univ. Press (2008)*, citing *Villepin enterre le redécoupage électoral*, **Le Figaro** (June 17, 2005) and *Le gouvernement renonce au redécoupage de la carte électorale*, **Le Monde** (June 17, 2005. *See*, Decision No. 2008–24 ELEC of May 29, 2008, Observations of the Conseil Constitutionnel on the parliamentary elections of 10 and 17 June 2007; and Decision no. 2008–573 DC, Conseil Constitutionnel (January 8, 2009). The English version of the opinions have no page numbers. (@ https://www.conseil-constitutionnel.fr/en).

drawn. The latest review (Sixth Periodic Review of Westminster Constituencies) is discussed elsewhere in this Chapter.

8.6 Untimely Action Is Common

Many nations have found reasons for postponing redistricting or the reallocation of constituencies. Examples of this inaction can be found in Europe, Asia, Africa, and the Americas. Politicians, but also voters, often see maintenance of the status quo as more attractive than change. The following are a few examples.

8.6.1 India: A Moratorium on the Reallocation of Seats

After redistricting in 1973, India[20] placed a moratorium on the reallocation of seats among the states until 2000. This moratorium was later extended until after the first census (2031) following 2026. As a result, there is already a severe malapportionment among the states, which appears to favor the slower-growing Southern states.[21]

The situation is complicated as a policy matter because the Indian government had asked the nation's states to get theie inhabitants to reduce population growth. This policy was followed unevenly around the country. Advocates for a moratorium on reallocating seats among the states argued in part that such a reallocation of seats in the national legislature would unfairly penalize those regions of the country that were the most successful in reducing population growth. Critics said that this argument was only "a smoke screen" for baser political objectives.

It is clear that any reallocation of seats now would mean very major political changes. The task almost certainly will only become more difficult in the future and will exact even greater political changes later (e.g. an estimate is that by 2026, one state will have 12 too many seats in the national legislature and another will have 17 too few seats). A further extension of the moratorium seems likely.

Supporters of the moratorium urge that any unfairness in the moratorium on the reallocation of seats is offset to some extent by the recognition of new states, dissolution of some constituencies, and the continued redrawing of some individual constituencies within the states on the basis of the existing allocation. However, this is very confused, is a slow process, and is piecemeal. One source says delimitation within a state occurs only with the President's assent,. Some states have differed the redrawing of constituencies until after 2031. The last nationwide delimitation of

---

[20]*See, The Paradox of Political Representation (in India)* by Yogendra Yadav (2008) available @ www.india-seminar.com

[21]*See, Delimitation in India by Alistair McMillan* at page 75 in **Redistricting in Comparative Perspective** *by Lisa Handley & Bernard Grofman, eds., Oxford Univ. Press (2008).*

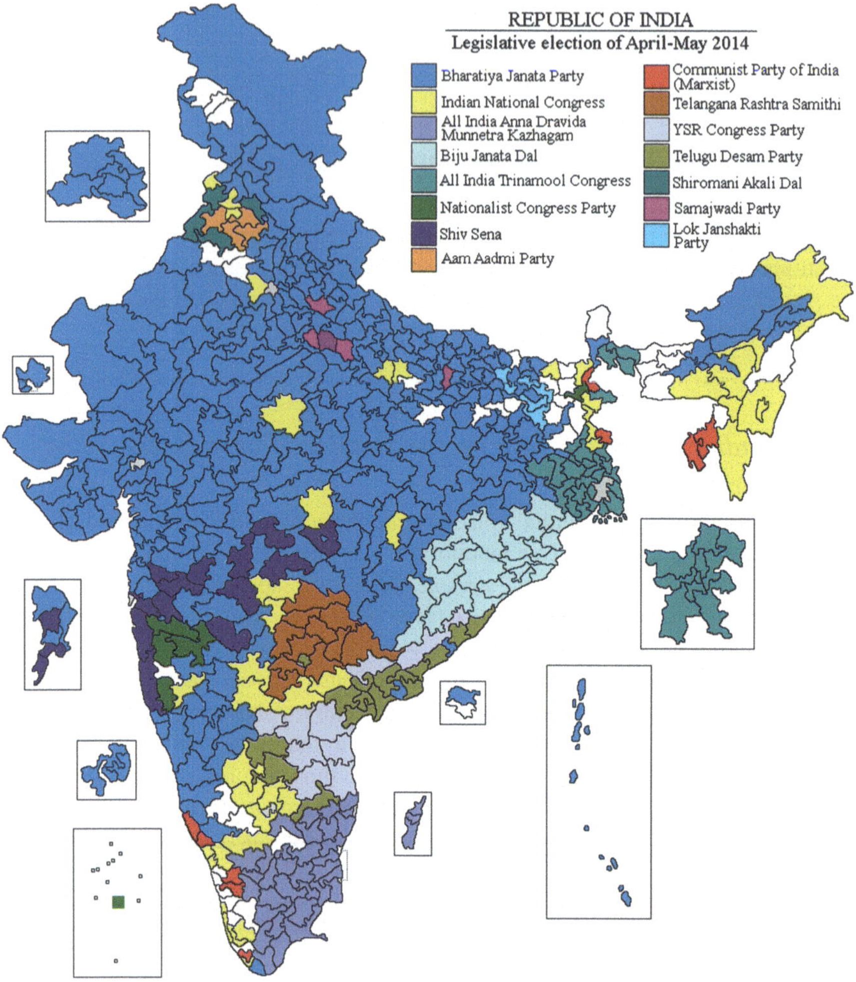

Fig. 8.2 Single-member electoral districts in India. The map is courtesy of Dr. Adam Carr @ http://psephos.adam-carr.net

parliamentary constituencies occurred in the 1970s, but many constituencies were drawn on the basis of 2001 census and will continue to be used until after 2031. Critics dispute the value of such redistricting and claim that it too has been marred by confusion, delays, and extensive gerrymandering of the nation's single-member districts (Fig. 8.2).

8.6.2 *The United Kingdom*

For several decades, the redistricting process in the U.K. has been unnecessarily long and drawn-out and has utilized old data. Moreover, the Parliament has often delayed or postponed changes with the effect of leaving members of the House of Commons to run for reelection in the same constituency as the one in which they were elected even though the constituency's demographics have changed.

For example, the Fifth Periodic Review of Westminster Constituencies was based on the Roll of Electors for 2000. The new constituencies were first used for 2010 elections. Scotland implemented the changes for the election in 2005, but Parliament postponed the changes for the remainder of the U.K. These constituencies remain in effect today.

The Parliamentary Voting System and Constituencies Act of 2011 was originally scheduled to take effect after the completion of the Boundary Commissions' next review of constituencies. The Boundary Commissions submitted new reviews to Parliament in 2013. However, only Parliament, with royal Assent, has authority to enact or repeal legislation, including implementation of the recommendations of these commissions. Implementation of the Act stalled, with the Boundary Commissions cancelling their review in the face of opposition in Parliament. Parliament voted to postpone these changes. This postponement was beneficial for the party in power and the incumbents of all parties. It was in effect a gerrymander for the benefit of incumbents and the Conservative Party.

The Boundary Commissions restarted their review process in 2018, with the change in the number of constituencies postponed by Parliament until the 2020 election. In proposing the new constituencies, the Boundary Commissions are forbidden from considering any demographic information generated after January 1, 2015.[22]

England's number of electors continues to grow faster than its sister entities so that the inequality among constituencies has worsened as the redrawing of constituencies has been delayed. After observing the 2015 elections, the OSCE concluded:

> Significant population changes have occurred since the last boundary review, consequently, the number of registered voters in each constituency for the 2015 general election varied widely. The Boundary Commission for England noted that the number of registered voters per constituency ranges from 53,877 to 107,572, with an average of 75,774 voters. Out of the 533 constituencies in England, 343 constituencies deviate by more than five per cent from the electoral quota. . . .The most recent constituency reviews were completed in 2007 (England and Northern Ireland), 2004 (Scotland) and 2003 (Wales).[23]

In the meantime, elections have continued to be held in the constituencies drawn by the Fifth Review based on the Roll of Electors for 2000. This delay has had added

---

[22]This makes the data already at least 3 1/2 years old. It will be at least seven plus years before any new constituencies are used in U.K.-wide (Scotland may be an exception) Parliamentary election.

[23]UNITED KINGDOM OF GREAT BRITAIN AND NORTHERN IRELAND, GENERAL ELECTION, Final Report, at pages 2–3, **OSCE/ODHIR** (May 7, 2015).

importance because these are the members of Parliament dealing with the exit of U.K. from the E.U.

8.6.3 Germany

In Germany, an Electoral Districts Commission (EDC) (Wahlkreiskommission) is appointed at the beginning of each parliamentary session (approximately every 4 years) by the President, but it is not independent. It has 15 months to review and report on the need to reallocate seats among the states (Länders) and to redraw single-member districts in Germany's mixed system. The commission's report, however, is merely a recommendation to the German national legislature.

The Bundestag receives the report and decides whether to approve any or all of the changes. Historically, the Bundestag has been reluctant to accept the changes recommended by the commission except when the malapportionment of a specific district exceeds legal limits. Ostensibly redistricting of an electoral district is required if malapportionment of the district is 25% or greater (previously 33%) than the national average or quota.

In its assessment of German election practices, ACE in 2004 concluded,

> Länder governments – particularly if they are due to lose a seat – do not relish a change in constituency boundaries. Members of Parliament are also likely to object to changes in constituency lines: new constituency boundaries could make it more difficult for incumbent legislators to win and could lead to the loss of a party seat. Therefore, Parliament often simply accepts only those changes that are mandated by law, retaining the status quo as much as possible.[24]

The national legislature not only rejected reallocation recommendations in 1983, 1987, and 1990, but also rejected the EDC constituency delimitation plan for a united Germany in 1994. In 1995, the Bundestag voted to reduce its size, effective in 2002. This major reform reduced the number of single-member constituencies to the current 299 and caused several Länder to lose constituencies.

A proposal in 2004 to reduce two states by one seat and to increase two others because of population changes was rejected. Amendments in 2005 reduced some of the deviation among Länders and redrew several direct constituencies, but left 53 districts over 15% from the national quota or average.[25] These deviations worsened.

---

[24] *Annex, Case Study, Germany, Delimiting Districts in a Mixed Member Proportional System,* at *Conclusion,* **ACE** available at https://aceproject.org/ace-en/topics/bd/annex/bdy/bdy_de

[25] FEDERAL REPUBLIC OF GERMANY ELECTIONS TO THE FEDERAL PARLIAMENT (BUNDESTAG), **OSCE/ODIHR** Election Assessment Mission Report (September 2009). Following 2005 ELECTION, the CEC prepared proposals for amending some boundaries. As a result of the review, Niedersachsen and Baden-Württemberg each gained one SSED seat and Anhalt and Sachsen each lost one seat. In addition, the boundaries of 31 single-member districts were redrawn prior to the 2009 federal elections. However, the finalized districting plan includes some 53 districts

By 2012 the Bundestag had acted to overcome the worst disparities among the Länder, but significant disparities remain. In the view of one German political scientist (in a dig at their oft rivals), the necessary changes in Germany are "merely delayed," not totally rejected "as happens with the French."[26]

8.6.4 *France*

France redistricted and reallocated seats in 1986 based on the 1982 census. The Conseil Constitutionnel, the nation's highest constitutional authority, reluctantly approved the legislation after earlier cautioning about its degree of population deviation.[27] Over time the population deviation among districts and administrative units (départements) worsened. The Conseil prodded the national legislature to act to redistrict and reallocate seats.[28] The French Parliament failed to do so. In 2002, the legislature even did away with the national census and statutory obligation to periodically redistrict and reallocate seats. The Conseil began to show its impatience and in 2008[29] explained:

> For more than twenty years, the Constitutional Council has recalled that the National Assembly, designated by direct universal suffrage, must be elected on essentially demographic bases. . . . It is now imperative to proceed with this division.

France's Parliament finally acted in 2010,[30] but concerns about malapportionment persisted. The Conseil allowed a deviation of ±20%, but emphasized that this deviation was only for special circumstances.

8.6.5 *The United States: Learning a Lesson*

Although each member of the U.S. House of Representatives is ultimately elected from a single-member district drawn by each state's legislature, each state may be

---

which deviate from the federal average by more than ±15%, of which some 18 deviate by more than ±20%.

[26]This statement was made in jest by the renowned German Professor Friedrich Pukelsheim in an e-mail to the author on June 16, 2016.

[27]*See, Decision No. 86-208 DC,* Conseil Constitutionnel [CC] (July 2, 1986); and *Decision No. 86–218,* Conseil Constitutionnel [CC] (Nov. 18, 1986).

[28]Decision no. 2008–573 DC, 8 January 2009. The Conseil even declared the guarantee of two seats for each département unconstitutional.

[29]OBSERVATIONS DU CONSEIL CONSTITUTIONNEL SUR LES ECHEANCES ELECTORALES DE 2007, Conseil Constitutionnel (July 7, 2008). *See* Chap. 14 for more of this opinion.

[30]This redistricting was upheld, but claims of gerrymandering and population imbalance persisted.

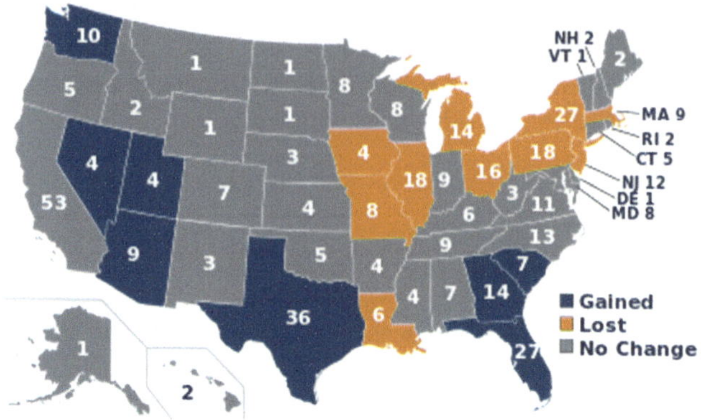

Fig. 8.3 2011 United States apportionment. The map is from Wikipedia

seen as a multi-member fixed district that every 10 years is apportioned seats in the U.S. House of Representatives. The critical apportionment of seats among the states is done by Congress. A state can create only as many districts as it has been apportioned. Every 10 years the U.S. Congress apportions the 435 seats in the House of Representatives anew among the states, according to the population of each state as determined by the new decennial census (conducted in the last year of the previous decade) and with the guarantee of a minimum of one seat for each state.

This necessarily means that some states gain seats in the House of Representatives and that other states lose an equivalent number of seats in that body (Fig. 8.3).[31]

Previously, this decennial apportionment was left largely to Congress. In 1921, however, Congress was confronted by a political gridlock and failed to adopt an apportionment act. Congress ultimately addressed the reapportionment issue by removing its discretion and making the reapportionment essentially automatic based on the results of the decennial census.

For slightly under 100 years, the apportionment process has been strictly controlled by a statutory formula[32] and the calculation for each state made automatically by the Bureau of Census, a federal agency, based on the decennial census and the prescribed formula. The agency reports the results to the President and through him to Congress. Congress has never interfered with this apportionment since 1921.

As for the states themselves, the courts have been the driving force. Many state legislatures in the United States for decades avoided redistricting congressional and state legislative districts even though required by their state constitution to do so. The failure of states to redistrict ended only when the federal courts intervened

[31]For example in 2011, a total of 12 additional seats were apportioned to Texas (4), Florida (2), Arizona (1), Georgia (1), Nevada (1), South Carolina (1), Utah (1), and Washington (1). An equivalent number of seats were lost at the same time by New York (2), Ohio (2), Illinois (1), Iowa (1), Louisiana (1), Massachusetts (1), Michigan (1), Missouri (1), New Jersey (1), and Pennsylvania (1).

[32]The United States apportions using the method of equal proportions.

in 1963, 1964, and 1968 to require congressional, state, and local legislative districts within a state to be roughly equal in population. The standard for congressional districts was essentially absolute equality in population, but was less rigid for state and local districts.

The release of the federal decennial census at the beginning of each decade provides the means for states to redraw their congressional and state legislative electoral districts, and the data by which a state's redistricting, or failure to redistrict may be challenged in court.

8.6.6 *Others*

It appears from my research that many nations have never redrawn their single-member electoral districts or reallocated their seats in the national legislature. Some, like Iran, with a combination of MMDs and SMDs, have enlarged the national legislature and added seats to existing districts to overcome the worst imbalances, but this tactic has proven to be an imprecise and ultimately unsuccessful effort.

Other nations have simply ignored the need. Examples can be found throughout the world, but especially in Southeast Asia, Latin America, Africa, and Eastern Europe.

8.7 Examples of Timely Action

There are a few nations, however, where the processes of redistricting and reallocation of seats seem to have proceeded in a timely manner in the past. English-language writers often identify the United States, New Zealand, Canada, and Australia as examples of systems in which the reallocation and redistricting processes occur regularly and are largely unaffected by political bias. They suggest that a major reason for this success is that three of these countries have independent redistricting commissions that act without legislative approval.

8.7.1 *The United States*

The United States is discussed above. The requirement for the decennial apportionment of seats in the U.S. House of Representatives to the states according to the number of persons in each state is in the U.S. Constitution. Congress has complied except in 1921 when congressional gridlock prevented passage of a reapportionment act. Since the 1930 census, reapportionment according to the decennial census has become an essentially automatic task. Federal law requires the Clerk of the House of Representatives to notify each state government no later than January 25 of the year immediately following the census of the number of seats to which it is entitled. The states are responsible for drawing the boundaries of these electoral districts. The federal courts make certain that promptly they do so. State laws generally require that the new districts be drawn in the same year that the census is released (i.e. the first year of the decade; the year after the census is taken), but some state laws allow until the following year.

8.7.2 New Zealand

New Zealand[33] first adopted a requirement for an equal number of "votes" among electoral districts in 1852. It conducts a census every 5 years and some of its single-member district lines are redrawn as necessary after each census on the basis of total population and are required to meet a standard of $\pm 5\%$ deviation from the quota, subject to certain "neutral" considerations.

Since 1994 the country has used a MMP voting system that combines these single-member districts with national PR voting. The South Island has a fixed number of single-member districts or constituencies (16). The number of such districts allocated to the North Island is determined by the number necessary to make the average number of persons in each district in the North equal to the average number of persons in the South Island constituencies. A separate set of districts nationwide is established for Māori inhabitants using the same formula.

In 2007 there were 16 districts for the South Island; 47 for the North Island; and seven for the Māori. The remainder of the usually 120 member national legislature, including possible additional "overhang" members under the MMP system, is determined based on a national PR election. Each party receiving at least 5% of the national vote chooses these additional members from a closed party list.

An independent commission, which was first created in 1887, is responsible for redistricting the single-member constituencies. Although there have been occasional claims of gerrymandering, the commission's plans have generally been seen as lacking political bias. Interestingly, New Zealand law bars any legal challenge to the commission's redistricting because such challenges are seen as usually having a political objective. New Zealand has the advantages of having a relatively small population to count and a rich history of relatively gerrymander-free redistricting.

---

[33] *See, An Independent Commission with Political Input: New Zealand's Electoral Redistribution Practices* by Alan McRobie at page 27 in **Redistricting in Comparative Perspective** by Lisa Handley & Bernard Grofman, eds., Oxford Univ. Press (2008).

8.7.3 Australia

Australia has an election system dependent on single-member districts allocated among the country's eight states and territories. The Electoral Commissioner allocates the seats based on a statutory formula. Although total population is used for allocation of the seats, redistricting of the states and territories is based on eligible voters. Voting registration is mandatory in Australia for all qualified persons. Therefore, the number of registrants per district should equal the number of persons eligible to vote and, unlike nations dependent on a decennial census; Australia theoretically has an ongoing and current count of the number of eligible voters in each district.

Australian law requires periodic redistricting (every 7 years), but also has several other triggers for when redistricting or reallocation of seats must occur. These include when more than 1/3 of the districts within a state vary by more than 10% from the ideal number of registrants.

A Redistribution Commission is appointed for redrawing the districts. Australia is unique in requiring that districts be drawn utilizing projected numbers of registrants based on rates of fertility, mortality, and interstate migration. As a result, although districts may legally be as high as 10% from the ideal when drawn, the objective is that they will vary no more than 3.5% from the ideal number of registrants after 3 ½ years.

Australia, however, guarantees each of its eight states and territories at least five representatives in its lower house regardless of population. As a result of this guarantee of seats, the average constituency in the least populated state, Tasmania, is over 20% smaller than the average constituency in the most populated state, New South Wales.

8.7.4 Canada

Canada is another nation where the reallocation and redistricting processes seem to be timely, but the limitations on voting equality are lax. The redistricting is done in each province by independent commissions.[34] Following the 2011 census, however, constituencies ranged in population from 26,728 to 132,443, with an average of 99,043. Of the 338 constituencies, 156 deviated more than 10% from the national average and 91 deviated by more than 15%.

---

[34]*See, Understanding Electoral Reform: Electoral Reform and Direct Democracy in Canada: When Citizens Become Involved by Lawrence LeDuc, 34* **West European Politics** *551–567 (Issue 3, 2011), available online* at *www.tandfonline.co*; and *The Electoral Boundary Revolution in Canada* by R. K. Carty, *15* **American Review of Canadian Studies** 273 (Issue 3, 1985), published online: November 10, 2009. These commissions consist of judges and politicians.

8.7.5 Turkey

A well-functioning process for reallocating seats among electoral districts may also be found outside the English-language nations. Turkey is an example.

Representatives in the national legislature are elected by proportional representation from the nation's 85 electoral districts, including two or more multi-member districts in three large cities, Istanbul, Izmir, and Ankara, situated in its 81 provinces. Before each legislative general election, an independent judicial commission reviews the number of registrants in each province and determines whether the number of representatives in the multi-member districts should be reallocated.

The urban districts in Istanbul, Ankara, and Izmir have higher numbers of registered voters per representative than the smaller, rural districts (about 15% above the national average). However, given the continuing and sometimes violent dispute between the nation's government and the Kurdish minority, I expected to find that the predominately Kurdish southeastern provinces would be overpopulated, but failed to find this imbalance. Moreover, I did not find an occasion on which the otherwise very vocal Kurdish activists criticized the allocation of seats among the provinces. My conclusion is that the seat reallocation process in Turkey has been timely and fair and that the judicial commission has done its job well.

8.7.6 Uruguay

Uruguay has a PR system in which the elections are at the fixed district level. The country has reallocated seats among those fixed districts every 5 years for at least 60 years.[35]

8.7.7 Others

Many nations refuse to reallocate seats, such as Croatia.[36] Others are generally timely about reallocation or at least have reallocated seats in recent years, including Greece, Finland, Bolivia, and Iceland.

[35] *See, Appendix C, A Case Study of Uruguay.*

[36] *See*, Chaps. 9 and 14.

8.8 Conclusion

A failure to timely and fairly reallocate seats in a national legislature among a country's fixed or multi-member districts is a form of gerrymandering and is not remedied by the use of proportional representation. The same self-serving political forces of incumbency, party interest, and personal bias that affect the drawing of single-member districts also affect the decision of whether to reduce the number of seats allocated to one state or province in order to increase the number allocated to another state or province because of demographic changes, or to maintain the status quo.

Some of the oldest and largest representative democracies in the world have avoided timely redistricting and reallocating seats in the national legislature. This inaction is at least partially based on the ostensible benefit of the status quo to incumbents and the government in power. This is gerrymandering. Sometimes it works; sometimes not.

According to my research, a clear similarity among the nations that have regularly reallocated seats is that each nation is using an automatic method or an outside commission to make the reallocation. Allowing the reallocation decision to rest with the legislature is to subject it to the uncertainties of political self-interest, even if the reallocation plan has been proposed by an outside commission.

The only legitimate basis for the allocation of seats in the national legislature is equality in total persons or electors. There should be a reallocation of seats on a periodic basis to fixed or special multi-member districts according to a fair formula. The reallocation should be automatic or through an independent commission of qualified persons.

Triggers, such as the reallocation of seats before each general election or the redrawing of a district's boundaries when it exceeds a specified deviation, are beneficial if the nation has reliable data on which to act. However, such triggers should supplement a requirement for periodic redistricting and reallocation of seats. Triggers for limits of deviation for individual districts must not be in lieu of a review of all districts in the nation as a whole and the requirement to equalize population or electors per representative, preferably nationwide.

Chapter 9
Gerrymandering Within Fixed Districts

Once seats in the national legislature are allocated to a fixed or special multi-member district, the manner of electing persons to fill those seats can take many forms.

In many countries, the fixed district is subdivided into single-member districts, or a PR system is used to elect representatives from the fixed district as a whole or in a special multi-member district. There are variations of these two systems and other election systems as well. Several states, such as Ireland and Australia, have single-member districts, but use an alternate vote system (AV). Iran uses a modified TRS system in a mix of single-member and multi-member districts.[1]

9.1 Gerrymandering

Each system is susceptible to gerrymandering. As discussed in the previous chapter, gerrymandering in a nation using elections within fixed or special multi-member districts can be achieved by controlling the allocation of seats to these districts. Each district should have a roughly equal number of persons or electors per representative. The presence of a significant difference in this figure among districts probably indicates a failure to timely reallocate seats to reflect demographic changes or a purposeful effort to disadvantage a political party or group. This action or inaction is a gerrymander to benefit incumbents and the parties in power.

9.2 Treating the Fixed District as a Single-Member District

It is possible to elect some representatives from the fixed district as a whole. The U.S. Senate is an example of such districts using FPTP elections. Each of the 50 states elects 2 senators statewide. Several other countries elect members of their

[1] *See,* Appendix C, A Case Study of Iran.

S. Bickerstaff, *Election Systems and Gerrymandering Worldwide*, Studies in Choice and Welfare, https://doi.org/10.1007/978-3-030-30837-7_9

upper or lower chamber in fixed district wide elections (see below and Chap. 6). Although these elections are not themselves subject to gerrymandering, the decision to hold certain legislative elections in the fixed district as a whole can handicap voters and candidates from less populated areas or political minorities within the fixed district by allowing them to be submerged in and consistently outvoted by an opposing and polarized majority.

9.3 Electing Members of the National Legislature by Proportional Representation Within Special Multi-Member Districts

A few nations allocate seats to special multi-member districts instead of traditional fixed districts.[2] These special multi-member districts usually do not have general governmental powers, but instead are used primarily or wholly in the election system. The boundaries of these districts seldom change.

For example, in Iceland the 63 members of the national legislature (Althing) are elected primarily using six closed list PR multi-member constituencies of 8–13 seats into which the nation's 23 counties and independent cities are incorporated. Of the 63 seats, 54 are elected using constituency results. The remaining nine seats are awarded to parties that crossed the 5% national electoral threshold, but failed to win an equivalent number of constituency seats.

In Finland, there are 15 multi-member constituencies, each electing from 1 to 35 representatives under a PR open list system that is based on pooling the votes for candidates of each party at the district level. The nation's provinces were abolished in 2010. The national legislature (Eduskunta) has 200 members. The Finnish constituency boundaries have remained essentially unchanged since 1906, but the number of seats has been regularly reallocated about 6 months before each election (Fig. 9.1).[3]

[2]Nations that use PR elections in fixed districts or special multi-member districts include Albania (changed to PR in 2008), Angola, Albania, Argentina (DSV in some states), Algeria, Aruba, Austria, Belgium, Benin, Bosnia & Herzegovina, Bhutan, Brazil, Bulgaria, Burkina Faso, Cape Verde, Cambodia, Chile (changed to PR in 2017), Columbia, Costa Rica (DSV), Croatia, Cyprus (North and South), Czech Republic, Denmark, Dominican Republic, El Salvador, Equatorial Guinea, Estonia, Finland, Faroe Islands, Greece, Greenland, Guatemala, Guyana, Hong Kong, Honduras, Iceland, Indonesia (some provinces divided into MMDs), Iraq, Ireland (STV), Kosovo, Latvia, Liechtenstein (Two MMD constituencies), Luxembourg (Four MMD constituencies), Malta (STV), Mauritius (BV), Macedonia, Mongolia, Moldova, Morocco, Montenegro, Mozambique, Namibia, Nicaragua, Norway, Palestine, Peru, Poland, Portugal, Palestinian Territories (BV), Romania (changed to PR in 2015), Rwanda, San Marino, Slovenia, South Africa, South Sudan, Spain, Sri Lanka, Sweden, Sudan, Switzerland, Tunisia, Turkey, and Uruguay (DSV).

[3]**Electoral Systems in Context** by Åsa von Schoultz (2016).

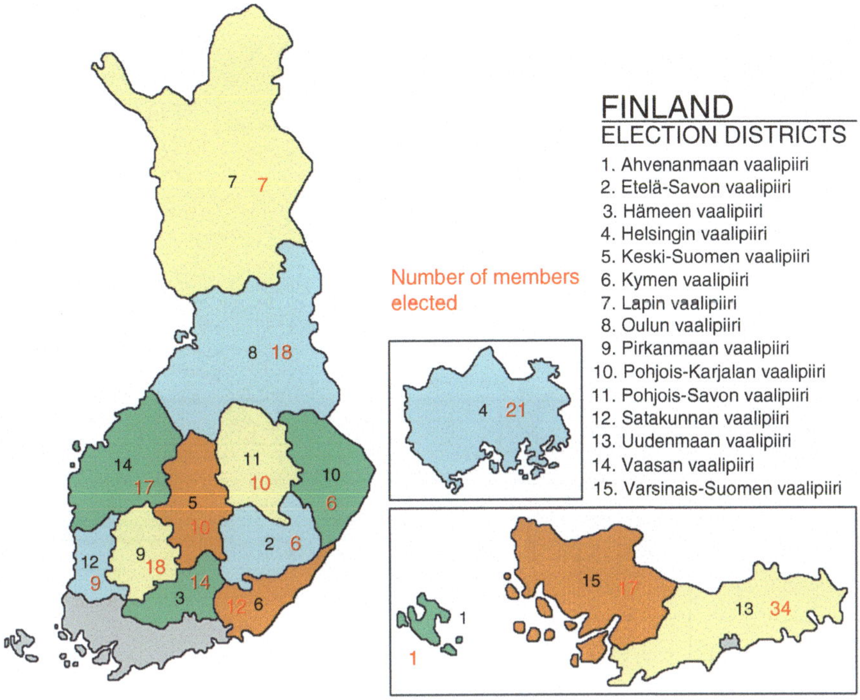

Fig. 9.1 Special multi-member districts in Finland. The map is courtesy of Dr. Adam Carr @ http://psephos.adam-carr.net

Sweden has a somewhat unique approach. It has 29 special multi-member electoral districts, which generally follow county lines except in the major cities. Of the nation's 349 members in its unicameral parliament, 310 are elected through a proportional system with open lists from these multi-member districts. The remaining 39 seats are "adjustment" seats. These seats are awarded based on the difference between a party's number of seats won in the multi-member districts and the number of seats that the party would have won in a proportional contest held in a single, nationwide constituency. Voters can choose between three different ballots to indicate both party and candidate preference, including a blank ballot paper where a voter can write in the party and a candidate's name. To be elected on a basis of personal votes, a candidate must receive at least 8% of the party votes in the respective constituency (Fig. 9.2).

As mentioned above, Iceland reserves nine seats for parties that receive at least 5% of the vote nationwide, but fail to win an equivalent number of constituency seats. Norway has "leveling" seats based on the party's performance nationwide.

Some of the nations that use PR elections in these special multi-member districts make little attempt to equalize voting power for voters within these districts through reallocation as the population changes. For example, in Croatia, representatives are

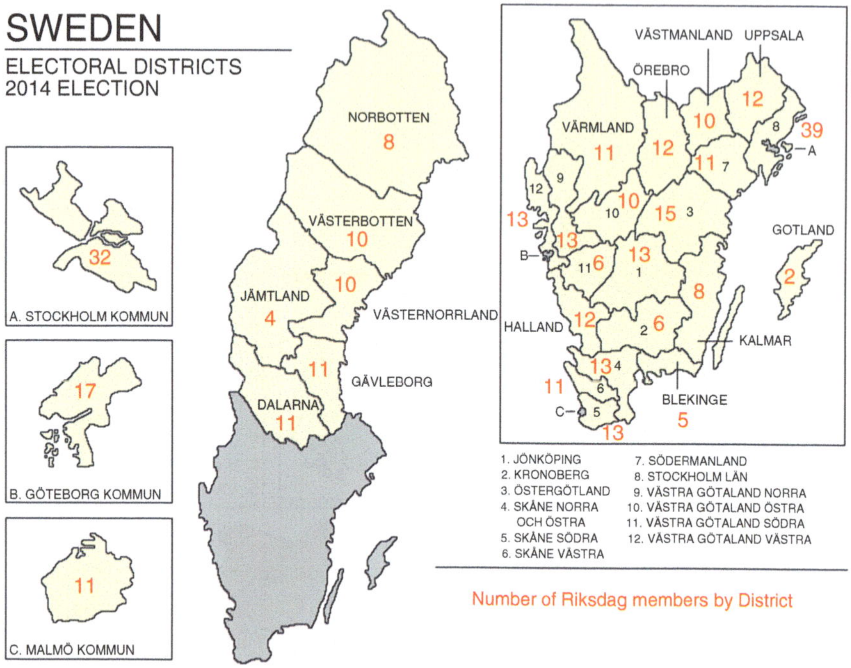

Fig. 9.2 Special multi-member electoral districts in Sweden. The map is courtesy of Dr. Adam Carr @ http://psephos.adam-carr.net

elected to a single chamber of Parliament (Sabor) by PR in 12 multi-member constituencies. Ten of the constituencies elect 14 representatives apiece, while the diaspora constituency elects up to 14 representatives, and a constituency for national minorities elects eight nationwide. In December 2010, the Constitutional Court of Croatia[4] ruled that an update to the layout of the ten primary electoral districts was necessary, as the differences in the number of voters per representative among the domestic districts, limited by law to a 5% deviation from the average, had grown to at least 25% (Fig. 9.3).

The Court requested data on the number of eligible voters in each constituency, but was told by the government that such data was unavailable; so the Court used the number of votes cast in the last election to show the probable imbalance in the number of voters among the districts.

In its opinion[5] the Court noted:

[4]THE CONSTITUTIONALCOURT OF THE REPUBLIC OF CROATIA No. U-X-6472/2010 Zagreb (December 8, 2010) available at https://www.usud.hr

[5]THE CONSTITUTIONALCOURT OF THE REPUBLIC OF CROATIA No. U-X-6472/2010 Zagreb (December 8, 2010) at para 5 available at https://www.usud.hr

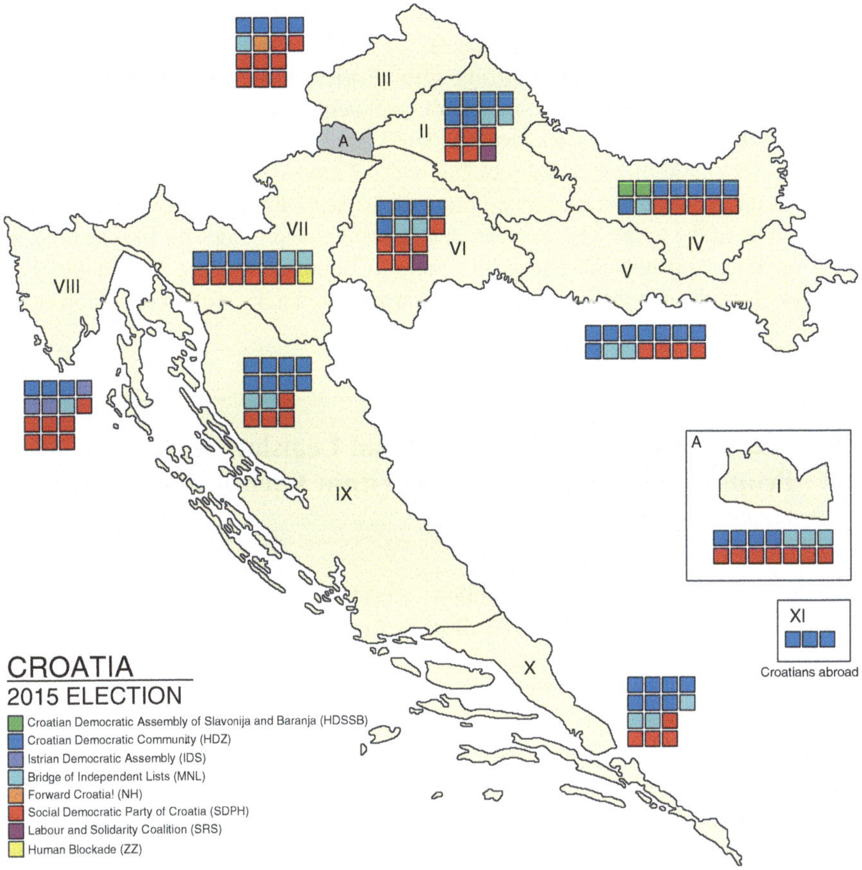

Fig. 9.3 Special multi-member electoral districts in Croatia. The map is courtesy of Dr. Adam Carr @ http://psephos.adam-carr.net

> Thus both the legality and the general democratic character of the elections depend on the equal distribution of the voters in the general constituencies (the equality of votes directly depends on this distribution). . . . In other words, constituencies that are once determined undergo changes by the nature of things. It is especially important that the division into constituencies cannot be regulated once and for all. Migration processes demand that constituencies should be constantly adapted to changing relations, by geographically changing their boundaries or by changing their number of seats.

In April 2011 the parliament discussed a proposal to change the constituencies, but no change was made in time for the 2011 elections. These ten multi-member districts remain unequal today, with one constituency regularly having over 70% more voters than another. Croatia faces pressure from the EU to change its election system as a condition for joining that body. Despite these pressures, the inequalities among constituencies remain unaddressed.[6]

Some nations with special multi-member districts make an attempt to balance voting power among these multi-member constituencies. Greece is an example of a nation that has reallocated seats recently. Until 2012 Greece elected representatives using mostly single-member districts, but with 12 representatives ("state deputies") elected nationwide and a majority bonus of 40 seats for the party receiving the largest share of the votes. The law was changed and now provides for PR elections in multi-member constituencies, but with a majority bonus of 50 seats. The country has 13 special multi-member constituencies, which generally following prefecture lines.[7]

9.4 Electing Members of the National Legislature by Proportional Representation Within Each Fixed District

The most popular system among nations worldwide is reliance on proportional representation (PR) within the fixed districts to determine their representatives to the national legislature.[8]

For example, Norway has 19 counties. Each county functions as a fixed multi-member electoral district or constituency. Candidates for the national legislature are elected by proportional representation within the constituency. The number of seats in each constituency is to be adjusted every 8 years, but the allocation is based on a consideration of both a county's population (one point) and geographic size (1.8 points per square kilometer). This has led to an imbalance in favor of the larger

---

[6]REPUBLIC OF CROATIA PARLIAMENTARY ELECTIONS 2015 OSCE/ODIHR NEEDS ASSESSMENT MISSION REPORT (September 2015); and *HDZ wins election in six constituencies,* **EBL News** (Croatia) (September 12, 2016).

[7]For the 2015 election, seats were reallocated by the Interior Ministry. The seats in the national legislature were increased by three in the electoral constituency of Attica (from 12 to 15 seats), by two in Athens second electoral constituency (which is the country's most populous, with a total of 1,428,759 voters), and by one in Piraeus first electoral constituency (from 5 to 6 seats), Thesprotia electoral constituency (from 1 to 2 seats), Magnesia electoral constituency (from 5 to 6 seats) and the Cyclades electoral constituency (from 3 to 4). At the same time, the parliamentary seats of Athens first electoral constituency were reduced by three (from 17 to 14 seats), while by one in Achaea electoral constituency (from 9 to 8 seats), Aetoloacarnania (from 8 to 7 seats), Boeotia electoral constituency (from 4 to 3), Karditsa electoral constituency (from 5 to 4), Serres electoral constituency (from 7 to 6) and Trikala electoral constituency (from 5 to 4). *The Greek Parliamentary Seats and Preference Crosses per Constituency* by Aggeios Skordas, at https://greece.greekreporter.com (January 16, 2015).

[8]A list of countries using PR in fixed districts or special multi-member districts appears in a previous footnote and in Appendix B.

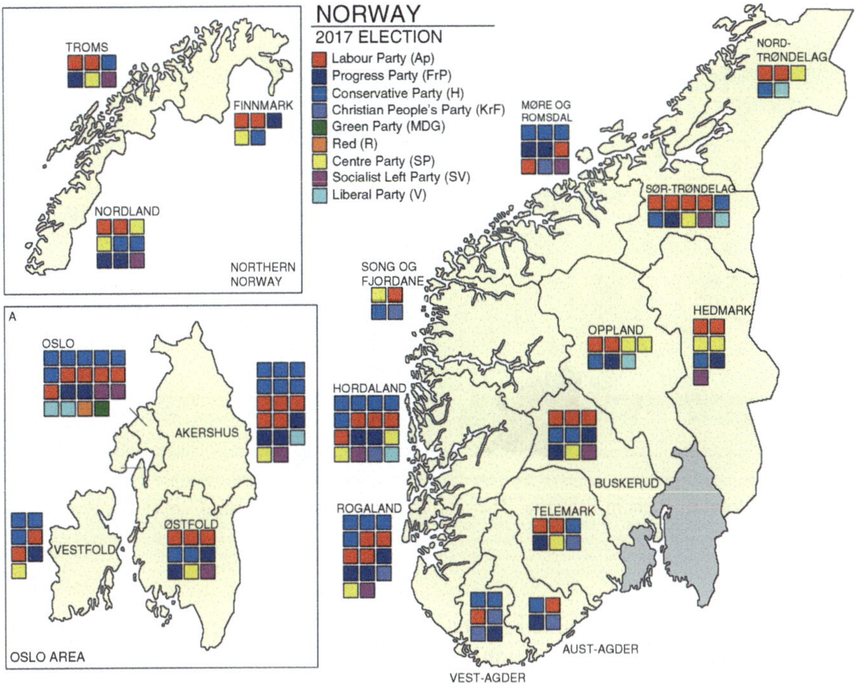

Fig. 9.4 Electoral districts in Norway. The map is courtesy of Dr. Adam Carr @ http://psephos.adam-carr.net

northernmost counties. In an effort to even out discrepancies between the number of votes received and the number of seats in the parliament (Storting), each constituency was given an additional "seat at large." Nevertheless, inequality has continued. For example, in recent elections, a vote in the northernmost county, Finnmark, has counted approximately twice as much as a vote in the capital Oslo or the surrounding county Akershus. Also, like Sweden and Iceland, Norway has "leveling" seats to reward parties that do not achieve representation through the constituency elections (Fig.9.4).

Portugal elects the 230 members of its unicameral national legislature (Assembly of the Republic) from 20 multi-member districts using proportional representation. These districts correspond to the nation's administrative units. An additional two districts are for Portuguese who live outside Portugal (the diaspora).

Each one of Bulgaria's 28 administrative regions is an electoral constituency, except for the city capital city of Sofia, which is split into three constituencies (Fig. 9.5).

Similarly, in Switzerland, each canton is a fixed multi-member electoral district. The members of the 200 seat lower chamber (Federal Assembly) are elected by proportional representation from within each canton. Switzerland, however, adds a

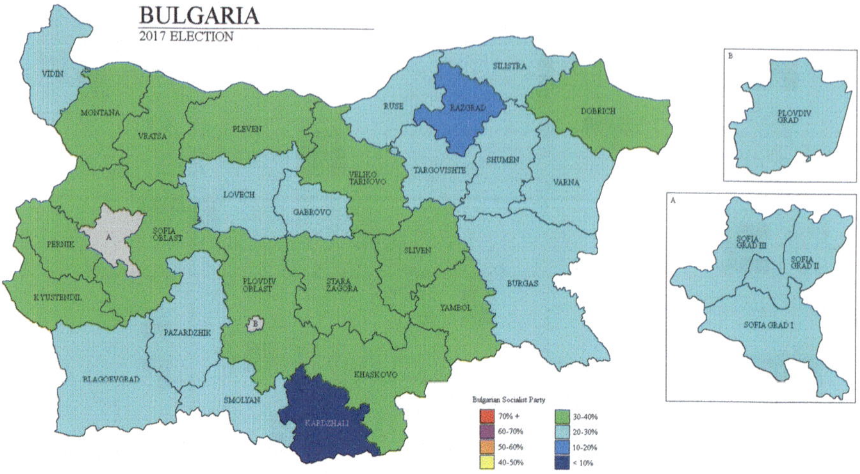

Fig. 9.5 Electoral districts in Bulgaria. The map is courtesy of Dr. Adam Carr @ http://psephos.adam-carr.net

twist. Its upper house (the Council of States) elects its 46 members from a mixture of 20 multimember and 6 single-member districts that correspond to cantons and ½ cantons.

9.5 Electing Members of the National Legislature in Single-Member Districts Within Each Fixed District

After allocating seats to fixed districts, several nations elect all of their representatives to the lower house of the national legislature exclusively from single-member districts or constituencies drawn within those fixed districts. The most notable examples of countries using only single-member districts are the United Kingdom, Ghana, France, India, Australia, Canada, and the United States.[9] Plurality elections, instead of PR elections, are also held in many other nations and are a component of mixed systems.

In most nations these single-member districts within fixed districts are drawn by the national legislature. The exceptions include the United States and Canada,[10]

[9]Although fewer countries use all single-member districts than use PR elections, there are more persons in these countries.

[10]*See*, www.elections.ca; *To End Gerrymandering: The Canadian Model for Reforming the Congressional Redistricting Process in the United States* by Anthony J. Gaughan, 41 **CAPITAL UNIVERSITY LAW REVIEW** 999 (2013). *Understanding Electoral Reform: Electoral Reform and Direct Democracy in Canada: When Citizens Become Involved* by Lawrence LeDuc, 34 West

where the state, provincial, or territorial legislatures or commissions draw the districts. This adds a new dynamic in which the self-interest of local legislators wanting to run for the national legislature may conflict with the self-interest of incumbents in the national legislature wanting to remain in office.

The manner of electing members varies within these districts. The two most common systems are FPTP and TRS.

First-Past-the-Post (FPTP) In some nations (e.g. United States, India, Canada, and United Kingdom), each representative from a single-member district (i.e. constituency) is elected using a first-past-the-post (FPTP) system, with a candidate needing only a plurality to win.[11]

India provides an example (Fig. 9.6).

Two Round System (TRS) Some nations, such as France and Iran, require that the winning representative receive a specific minimal percentage, perhaps even a majority of the votes in a district, so there often is a second election between the top vote-getters in the first election. This system is called a two round system (TRS).[12] Maps of France and Iran are in Appendix C.

In Iran, a form of the TRS is used in both single-member and multi-member elections. In Majlis (national legislative) elections, each elector has as many votes as there are seats at stake in the constituency (i.e. single or multi-member district) and may be voted as a block for a single candidate. After the first round of voting the candidates who have received the highest number of votes (at least 25%) are elected up to the number of seats at stake. If too few candidates meet the required minimum level of support, the unsuccessful candidates (up to twice as many as there are seats left to be filled) participate in a second round to fill the remaining seats.

There are other election systems at use in the world.

European Politics 551–567 (Issue 3, 2011), published online (April 11, 2011).*The Electoral Boundary Revolution in Canada* by R. K. Carty, 15 **American Review of Canadian Studies** 273 (Issue 3, 1985), published online: (November 10, 2009); **COMMISIONED RIDINGS DESIGNING CANADA'S ELECTION DISTRICTS** by John C, Courtney, McGill-Queen's Univ. Press (2001).

[11]The nations that use FPTP elections include American Samoa, Anguilla, Azerbaijan, Bahamas, Bangladesh, Barbados, Belize, Bermuda, Botswana, Canada, Cook Islands, Cote d'Ivoire, Dominica (nine appointed), Egypt, Eritrea, Ethiopia, Gambia, Ghana, Grenada, India, Jamaica, Japan, Kenya (12 appointed), Laos, Liberia, Maldives, Myanmar (25% appointed by military), Malaysia, Malta, Marshall Islands, Malawi, Monserrat, Mozambique, Micronesia, Nigeria, Niue, Northern Mariana Islands, Oman, Pakistan (with PR for seats set aside for women and non-Muslims), Samoa, St. Kitts and Nevis, St. Lucia, St. Vincent and the Grenadines (six appointed), Seychelles, Sierra Leone, Singapore (nine appointed by parties), Solomon Islands, Swaziland, Tanzania (with 75 seats set aside for women chosen by PR; and some members appointed), Uganda, United Kingdom, United States, British Virgin Islands, U.S. Virgin Islands, Yemen, Zambia, and Zimbabwe (some appointed).

[12]The nations that use a TRS include: Bahrain, Belarus, Republic of Congo (Brazzaville), Cuba, France, French Polynesia, Gabon, Haiti, Iran, Kiribati, Mali, New Caledonia, Tokelau (protectorate of New Zealand), Turkmenistan, Uzbekistan, Vanuatu, Wallis and Fortuna, and Viet Nam. Many of these are former French colonies.

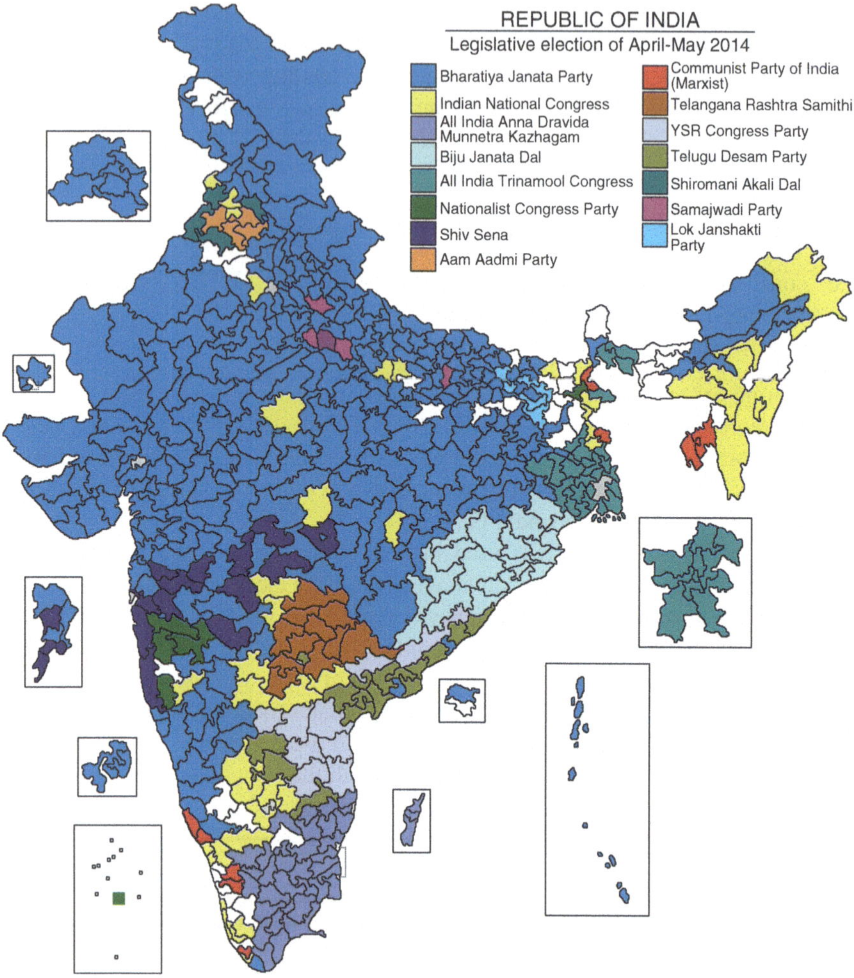

Fig. 9.6 Single-member electoral districts in India. The map is courtesy of Dr. Adam Carr @ http://psephos.adam-carr.net

9.6 Preferential Voting

There are several forms of preferential voting and different circumstances in which they are used.

One form of preferential voting is the alternative vote (AV). This manner of election is sometimes called "rank voting" or "instant runoff voting". It is a form of election that produces a single winner in a single-member district in a single election (i.e. no run-off), but allows the voter multiple choices. The voter receives a ballot with the names of all of the candidates for an office; Voters rank the candidates according to their preference. A formula is followed to allocate those votes among the candidates to produce a single winner.

Australia has single-member districts in its lower chamber, but uses AV voting within those districts. Papua New Guinea uses a similar system.

Another form of preferential voting is the Single Transferable Vote (STV). It is a voting system designed to achieve proportional representation through ranked voting in multi-member districts. Ireland, Nauru, and Malta are the only examples I could find of nations currently using this system for election to the lower chamber of the national legislature. Each has multi-member districts with three or more representatives.

In a few nations, however, such as Northern Ireland, Australia, Scotland, New Zealand, and even the United States, STV or AV is used for a few state or local elections. In some countries it is also is used within a few state legislatures as the method of choosing the state's representatives in the upper chamber of the national legislature.

Variants of the AV and STV systems include the Borda Count, Dowdall, Nanson and Baldwin methods of counting preferential votes to choose a winner. It may be used in single-member or multi-member elections. The nation of Nauru uses the Borda Count method in multi-member districts.

9.7 Single Non-transferable Vote (SNTV)

The Single non-transferable Vote (SNTV) method of selecting representatives in a national legislature is used in some nations with multi-member elections. Each voter casts only a single vote. The vote is cast for one candidate in a district in which there is more than one seat to be filled. Those candidates with the highest vote totals fill these positions.

SNTV is used in at least: Afghanistan, Pitcairn Islands, Vanuatu, 90 of the 150 seats of Jordan's Lower Chamber, the Senate elections in Indonesia, and in 6 of the 113 seats under the Parallel (P) system in Taiwan.

9.8 Block Voting (Blk)

Some sources classify the election systems in Singapore, the Palestine Authority, and Mauritius as having "block voting" systems, but this can be misleading. Each of these nations has several multi-member electoral districts. The political party obtaining the greatest number of votes in each multi-member district (usually 2–4 seats) takes all the seats allocated to the district. The block voting occurs only within individual multi-member districts, not nationwide.

Parties compete in each multi-member district as if in a PR election, but the winning party in each district gets all of the seats allocated to the district. Block

Voting is thought to aid minorities within a multi-member district by allowing them to concentrate their votes and elect their candidates within a district.

In Singapore, there are two types of districts. There must be no fewer than eight single-member constituencies. The remainder of the districts are Group Representation Constituencies (GRCs) contested by groups instead of individuals. These are essentially multi-member districts in which each group must include at least one person belonging to the Malay, Indian, Eurasian, or some other minority community. The party receiving a plurality of votes in a multi-member district wins all seats in the district.

In Mauritius, in addition to the 62 representatives elected from 21 multimember constituencies using block voting, there are a maximum of eight additional seats allocated to the "best losers." These "best loser" seats are appointed by the Electoral Supervisory Commission and are apportioned among four constitutionally recognized ethnic or religious communities (Hindus, Muslims, Chinese, and Creole) to ensure some representation for each of these minority groups.

In the Palestinian Territories, the West Bank and Gaza Strip are divided into 16 multimember electoral districts. Six seats across four districts (Jerusalem, Bethlehem, Ramallah, and Gaza) are reserved for the Christian population and one seat (in the Nablus district) for the Samaritans. In both Mauritius and the Palestine Authority, the political party obtaining the greatest number of votes in each multimember district takes all the seats allocated to the district.

9.9 Gerrymandering the Shape of Single-Member and Multi-Member Districts

In every nation that draws these single-member districts there are two opportunities for gerrymandering. The first opportunity occurs in the allocation of seats to the fixed districts. This form of gerrymandering was discussed in the previous chapter. The second opportunity occurs in the shaping of each electoral district itself.

The boundaries of single-member districts within a fixed district must be periodically redrawn to keep them equal in population or electors. The redrawing should occur long enough before an election to permit voters to be adequately informed of the changes and to avoid unnecessary confusion or instability.

9.9.1 The American Experience: Bizarre Shapes

Gerrymandering the shape of single-member electoral districts is often seen as a particularly American phenomenon because some of the U.S. congressional districts are bizarre in appearance. The U.S. redistricting process is usually and rightly criticized as being a haven for oddly shaped electoral districts drawn to favor or disfavor particular candidates or political parties. It is also appropriate, however, to observe that the shape of these districts is often bizarre in appearance because the drawer is simultaneously trying to create a politically advantageous districting plan and to comply with the nation's strict requirements for equality in population among districts and for non-discrimination against certain minorities.

These requirements are easily established by using census enumerations that are provided for each block or enumeration district in the country and are available to the government and every member of the general public. If the state legislature or commission does not use these tools to make certain its redistricting plan meets the strict court-imposed requirements for equality and legality, a dominant party's politically favorable redistricting plan will be struck down and may be redrawn by the courts. The political advantages in the original plan may be lost. Therefore, the bizarre shapes of the districts are often the result of an attempt by a plan's architects to use this census data to achieve certain political goals while insulating the plan from legal challenge. Sometimes they are successful, sometimes not.

9.9.2 Gerrymandering District Shapes Worldwide

If a nation permits districts to vary significantly in the number of persons, citizen population, or voters, the gerrymandered districts are less obvious and less bizarre in appearance than in the United States. Nevertheless, these districts can be drawn to favor or disfavor candidates or political parties by packing an unequal number of persons or voters among esthetically attractive districts that meet the historic neutral criteria for drawing districts, such as contiguous, compact, regular in shape, and respectful of political subdivision boundaries. The same may be achieved through "cracking" opposition strongholds. Both of these are gerrymanders regardless of their appearance.

Therefore, although gerrymandering single-member electoral districts is often seen as a particularly American phenomenon, it actually exists worldwide and is facilitated by the lax standard of equality of persons or voters found in most countries and the lack of court enforcement of even those existing standards.

Among the nations that have been explicitly accused of gerrymandering the shape or population of electoral districts are Australia, Canada, Chile (changed to PR in 2017), France, Germany, Greece (changed to PR in 2012), Hong Kong, Hungary, India, Ireland, Kuwait, Malaysia, Malta, Nepal, Philippines, Russia, Singapore, Sudan, Turkey, United Kingdom (including Northern Ireland), United States, and Venezuela. It is unfair, however, to pick on these particular countries because virtually every nation that allocates seats among fixed districts or has single-member or multi-member constituencies, including mixed systems, has examples of districts redrawn or seats allocated to achieve a political purpose.

A few of the most notorious examples of gerrymandering single-member districts include:

Canada—In 2006, the provisional government of Prince Edward Island replaced an electoral map drawn by a commission with one that ensured every current member of the legislative assembly from the premier's party with a district to run in for re-election.[13] Despite this obvious attempt at gerrymandering, only 7 of 20 incumbent members of the Assembly were re-elected (seven did not run for re-election), and the government was defeated.

France—Conservative governments took advantage of three opportunities to design favorable districts. These were in 1958, 1987, and 2010. The redistricting in 1987 was particularly effective, resulting in 80% of the seats going to conservatives with 58% of the vote in 1993. The Constitutional Council was asked twice to decide about gerrymandering, but, while it avoided the issue of partisan gerrymandering, it forced the national legislature to respect an 80–120% population ratio (20% from quota), ending a tradition in which départements, however small in population, would send at least two members to the national legislature.

As the national census was done away with by the French Parliament in 2002, the Electoral Code no longer provides for fixed redistricting. Some OSCE/ODIHR observers thought the process of redistricting in 2010 was politicized, leaving room for "gerrymandering" since the government controlled the process and the role of the Independent Commission was strictly advisory. This latest redistricting in 2010 is seen by critics as gerrymandered to continue to benefit conservatives, but supporters of Independent candidate Macron swept to a majority of the national legislature in 2016 despite the alleged gerrymandering.

Malaysia—The practice of gerrymandering has been around in Malaysia since its independence in 1957. The ruling coalition (National Front or Barinas Nasional) has been accused of controlling the election commission by revising the boundaries of constituencies. Most recently, in 2013, Barinas Nasional won 60% of the seats in the Malaysian Parliament despite receiving only 47% of the popular vote. Malapportionment has also been used at least since 1974, when it was observed that in one state alone (Perak), the parliamentary constituency with the most voters had more than ten times as many voters as the one with the fewest voters.

Philippines—The national legislature of the Philippines has never passed a national redistricting bill since the approval of the 1987 constitution. However, it has created 34 new districts, out of the 200 originally created in 1987. These new districts are carved from existing districts and allegedly gerrymandered to allow politicians from powerful families to avoid running against one another.

Singapore—Critics of the ruling People's Action Party (PAP) have accused it of unfair electoral practices to maintain significant majorities in the Parliament of Singapore. From Singapore's independence in 1965–1981, the People's Action Party won every single seat in every election, forming a parliament with no elected opposition for almost 2 decades. This dominance continues today. In

[13] *Reference re Prov. Electoral Boundaries (Sask)* [1991] 2 S.C.R. 158, 183 (Can.).

2015, out of 89 seats, the People's Action Party (PAP) contested all and won 83. The opposition attributes this PAP success to gerrymandering of the nation's single-member districts.

Sudan—In the election of 2010, there were numerous instances (according to a report from the Rift Valley Institute) in which constituencies were created that were well below and above the required limit of 15% greater or lesser than the average constituency size.

Japan—The nation has a mixed (P) system, with 360 SMD and180 PR in regional multi-member districts. The single-member component is notorious for respecting local government boundaries more than voter equality, with the most populous district being >200% larger than the least populous district. The Supreme Court held this disparity unconstitutional, but the Court refrained from intruding in the legislature's province and instead left the national legislature to fix the system. It did not do so.[14]

Russian Federation—The Russian Federation has a history of gerrymandering districts under different election systems.[15] In Chap. 7 I discussed how the new mixed system used for 2016 elections allowed the shaping of single-member districts and the unequal allocation of constituencies to facilitate the continued control of the national legislature by the *United Russia* party, which in the 2016 election won 77% of the seats in the Duma with 54% of the vote.

Northern Ireland—Gerrymandering was used after the establishment of Home Rule in Northern Ireland in 1921 to favor Unionists (who tended to be Protestant) over Nationalists (who were mostly Catholic).[16]

United Kingdom—Much has been written about how political parties in the U.K. try to influence the shaping of electoral constituencies to bias election results for Parliament.[17] Moreover, each redistricting takes years to complete—meaning that

---

[14]*See*, Chap. 14; and *The Politics of Redistricting in Japan: A Contradiction between Equal Population and Respect for Local Government Boundaries* by Tashimasha Moriwaki at page 107 in **Redistricting in Comparative Perspective** by Lisa Handley & Bernard Grofman, eds., Oxford Univ. Press (2008).

[15]*See, The Electoral System of the Russian Federation by Bill Bowring,* **DIRECTORATE-GENERAL FOR EXTERNAL POLICIES OF THE UNION OF THE EUROPEAN PARLIAMENT** *(2011); Russian Parliamentary Election Report on Duma Elections in 2016,* **OSCE/ODIR** *(2016);* and *Putin Changes September Election Rules To Prop Up His 'United Russia' Party* by Patrick Roderick Gregory, **Forbes** (Mar 14, 2016).

[16]*See, Electoral Redistricting in Ireland* by John Coakley at page *155* in **Redistricting in Comparative Perspective** by Lisa Handley & Bernard Grofman, eds., Oxford Univ. Press (2008).

[17]*Electoral Distortion Despite Redistricting by Independent Commissions: The British Case, 1950–2005* by Ron Johnston, Charles Puttie, and David Rossiter at page 205 in **Redistricting in Comparative Perspective** by Lisa Handley & Bernard Grofman, eds., Oxford Univ. Press (2008); **PUTTING VOTERS IN THEIR PLACE** by Ron Johnson & Charles Pattie, Oxford Univ. Press (2006).

the underlying data is outdated by the time it is used. For example, the last redrawing of constituencies in England began in 2001, but did not become effective until the 2010 election. In 2011, Parliament revised the redistricting criteria, reduced the number of constituencies (from 650 to 600), and directed the country's four boundary commissions to review and to report on new constituencies before October 1, 2013. This entire review of constituencies stalled in 2013 as the Parliament was unable to muster votes for adoption of the new constituencies. This review of constituencies was postponed until 2018 and the reduction in the number of constituencies was delayed until after 2020.

Southeast Asia—Several writers lament that Democracy is retreating in Southeast Asia.[18] The issues go far beyond the gerrymandering of electoral districts.

Latin America—Several countries are facing democratic regression. As in Southeast Asia, the issues go beyond the gerrymandering of electoral districts.

Africa—According to The African Election Database, in sub-Saharan Africa alone there are five countries that conduct elections that are not free and fair.

The gerrymandering of the shape of districts is also a factor when districts are drawn in mixed systems.

9.10 Conclusion

Gerrymandering is not solely an American phenomenon. It exists throughout the world and in every election system where decision-making about the allocation of seats or shape of electoral districts is susceptible to the influence of political self-interest. Any effort to limit gerrymandering lies in a nation adopting an effective means of eliminating or at least minimizing the opportunities for that influence, not through the choice of the election system itself. Some nations have been successful in finding such means; others have not.

[18]*See, South-East Asia: lots of elections, not so much democracy* by Banyan, Economist (May 26th 2018) *Democracy in Southeast Asia: Achievements, Challenges and Prospects, Electoral Integrity*, **a Kofi Annan Foundation Initiative** (Kuala Lumpur, Malaysia September 2–3, 2017); *East Asia and the Receding Tide of the Third Wave of Democracy* by Larry Diamond (Keynote Speech), International Conference on Democracy in East Asia and Taiwan, Global Perspective (2011) available at ldiamond@Stanford.edu

Chapter 10
Mixed Election Systems Combining Electoral Districts with Proportional Representation Elections

Several nations combine single-member electoral districts with proportional representation in a dual system for the election of members of the lower chamber of its national legislature or for its unicameral national legislature.[1]

The two electoral systems function separately. Usually each voter may cast two votes—one for the direct election of his or her favored candidate in the single-member district where the voter resides and one for a political party. These choices can appear on a single ballot, but usually appear on two separate ballots. The basic purpose of such a dual system is to combine the ostensible advantages of direct single-member elections (e.g. geographical representation) with the perceived fairness of proportional representation. The specifics of this dual system vary among nations.

10.1 Mixed Member Proportional (MMP) Elections

Germany is the leading example of a mixed system, but with a twist. The Bundestag has 299 members elected directly from single-member districts in each of Germany's 16 states (Lander). The Länder are allocated these constituencies based on their

[1]Nations that have mixed election systems include: Andorra (P), Armenia (P), Antigua and Barbados (P), Bolivia (MMP), Cameroon (P), Chad (P), Democratic Republic of Congo (Kinshasa) (P), Djibouti (P), Ecuador (P), Georgia (P), Germany (MMP), Guatemala (P), Guinea (P), Hungary (P, changed from MMP in 2012), Italy (P, changed in 2018), Japan (P), Jordan (P, with seats reserved for women, Christians, and Chechens/Circassians), Republic of Korea (P, South Korea), Lesotho (MMP), Lithuania (P), Libya (P), Madagascar (P), Mauritania (P), Mexico (P), Monaco (P), Nepal (P) (26 appointed), New Zealand (MMP), Niger (P), Panama (P), Pakistan (P), Philippines (P), Puerto Rico (P), Russian Federation (P beginning in 2016), Romania (MMP), Senegal (P), South Sudan (P),Taiwan (P), Tajikistan (P), Tanzania (P), Thailand (P), Ukraine (P), Venezuela (changed from MMP to P in 2010), and Zanzibar (MMP).

S. Bickerstaff, *Election Systems and Gerrymandering Worldwide*, Studies in Choice and Welfare, https://doi.org/10.1007/978-3-030-30837-7_10

number of German citizen population in each Land and the number ostensibly changes as the seats are reallocated because of changes.[2] A proportional representation system exists alongside the single-member election system. A map of the German single-member electoral districts is in Appendix C.

After World War II, Germany attempted to engineer a system (Zweistimmensystem, or as known Internationally—Mixed Member Proportional [MMP]) in which there were a fixed number of single-member electoral constituencies, but a political party's ultimate representation in the Bundestag was never greater than a party's percentage of the national vote. The respective states and parties, however, resisted giving up the seats derived from the district direct elections (i.e. single-member) even if the total number of seats for the party was greater than the percentage earned in the national vote. This led to excess seats in the Bundestag unfairly favoring certain political parties and states. In 2008, the country's Federal Constitutional Court held this system unconstitutional as violating the principles of equality and immediacy of choice.[3]

After two tries, the Bundestag in 2013 adopted a modified system intended to correct this failing. In the words of noted author Professor Freidrich Pukelsheim, the German System:

> serves three goals: to achieve proportionality between political parties across the whole country; to allocate the seats of a party among the party's state-lists of nominees, and to combine the system's proportionality component with plurality elections of individual candidates in single-seat constituencies.[4]

The new system continues to combine single-member district elections and proportional representation, but is designed to adjust representation in the Bundestag according to each party's ratio of votes nationwide by increasing the number of members from other parties. The Constitutional Court approved the new system. As a result, the Bundestag is expected to grow in size.

Several nations followed the German (MMP) model, including Bolivia, New Zealand (changed to MMP in 1993), Hungary (changed from MMP to parallel [P] in 2012), Lesotho, Venezuela (changed to Parallel in 2010), Zanzibar, and

---

[2]As discussed in Chap. 8, Germany has been slow to reallocate seats. In 2012 the average single-member constituency size nationwide was 268,293 persons, but Berlin with a population of 3.56 million had 12 constituencies (average 296,666); while Lower Saxony with a population of 7.79 million had 30 constituencies (average 259,666); and Thuringia with 2.181 million had 9 constituencies (average 242,333).

[3]BVerfGE 121 (2009) 266–317, Judgment of 3 July 2008 (2 BvC 1/07, 2 BvC 7/07). One of the Court's conclusions was that the "negative voting weights" characteristic of the system actually caused parties sometimes to win more seats by getting fewer votes—causing voters to speculate whether casting their vote for their favored party would help or harm it. On a personal note: while teaching in Germany in the early 2000s, I recall being startled by Chancellor Merkel's plea that supporters of her CDU party actually vote for another party to prevent CDU from losing seats.

[4]APPORTIONMENT METHODS AND THEIR APPLICATIONS by Friedrich Pukelsheim, (Springer International Publishing 2014); PROPORTIONAL REPRESENTATION at 247 (Second Edition 2018).

Romania (changed from MMP to FPTP in 2006 and then to PR in 2015). In some of these nations the election system is called "the Additional Member System," but the idea is the same—a party is limited in the total of its representatives in the national legislature from SMD and PR elections to its proportion of the national PR vote.

Italy in 2015 considered following the German lead, but settled instead for a Parallel system (P). Hungary had a MMP system for a while, but changed to a Parallel (P) system in 2011. Venezuela changed to a Parallel (P) system in 2010. Romania changed from MMP to a FPTP system in 2006, but went to a strictly PR system in constituencies in 2015. Bolivia modified the MMP system to avoid increasing its Chamber of Delegates by providing that if one party has more seats from the single-member districts alone than the proportion of list vote it received, the extra seats are taken from the last allocated list seats. The MMP system is used at below the national level in at least Scotland and London.

International agencies, such as ACE and OSCE/ODIR, have concluded that the German Lander do not relish a loss of seats or a change in constituency boundaries and that members of the German Parliament are also likely to object to changes in constituency lines because new constituency boundaries could make it more difficult for incumbent legislators to win and could lead to the loss of a party seat. "Therefore, [the German] Parliament often simply accepts only those changes that are mandated by law, retaining the status quo as much as possible."[5]

10.2 Parallel Election Systems (P)

Most of the 45 or more nations with a mixed system make no effort such as Germany's to limit a party's membership in the national legislature, including constituency victories, to the ratio of a party's percentage of the vote nationwide or to increase the size of their national legislature for equality. In this second category of a mixed system the two components—single-member district elections and national proportional representation elections—are unconnected. This is called a Parallel System (P).

In the nations using this parallel system, such as Japan, Mexico, Ecuador, Republic of Korea (South Korea), Niger, Pakistan, Philippines, The Russian Federation, Italy, and South Sudan, there are a fixed number of single-member and proportional representation seats. The seats won by a political party in the proportional representation election are merely added to the seats won by the party directly through the district single-member elections.

[5] *See,* Appendix C, A Case Study of Germany.

10.3 The Percentage of SMD and PR Seats

The relative number of seats that are decided in single-member or PR elections varies by country. The most common division is a roughly evenly split mix. Some countries, however, have a significantly uneven split. For example, in the Republic of Korea (South Korea) there are 253 members of the national legislature elected from single-member constituencies, while only 47 are elected through a national PR system. In MMP election systems, the number of single-member constituencies remains unchanged, but the number of PR seats fluctuates as necessary to equalize party representation in the national legislature.

10.4 Geographical Areas for the PR Component of MMP or Parallel Election Systems

The PR component of a mixed system election may be carried out on the basis of the nation as a whole, within specially designated multi-member districts, or within the country's fixed districts.

Nationwide

The Russian Federation is an example of a nation that combines single-member districts with a nationwide PR election. Russia had experimented with a nationwide PR election for all members of its lower chamber, but recently changed to a Parallel System.[6] In doing so, it kept nationwide elections for the PR component of the system.

Other nations that use nationwide elections for the PR component of their mixed systems include the Republic of Korea (South Korea), the Philippines, and Hungary. This is also true of some other countries, although many allow a party to submit a different list for each fixed district.

Specially Designated Multi-Member Districts

Several nations that use mixed systems conduct their PR elections using specially designated multi-member districts.

In Mexico,[7] both chambers of the national legislature use a Parallel election system. The PR component of the lower chamber (Cámara de Diputados) is based on the outcome in five super-sized multi-member, multi-state districts (Fig. 10.1).

Each multi-member district in Mexico elects 40 members to the national legislature. The electoral regions may be modified by the National Electoral Institute to

---

[6]See Chap. 7.

[7]*Mexico: Final Report, Observing the 2000 Mexico Elections* by Marcela Szymansic, Carter Center and ACE (2000); and *From Politics to Technicalities: Mexican Redistricting in Historical Perspective* by Alonso Lujambio and Horacio Vives Segi in **Redistricting in Comparative Perspective** by Lisa Handley & Bernard Grofman, eds., Oxford Univ. Press (2008).

Fig. 10.1 The special multimember PR electoral districts in Mexico. The map is courtesy of Dr. Adam Carr @ http://psephos.adam-carr.net. In this map, each of the five special multi-member PR (circumscription) districts is shown in a different color. The black lines show the states

maintain a roughly equal distribution of population among the regions. However, the current distribution has been in use since September 30, 2005. The PR component for the upper chamber (Cámara de Senadores) is decided on a nationwide basis.

Among nations that use regional multi-member districts as part of the PR component in their mixed electoral system are Italy, Mexico, and Japan.

Fixed Districts

Several nations with mixed systems determine each party's share of PR seats at the national level after an election, but then disburse those seats to party lists in its fixed districts. Such a dispersion allocation raises the issue of whether its goal is equality in the treatment of voters or political parties. This dilemma is discussed below.

10.5 Gerrymandering the Mixed System

A mixed system is susceptible to gerrymandering. While such a system enjoys the advantages of both single-member and PR systems, it also has the disadvantages of both systems. Some of the most famous examples of gerrymandered mixed systems are discussed elsewhere in this book, but include Germany, The Russian Federation, Mexico, and Japan.

The single-member component can be gerrymandered through both the reallocation and redistricting processes. Any PR component that is based on fixed districts or regional multi-districts can be gerrymandered through the reallocation or district redrawing processes. Both components can be manipulated through the failure to timely make the adjustments that are necessitated by demographic changes.

It is also meaningful that many of the nations that have mixed systems allow preferential voting and independent candidates in the PR component.[8] These aspects of the system theoretically diminish the power of the parties to control who serves in the national legislature and increase the potential for accountability of candidates to voters. Whether these aspects of the system actually have these effects varies by country.

10.6 Is the Goal A Fair Treatment of Persons (Voters) or Parties?

An issue for nations with PR, MMP or P systems that after an election disburse PR seats to their fixed or special multi-member districts is whether the objective is equality for voters or fairness for political parties.

In Germany, the Constitutional Court has endorsed the concept of "success value equality." This concept is based on the premise that "all voters shall have the same influence on the result of the election from the vote they cast."[9] This concept is an endorsement of these Post-Election adjustments to assure that parties receive seats equivalent to their national showing.

Formulas for the Post-Election dispersion of seats are complicated, but usually include the number of votes for a party in a fixed or special multi-member district as a factor. Using the number of votes instead of, or in addition to, the number of persons, citizen population, or electors in a fixed district for dispersion of seats in a PR component invariably adds some deviation from equality because of variations among fixed districts in turnout, invalid votes, and uncounted votes for parties that failed to meet the party threshold.

This problem also exists in circumstances in which a nation uses "leveling seats" or "adjustment seats" after an election to reward parties that met the national threshold, but did now win sufficient votes to gain enough seats in the constituencies to equal its share of the vote nationwide. The underlying principle is that the number

---

[8]For example, both Mexico and Japan allow a voter's preference to affect the ranking of candidates on a party list.

[9]APPORTIONMENT METHODS AND THEIR APPLICATIONS by Friedrich Pukelsheim, (Springer International Publishing 2014); PROPORTIONAL REPRESENTATION at 247 (Second Edition 2018).

of seats a party gets in the national legislature should be as close as possible to the relative number of votes that the party got in the election countrywide.

These Post-Election adjustments in a PR system or in a mixed system almost make the pre-election distribution of seats on the basis of total population or the number of citizens or registered voters largely meaningless. They benefit the parties at the cost of voter equality.

Whether this deviation works over time to provide significant unequal treatment for voters in certain countries is unclear to me.

10.7 Conclusion

Several nations, such as Italy, the Russian Federation, and Hungary, have changed to a mixed system within the past decade. Combining direct election and PR election systems is attractive, but it has advantages and disadvantages. Having a mixed system does not mean avoiding the opportunity for gerrymanders. Such a system has multiple ways in which it can be manipulated for political self-interest.

The key to true representative government lies not in the choice of a specific election system, but in how the redistricting and seat allocation decisions are made. Are there clear criteria to identify the public interest? Are the decision processes insulated from political self-interest? These issues are addressed in the following chapters.

Chapter 11
Protecting Access by Minorities and Women to the Political Process

Many nations now provide by law for a means for advancing or protecting the interests of groups when those persons or voters might not otherwise be able to win election to the national legislature. These provisions are the result of the work of many organizations.[1] International treaties and standards allow special measures for advancing ethnic minorities or groups that have suffered past discrimination, and such measures are not considered necessarily discriminatory themselves. Many organizations have pushed for greater representation of women on party lists or in the national legislature.

Single-member districts can discriminate against minorities if drawn to crack or pack cohesive areas of predominately minority population. The districts may also effectively prevent minority success at the polls even when gerrymandering has not occurred, if voting in the district is polarized against the minority.

Multi-member districts, such as used in PR elections, can present several impediments to minority access. If voters are polarized along racial, ethnic, religious or political lines, all seats in a district may consistently be won by the same electoral majority unless the election system overcomes such bloc voting. For some observers, this means that minority voters are "submerged" in the political majority and are unable to elect a person of their choice.

There are many methods, however, that can be used to increase minority representation.

At least 40 nations set aside seats in the national legislature for designated racial, ethnic, language, or religious groups, have power-sharing arrangements (e.g. Bosnia), or allow race conscious redistricting to assure minority representation

[1]*See*, e.g. *Statement of Gay J. McDougall, United Nations Independent Expert on Minority Issues,* Hearing of the U.S. Helsinki Commission available @ www.csce.gov/sites/helsinkicommission. Reports of the U. N. Independent Expert on minority issues based on her observations are available for many different countries.

S. Bickerstaff, *Election Systems and Gerrymandering Worldwide*, Studies in Choice and Welfare, https://doi.org/10.1007/978-3-030-30837-7_11

in the national legislature.[2] The definition of the protected minority and the methods of achieving minority representation vary widely among countries.

11.1 Methods of Aiding the Representation of Identified Minority Groups

The following are the methods I identified that nations are using to aid minority representation in their national legislatures and a few examples of the nations using the method. It is not intended as listing of all nations that aid minority representation.

11.1.1 Consideration in Redistricting

One method is to specify that minority communities are communities of interest to be considered in redistricting. In Panama concentrations of indigenous populations must be considered. Kazakhstan is bicameral, with the lower chamber (Mazhilis) having 107 seats. Most (98) are directly elected nationwide, but nine are chosen by the Assembly of Kazakhstani Nation, which is a presidentially appointed advisory body designed to represent the country's ethnic minorities. In Italy's mixed system, separate districts are formed where recognized linguistic minorities reside. In Ukraine, the density of national minority populations is to be taken into account. Criteria requiring due consideration of a minority population is often unlikely to have any significant effect on the election of minorities. On the other hand, in at least two countries, U.S. and Canada, the splitting of a minority community can be a basis for a court challenge to the redistricting plan.[3]

11.1.2 Guaranteed Seats for Minority Groups

A surer method for guaranteeing that the views of named minorities are part of a nation's law-making is to set aside a certain number of seats in the national legislature for designated minorities. The definition of a protected minority varies by nation and circumstance. In some cases it is a racial or ethnic group. In others it is

---

[2]*See, Reserved Seats in National Legislatures: A Comparative Approach by Andrew Reynolds* at 115 in **Redistricting in *Comparative Perspective*** *by Lisa Handley & Bernard Grofman, eds., Oxford Univ. Press (2008).*

[3]*See, e.g.* Reference re Prov. Electoral Boundaries (Sask) [1991] 2 S.C.R. 158, 183 (Can.); Thornberg v. Gingles, 478 U.S. 30 (1986).

a religious group. Some countries even reserve seats for certain occupations such as farmers, students, or laborers or for disabled persons.

In the Middle East the emphasis is on religious groups. For example, Iran's national legislature includes five seats reserved for non-Muslim minorities; specifically the nation's Jewish, Zoroastrian, and Armenian Christian populations. Pakistan reserves categories of seats for women and non-Muslims. The State of Palestine reserves seats for religious minorities. Jordan is a constitutional monarchy, but it too reserves seats in its national legislature for Christians, Chechens/Circassians and women. In addition, Jordanian law requires three multi-member districts drawn for the probable election of Bedouins. Lebanon divides the national legislature equally between Christians and Muslims, and further divides the nation into districts and sub-districts designed to elect representatives of different sects of these two religions.

By contrast, the emphasis in Eastern Europe is on racial or ethnic groups and is largely the result of past conflict among these groups. In Croatia, for example, separate seats are reserved for the Hungarian, Czech and Slovak, Rumanian and Ukrainian, and Austrian and German minorities. In addition, Croatian law specifically reserves three seats in the national legislature for the Serbian minority. In Slovenia, two seats are reserved for the Hungarian and Italian minorities. Kosovo reserves 20 seats in its 120 member national legislature split between ten for Serbs, four for Roma, Ashkali, and Egyptian, three for Bosnians, two for Turks and one for Goranis. Since 2014, Hungary has allowed each of the Armenian, Bulgarian, Croatian, German, Greek, Polish, Romani, Romanian, Rusyn, Serbian, Slovakian, Slovenian, and Ukrainian ethnic minorities to win one of the 93 PR seats in its parallel system if they register as a specific list and reach a lowered threshold.

In Central and South America, the dominant issue is representation of indigenous persons. Columbia reserves a single seat for indigenous people. Venezuela reserves three. Panama requires that concentrations of indigenous people be considered in redistricting. In several nations the seats are filled by the "indigenous" persons using usos y costumbres practices, which are a less formal and more "community-based" method for resolving disputes selecting representatives.

In Africa, many of the governments continue to face economic and political challenges, including the representation of minority groups. Guaranteed seats are primarily for tribal groups and women. In Burundi, approximately 60% of the seats in the national legislature are allocated to Hutu and 40% to Tutsi, with three 3 seats reserved for Twas. Women must occupy 30% of the total seats. Appointments are made to "co-opted" seats as required to assure that the quotas are met. In Rwanda, one authority says that there are 45 Hutu and 13 Tutsi seats in the lower house,[4]

[4]See, *Reserved Seats in National Legislatures: A Comparative Approach* by Andrew Reynolds at page 115 in **Redistricting in Comparative Perspective,** Lisa Handley and Bernard Grofman, Eds. (Oxford Press 2008). Another authority says that the tribal distinctions between Hutus and Tutsi have been abandoned and all are Rwandans.

but other sources disagree. Twenty-four women are elected by electoral colleges[5] formed in the provinces and three members of the national legislature are appointed by mini-committees, two representing youth (selected by the National Youth Council) and one representing disabled people (selected by the Federation of the Associations of the Disabled). Niger sets aside eight seats for the Taurag, a nomadic people inhabiting the Sahara. At least one nation, Zimbabwe, once reserved 20 seats for "Whites" elected nationwide using preferential voting. Zimbabwe eliminated this reservation of seats in 1987.

In Asia, the protected groups are more diverse. The Philippines reserves 20% of the seats in its national legislature for "marginalized groups or parties", with a three seat cap for such groups or parties. Papua New Guinea has single-member constituencies with an Alternative Vote (AV) election system, but has separate sets of communal seats to guarantee representation of the major ethnic groups. Samoa has seats for non-Samoans.

There are several methods by which these countries fulfill their guarantee in regard to minorities and women in the national legislature. One common method is by appointment. For example, in some nations, if elections fail to produce the desired result, someone (usually the president) is authorized to appoint as necessary to meet the prescribed membership.[6] Another method is by the use of nationwide elections in which only certain minorities or women are eligible to become candidates or to vote. For example, Pakistan uses primarily single-member districts, but it uses PR elections to fill 60 additional seats for women (PR by province) and 10 seats for non-Muslims (PR nationwide).

Specific examples include:

11.1.3 Creation of Districts Designed to Elect Minority Candidates

In New Zealand,[7] a separate set of Maori electoral districts exists alongside the general districts; with only Maoris allowed to vote or to seek election in these electorates.[8] These Maori districts cover the entire country and exist as an overlay of the general electoral districts. Maoris have been represented in the New Zealand parliament in roughly the same proportion as their percentage in the population

---

[5]Encarta Dictionary defines a college in this context as "A group of people, usually of the same profession, who have agreed duties and rights."

[6]For example, in Mauritania so-called "best loser" seats are appointed by the Electoral Supervisory Commission and are apportioned among four constitutionally recognized ethnic or religious communities (Hindus, Muslims, Chinese, and Creole).

[7]*See, An Independent Commission with Political Input: New Zealand's Electoral Redistribution Practices* by Alan McRobie in **Redistricting in Comparative Perspective** by Lisa Handley & Bernard Grofman, eds., Oxford Univ. Press (2008).

[8]Maori voters and candidates are not prohibited from instead participating in the general election.

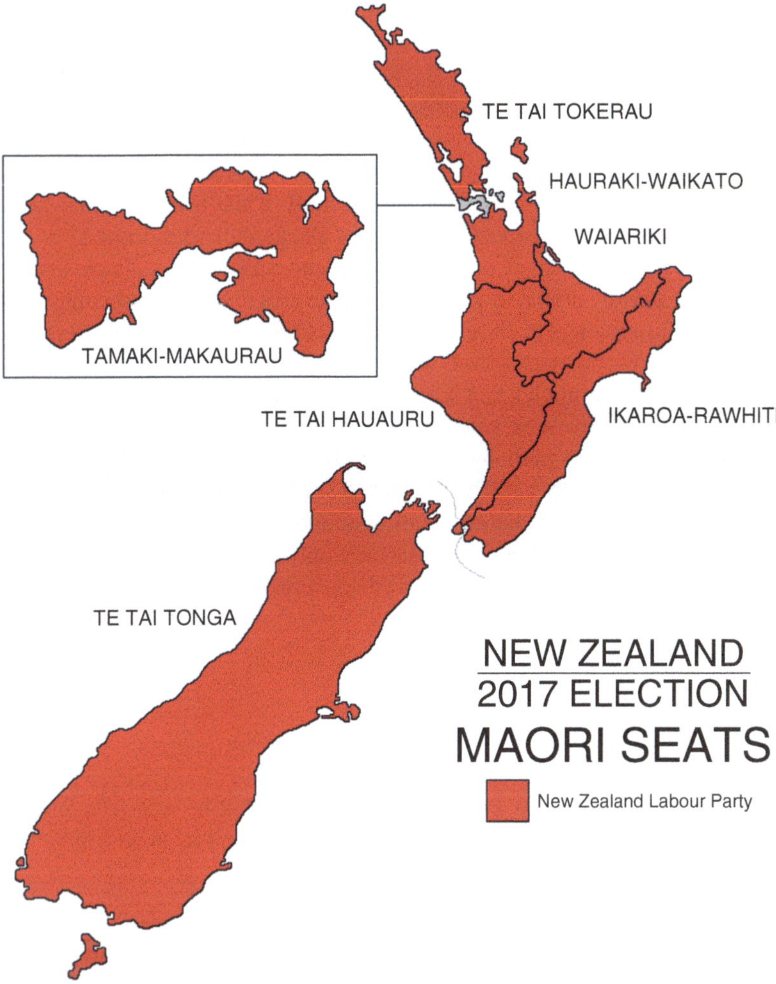

Fig. 11.1 New Zealand 2017 election: Maori seats. There have been seven Māori electorates in each of the 2008, 2011, 2014, and 2017 general elections. The map is courtesy of Dr. Adam Carr @ http://psephos.adam-carr.net

(Fig. 11.1). Registration on the Maori electoral roll is optional; Maoris can choose to register on the general roll instead.

In Italy the new system calls for separate constituencies to be formed where recognized linguistic minorities reside.

Lebanon probably carries the idea of creating districts to assure religious equality further than any other country.[9] The 2008 Lebanon Constitution requires that the

[9]*See, The Lebanese Electoral System,* **IFES** (2009) available at *www.IFES.org; Lebanon's Unique Democracy: 7 Things to Know About Today's Elections, A complex new election law, sectarianism, Palestinian refugees, and the 'selfie prime minister': Your guide to Lebanon's first general election in 9 years,* **The Associated Press** *(May 06, 2018).*

seats in the national legislature must be divided evenly between Christians and Muslims. The two religions are sub-divided into four Muslim and seven Christian sub-groups[10] called "confessionals".[11] The nation's legislature became gridlocked and elections were postponed three times for a total of nine years. A new election law was implemented in 2018. The Constitutional mandate for an even split between Muslims and Christians remains, but the new law implements a PR system that awards seats by the share of vote received, instead of the former winner-takes-all system in each district. It reduces the number of electoral districts from 23 to 15, but many districts are unchanged or are divided into sub-districts. Each district or sub-district is carefully drawn to give voting majorities to the various confessionals. The new law allows voters to choose both an electoral list and a preferred candidate from that list. A general election was held under the new law on May 6, 2018. The new election law is so complex that some say they would rather stay at home because they can't figure out how their vote will be computed.[12]

In India, there are 79 parliamentary seats reserved for Scheduled Castes, and 41 seats for Scheduled Tribes.[13] These reserved single-member districts are allocated to each state (fixed district) based on its proportion of the protected class in the national population. In reserved constituencies, only candidates from these communities can stand for election. These reserved constituencies shift among states from one election to the next.

11.1.4 Allowing Self Government

Recently the President of the Philippines announced that he was recognizing the right of the Southern Philippines to limited self-government in an area to be known

[10]Muslim sub-groups were Sunni, Shia, Alawite, and Druze.

[11]Under the previous law, the nation's 128 parliamentary seats were allocated among 26 multi-member districts (2–10 seats in a district), with seats in a district assigned to specific confessionals. Although candidates for a particular seat had to be from that confessional, all voters in the district could vote for each seat allocated to the district.

[12]*See, Lebanon's Unique Democracy: Seven Things to Know About Today's Elections, A complex new election law, sectarianism, Palestinian refugees, and the 'selfie prime minister': Your guide to Lebanon's first general election in 9 years,* **The Associated Press** (May 06, 2018); *The Lebanese Elections and Their Consequences* by Rayan El-Amine, Middle East Research and Information Project (June 14, 2018); Is Lebanon's New Electoral System a Path Out of Sectarianism? By Elias Muhanna, **The New Yorker** (June 29, 2017); *7 Things to Know About Today's Elections, A complex new election law, sectarianism, Palestinian refugees, and the 'selfie prime minister': Your guide to Lebanon's first general election in 9 years,* **The Associated Press** (May 06, 2018); *The Lebanese Elections and Their Consequences* by Rayan El-Amine**, Middle East Research and Information Project** (June 14, 2018); *Is Lebanon's New Electoral System a Path Out of Sectarianism?* by Elias Muhanna, **The New Yorker** (June 29, 2017).

[13]*See, Delimitation in India* by Alistair McMillan at page 75 in ***Redistricting in Comparative Perspective*** by Lisa Handley & Bernard Grofman, eds., (Oxford Univ. Press 2008).

as Bangsamoro. The area is predominately Muslim, while the remainder of the Philippines is primarily Christian. The action followed many years of fighting by the Muslims for independence. A similar recognition of self-government applies in the relationship of Zanzibar to Tanzania and in a few other situations around the world.

11.1.5 Exemptions in a PR System

An approach for aiding certain groups to become represented in the national legislature in a country using proportional representation elections is to waive the required threshold of votes that the group as a "racially or ethnically minority" party must receive nationwide. For example, Serbia, Germany, and Poland make an exception to their 5% proportional representation threshold for qualifying minority parties. These parties are only required to meet a threshold of .04% of the national vote in Serbia, the equivalent of a single member in the national legislature. Another approach is to require party lists to contain a certain percentage of identified minorities.

11.1.6 The Upper Chamber

Many nations have similar measures to assist minorities in becoming members of the nation's upper chamber. For example, Belgium reserves seats for French, Flemish, and German in its upper chamber.

11.2 Representation of Women

It has become increasingly common for countries to advance the election of women. In countries using PR elections, this may be accomplished by requiring parties to include women on their party list, or even to require them to alternate men and women on the list. In Burundi, the election in the lower chamber is PR in MMD, but there is a quota of 30% women. If the quota is not met in the election, the president appoints women to fill the gap.

The PR component of the new mixed system in Italy is an example of how a PR system can be designed to assure female representation. Each party list is closed and must alternate male and female candidates. Some preferential voting exists, but is limited. This limit is intended to prevent voters from skipping over the female candidates. Also, no party list can have over 60% of same gender, nor can any party have over 50% of one gender among its leaders.

In countries that rely on single-member elections, seats may be set aside for women. For example, in Pakistan, 272 members of the national parliament are elected from single-member districts, but an additional 60 seats are reserved for women and 10 for non-Muslims. The women candidates for these reserved seats are chosen from closed lists filed by the political parties and the seats are filled under a PR system based on the number of general seats won by each political party by province. The seats reserved for non-Muslims are filled under a PR system, but based on results in the country as a whole. Morocco has a similar system, with 30 seats reserved for women and filled by national PR elections.

An alternative for increasing the number of women in the national legislature's Upper Chamber is by requiring the appointment of women. In Afghanistan the President appoints 34 persons to the Upper Chamber, half of whom must be women. This same approach exists in Swaziland, where the King appoints ten Members of the Upper Chamber, half of whom must be women.

11.3 The United States

The United States makes no special provision for aiding women to secure seats Congress. After the 2018 mid-term elections, there are 25 female senators out of 100 members of the Senate and 102 women out of 435 members in the U.S. House of Representatives.

Nor does the U.S. expressly set aside any seats for minorities or (contrary to some descriptions) require that districts be created for the election of minorities. Instead, the Voting Rights Act of 1965 and Constitution have been interpreted to prohibit districts that dilute minority voting strength by gerrymandering (i.e. packing or fracturing) large, cohesive minority communities in the presence of polarized voting by a majority.[14]

The Act has aided certain minorities to win election to Congress. After the 2018 mid-term elections, there were two Hispanic-American, three Asian-American, and three African-American members of the U.S. Senate, and 35 Hispanic-American, 12 Asian-American, and 52 African-American members of the U.S. House of Representatives. The biggest growth has been among Hispanic-Americans and Asian-Americans, both of whom have doubled their representation in the national legislature since 2001.

Court decisions enforcing these Voting Rights Act prohibitions have had the general effect of creating districts in which the protected racial or language group (Black, Latino, Asian, or Native American) has the "opportunity to elect the person of their choice." As a practical matter, this has meant the creation of electoral districts under the Voting Rights Act in which the minority voters are a majority of

[14]Thornberg v. Gingles, 478 U.S. 30 (1986). The case also emphasizes the importance of the residual effects of past discrimination.

the qualified voters and thus have the ability to outvote any racially "polarized" opposition.[15] In some such districts, the minority voters have elected white representatives.

These districts are also often seen as form of gerrymander because designed to achieve a specific purpose and are some of the most bizarre in appearance of all districts as the map drawer searches by computer for election precincts or census blocks that have the desired demographics, while avoiding other precincts and staying within the strict one person, one vote requirement. I dislike the bizarre shapes of some of these districts and think that the desired result can be achieved without such contortions, but I disagree with the classification of these districts as gerrymanders because (if done correctly) they are created to meet a legally recognized public need or approved criteria, not the self-interest of politicians.

The following congressional districts were created in the center of Harris County (Houston), Texas by a Democratically-controlled state legislature in 1991. They were designed to allow both Black and Hispanic voters in Harris County to elect a person of their choice to Congress. I applaud the goal, but deplore the largely unnecessary disregard of traditional redistricting criteria.

The districts were drawn so that Black voters were a majority of the voters in the light blue district (Congressional District 18) and Hispanic voters were a majority of voters in the red district (Congressional District 29).[16] The underlying assumption was that these minority groups could not be assured of the ability to elect the person of their choice as required under the then existing law unless they constituted a majority of the eligible voters in the districts. A majority of persons was thought insufficient because of the higher rate of non-citizens and underage persons within these groups, especially among Hispanics.

The districts were created using census blocks (shown by the solid lines) which provided the population and racial composition of each block. These small census blocks, sometimes containing <50 persons, were used in an effort to achieve the designed objectives while also meeting all perceived legal requirements of the U.S. Constitution and Voting Rights Act (Fig. 11.2).

There was also a partisan component to the redistricting as the race of the voters was used as a proxy for the voter's partisan tendency.[17] The pink and orange districts were expected to favor Republican candidates.

The bizarre district shapes were the result of the drawer's efforts to meet the political and racial objectives while also keeping the districts contiguous and equal in population. Although the districts met these legal requirements, the redistricting

---

[15] *See, e.g.*, League of United Latin American Citizens v. Perry, 548 U.S. 399 (2006). It should be noted that there are some districts with a majority of white voters which have elected a minority candidate and some districts with a majority of minority voters which have elected a white candidate.

[16] District 29 elected a white candidate, who continued to win reelection in the district until retiring in 2018. An Hispanic Democrat won election in 2018 when the white incumbent retired.

[17] Texas does not register voters by party, but it was assumed that Black and Hispanic voters were likely to favor Democratic candidates.

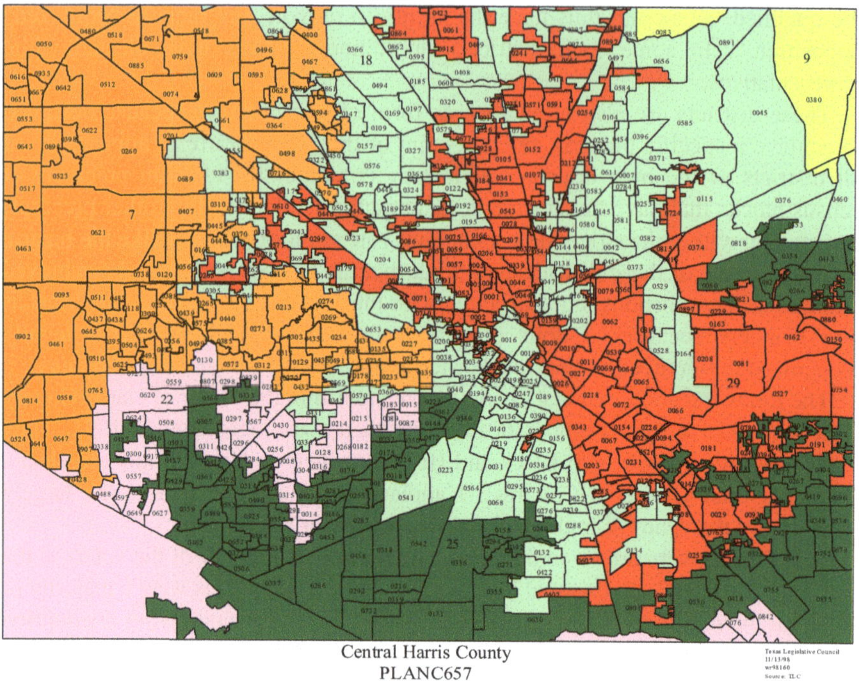

Fig. 11.2 Texas 1991 districts in Harris County. The map is courtesy of Bickerstaff, Heath, Delgado, Acosta LLP

plan for these congressional districts in central Harris County were struck down as racial gerrymanders[18] and redrawn by a federal court. The redrawn districts still accomplished the purposes of the Voting Rights Act and created congressional districts that enabled Black and Hispanic voters to elect the person of their choice.

11.4 Conclusion

The legitimate objective of provisions designed to aid the representation of minorities and women in a nation's national legislature is to build inclusiveness in a democracy and to encourage multi-ethnic coalitions. Overall the willingness of a

[18]Bush v. Vera, 517 U.S. 952 (1996). At the same time, my law partners and I were representing the City of Houston in redrawing its city council districts. We made certain that the city's districts were drawn correctly to comply with the U.S. Constitution and the Voting Rights Act without being influenced by politics. The same organization that had successfully challenged the congressional districts (and the state legislative districts) also filed a suit challenging the Houston City Council districts, but lost. Chen v. City of Houston, 9 F. Supp. 2d 745 (S.D. Tex. 1998). Redistricting can be done correctly.

nation to acknowledge the presence of minorities and women and to provide some means for their views to be heard in the national legislature is a positive development.

It is appropriate, however, to question whether in the long term any of these provisions for racial and ethnic minorities or women are ultimately beneficial, or merely a means for separating these voters and candidates, capping their presence in the national legislature, and making them a permanent and largely powerless underclass.

From my research for this book, I have been pleasantly surprised at the large number of nations that make some provision for minority or female representation in their national legislatures, but distressed at the negative assumptions that underlie the need for such provisions. I wish we lived in a world where it was assumed that the member of a group can fairly represent all of his or her constituents, and that everyone can be fairly represented by his or her member of the national legislature regardless of that person's race, ethnicity, gender, or religion. We are not there yet.

The assumption underlying the Voting Rights Act in the United States is that as more and more persons from a minority group are elected, the barriers of bias will lessen. The Act has had a significant effect. The number of minorities and women elected to Congress, state legislatures, and local government governing bodies has soared. Many observers suggest, however, that this effort at achieving minority representation and proportionality in an electoral system where the number of persons is equal in each district has had the unintended consequence of increasing the number of conservative nonhispanic white office-holders, bizarre shaped electoral districts, and the degree of voter, racial and political polarization that is being experienced today.

Is a provision for minority representation in Iran or these strangely shaped "minority" districts in the U.S. gerrymanders? Not always! They are for an approved public purpose, not for the self-interest of the dominant party or an incumbent. Their legitimacy is recognized in international law when a minority has been subject to past discrimination.

Certainly in the U.S., these districts are a result of the manipulation of district boundaries and can be bizarre in appearance, but if genuinely created for the purpose of securing the representation of groups that have suffered past discrimination and have been denied an equal opportunity to affect a nation's policy, they fail to meet the definition of a gerrymander.

As I noted earlier, however, the purpose behind the manipulation of district lines or the guarantee of a seat is not always obvious. Some of the worst gerrymanders to reduce minority election influence are disguised by the majority as districts drawn or seats ostensibly reserved for the protection of minorities.

Chapter 12
Criteria for Determining District Boundaries

The technical processes of redrawing districts or reallocating seats among districts has always been relatively simple,[1] but it has become even easier in most nations because of technological advances and improved data. The greatest difficulty, however, is political. Even the simplest change necessarily affects two or more districts, meaning two or more incumbents and potential election outcomes.

Every change has a political effect, even if that effect is not foreseen or intended. Incumbents, potential candidates, communities (e.g. states), racial, religious or ethnic groups, political parties, and individuals are all affected. As a result, it is common for redistricting single-member districts or reallocating seats among single-member or multi-member districts to be compromised, delayed, or abandoned altogether because of politics.

The redistricting process is not about finding a pre-existing "ideal," but about creating districts that can serve one of two purposes. The districts can be drawn to serve the self-interest of political parties and politicians, or they can be drawn to serve the public interest according to criteria established by law.

There are several criteria traditionally considered "neutral" in drawing electoral districts and often mentioned as appropriate guidelines for how districts should be drawn. These are discussed in this chapter.

These factors serve several purposes. The first is to provide legal and neutral guidelines for line-drawing that can minimize the effects of politics and, if followed, keep the most extreme partisanship at bay. A second purpose is to make each electoral district an area where most of the inhabitants share some common interests. A third purpose is to make each district one where transportation options and media

[1]The basic criteria for drawing electoral districts have changed little in the past 40 years. *Compare: Reapportionment by State Legislatures: A Guide for the 1980s* by Steve Bickerstaff, 34 **Southwestern Law Journal** 607 (1980) with *A Comparative Survey of Structures and Criteria for Boundary Delimitation* by Lisa Handley at page 265 in **Redistricting in Comparative Perspective** by Lisa Handley & Bernard Grofman, eds., Oxford Univ. Press (2008).This Book also contains in Appendix C a list of 60 nations that claimed to delimit districts and their criteria.

S. Bickerstaff, *Election Systems and Gerrymandering Worldwide*, Studies in Choice and Welfare, https://doi.org/10.1007/978-3-030-30837-7_12

are shared by all inhabitants and allow communication among candidates and voters throughout the district. A fourth purpose is potentially to provide a reason for any deviations in the equality of persons or voters among districts.

The following are common criteria for discerning the public interest in how districts are drawn. ACE is a good source of information on the redistricting delimiting) process.[2]

12.1 Equality in Population or Electors

Voter equality as a criterion is discussed in a Chap. 4. Most countries use a census or the latest count of electors as the base for drawing districts. A few nations, such as Canada and Australia, allow the use of projections of population or electors. Many nations, however, ignore this requirement or use a lax standard of equality.

12.2 Contiguity of Districts

An electoral district envisions a constituency that shares some common geographical location. Basic to this concept is the notion that each district should be a whole—i.e. not divided into disconnected parts.[3] Although this concept is generally accepted,[4] several issues have emerged such as: (1) is a district contiguous if it and another district cross (i.e. make an X)? (2) is a district contiguous if it is divided by a body of water? (3) Is a district contiguous if it is divided by a natural feature, such as a mountain, that makes it impossible to go directly from one part of the district to another? and (4) is contiguity important today given the advance of media technology?

12.3 Compactness of Districts

Compactness is often mentioned as a neutral factor, but efforts to define it using a mathematical formula have been unsuccessful. Still, many countries claim compactness or the uniformity in the shape of districts as a desirable goal for drawing district boundaries.[5] For example, the applicable law of Mexico specifies a preference for

---

[2]http://aceproject.org/ace-en

[3]In the U.S., however, some districts are contiguous only in the technical sense of being connected by thin areas with few or no inhabitants.

[4]At least one country, Mongolia, has some non-contiguous electoral districts.

[5]These nations include Mexico, Albania, Armenia, Bangladesh, Barbados, Belarus, Dominican Republic, India, and Pakistan.

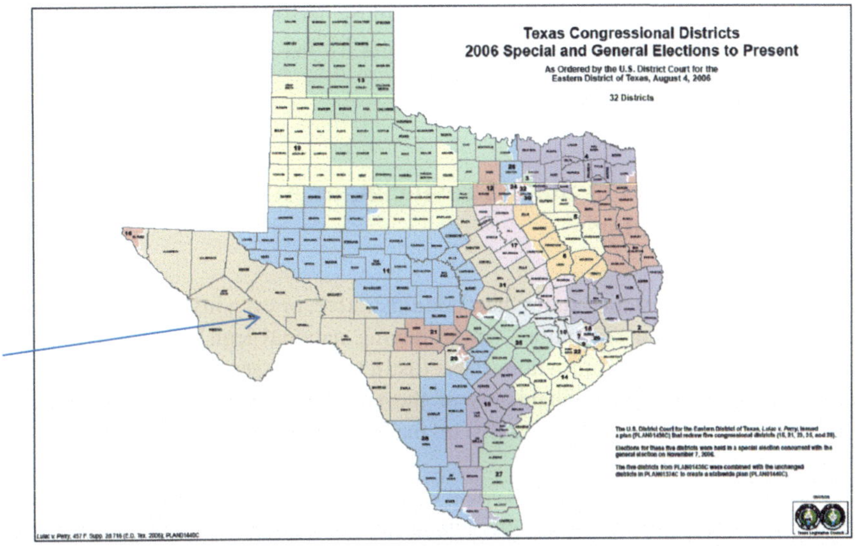

Fig. 12.1 Congressional District 23 in Texas. The map is available courtesy of the Texas Legislative Council @www.tlc.gov. The arrow points to Texas Congressional District 23. This is an old map. The districts were redrawn in 2011, but District 23 still stretches across West Texas

regular geometrical patterns, such as polygons. Even many states in the U.S. include compactness as a factor.

The reality in the U.S. and most other countries, however, is that this criterion of compactness is often lost among other criteria. There are good reasons, such as population inequality, sparsity of population, irregularity in administrative unit or community borders, and bad reasons, such as political advantage, for drawing non-compact electoral districts.

The problem is epitomized in Texas by Congressional District 23 which stretches from urban San Antonio westward to the outskirts of El Paso—a distance of over 500 miles (Fig. 12.1). Yet, it is absolutely equal in population with some Texas congressional districts in the urban counties that are barely 5 miles across. It is common for an uninformed observer to spot District 23 as bizarre and dismiss it as a gerrymander. However, most of the district is composed of rugged, largely barren and mountainous land that has few inhabitants. Under U.S. law, this land must be included in an electoral district. The only way to achieve population equality is to have the boundaries of the district stretch to include densely populated areas far distant from these remote lands. However, the district is gerrymandered for political and racial advantage by less obvious boundary changes on the eastern end to include or exclude areas of Hispanic voters. It has been at the center of major federal litigation for 3 decades.

There is no way to make the district compact while equalizing its population with other districts in the state. It might be possible to let the district's population drop and become unequal with the other districts by removing one or both of the population centers at either end of the district and adding those persons to other districts. Would this inequality be justified by the district's size? Since such inequality would be challenged in court, no legislature has tried.

12.4 Recognition of State, Provincial, or Administrative Unit Boundaries

The Code of Good Practice states that "administrative, or even historical, boundaries may be taken into consideration"[6] in redrawing national legislative districts. The representatives elected from within these districts can be seen as also representing the interests of all of the inhabitants of the state, province, city, ward, or other governmental unit even if it results in malapportionment. This criterion has a significant effect worldwide.

The starkest evidence of the historical importance of this criterion is, as discussed earlier, the reality that many nations guarantee one or more seats in their national legislature to each state, province, or administrative département or a specific area, such as an island, regardless of the number of persons or voters in the area. This guarantee usually creates an inequality that is not overcome even if the remaining seats are allocated on the basis of the number of persons or voters. The resulting inequality is regrettable and, although widespread and possibly justified at the time of its origin, is less necessary today because of the inclusive effects of nationwide communication. The French Constitutional Council has taken on this issue by reducing each département to one guaranteed seat rather than two.

The recognition of government or administrative boundaries is an important factor in the redistricting of single-member constituencies. Some national laws expressly require the consideration of ward or city boundaries in the shaping of single-member district lines.[7] For example, in France, cantons with fewer than 40,000 inhabitants and cities with fewer than 5000 must be kept intact. U.K. law requires that ward lines remain intact when possible; any split must be justified and, if the ward line is split, it is necessary for the boundary commissions to use polling districts (i.e. voting precincts). Japan has shown a particular interest in the recognition of local government boundaries in the design of single-member districts.[8]

---

[6]*See,* Appendix A.

[7]These countries include: Albania, Bangladesh, Barbados, Botswana, Cameroon, Canada, Croatia, Czech Republic, Dominica, Dominican Republic, France, Germany, Hungary, India, Indonesia, Italy, Japan, Kenya, Republic of Korea, Kyrgyzstan, Lithuania, Malaysia, Mauritius, Mexico, Namibia, Pakistan, Panama, Poland, Saint Lucia, Saint Vincent and the Grenadines, Seychelles, Tanzania, Turkey, Uganda, Ukraine, United Kingdom, United States (some states), and Yemen.

[8]*See, The Politics of Redistricting in Japan: A Contradiction between Equal Population and Respect for Local Government Boundaries by Tashimasha Moriwaki at page 107 in* **Redistricting in Comparative Perspective** by Lisa Handley & Bernard Grofman, eds., Oxford Univ. Press (2008).

12.5 Recognition of Communities of Interest

The objective of this criterion is desirable—that the boundaries of an electoral district should combine, not separate, persons that share common interests. It is, however, a criterion that provides little or no real guidance. People often perceive any interest or community in question differently.

Some countries define the community of interest in terms of common economic interests or racial or ethnic factors. For example, Botswana defines districts in terms of tribes. Others perceive a community of interest in terms of a common religion or merely as inhabitance of the same geographical area. In Hungary, for example, the boundary authority is to take account of ethnic, religious, historical, and other local characteristics when creating electoral districts. ACE indicates[9]:

> German electoral law states that constituencies should form a coherent area. Nepal, Pakistan, and Papua New Guinea electoral laws instruct the boundary authority in each nation to "consider community and diversity of interest" or "homogeneity and heterogeneity of the community." Australian electoral law states that the Redistribution Committee shall give due consideration to "community of interests within the proposed Electoral Division, including economic, social and regional interests."

In most nations, however, the law leaves the community to be defined by the national legislature or commission responsible for the redistricting. This discretion allows the entity to engage in widespread gerrymandering by defining its actions as justified by what it sees as an area of common interests.

12.6 Recognition of Remote or Sparsely Populated Areas

The laws of several nations specifically mention remoteness, sparseness of population, or inaccessibility of an area as factors to be considered in drawing district boundaries. This criterion is used to justify districts with fewer voters or persons as needed to protect rural or sparsely populated areas. In Malaysia, the Election Commission is expressly required to weigh sparsely populated rural constituencies in a manner to guarantee their over-representation in the legislature.

Norway is an example of a nation in which the law recognizes the need to represent underpopulated, rural areas even if it means inequality in population. As explained by the OSCE, "Rural, sparsely-populated constituencies get more seats than the population would otherwise dictate. This is to maintain a representative feeling in assemblies and to prevent the preferences of urban areas always overruling those of rural areas."[10]

---

[9] *Structure and Rules for Delimiting Districts, Establishing Criteria, Communities of Interest; Delimiting Boundaries, Defining Communities of Interest,* **ACE** @ http://aceproject.org/ace-en

[10] NORWAY, PARLIAMENTARY ELECTIONS 14 September 2009, Final Report at page 5, **OSCE/ODHIR** (NOVEMBER 2009). *See* NORWAY, PARLIAMENTARY ELECTIONS

The large physical size of the district can also be an issue. Both Canada and Australia have wrestled with this issue because each has significant tracts of largely uninhabited land. It is very difficult in these areas to make districts equal in persons with other districts without also making the districts huge. A huge district is undesirable because it is likely to combine communities in which the persons have little in common and travel and communication across the district is difficult. For example, in Western Australia, the state and electoral district of Kalgoorli was 3,295,354 sq. km. in size until abolished in 2008. Other countries have addressed the size issue. For example, UK limits the size of its constituencies to 12,000 sq. km.

12.7 Recognition of Natural Features

Natural features, such as a river or mountain, often provide the clearest and most easily determined boundaries of electoral districts. The Code of Good Practice states that "geographical criterion ... may be taken into consideration."[11] Even these boundaries can be problematic. A common difficulty is the manner in which an island is to be treated. The water surrounding an island is clearly a recognizable natural feature and persons separated by significant bodies of water may have few common interests, but making the island into its own electoral district, or districts may cause its residents to be underrepresented or overrepresented in the national legislature.

The Isle of Wight is an example. It is in the English Channel and a part of England, but It has only one member of the U.K. parliament, while other constituencies, with less than half as many eligible voters, also have a member.[12] The last, but unfinished redistribution of constituencies in the U.K. saw the Isle of Wight allocated an additional district—the two districts having 56,000 and 55,000 eligible voters, respectively. By comparison, the average constituency in England is over 70,000. Likewise in the postponed review, the boundary commissioners in Scotland granted the Western Isles, with 22,000 registrants in 2011, and the islands of Orkney and Shetland, with nearly 36,000 registrants in 2011, their own representatives. These islands are exceptions in an otherwise nationwide set of districts. Similar exceptions may be found for islands worldwide, such as Zanzibar (Tanzania), Rotuma (Fiji), Aland (Finland), and Banaba (Kiribati). What if the nation itself (e.g. Indonesia, see Appendix C) consists largely of islands?

---

9 September 2013, Election Assessment Mission Final Report, **OSCE/ODHIR** (December 2013) and NORWAY, PARLIAMENTARY ELECTIONS 11 September 2017, Final Report, **OSCE/ODHIR** (December 2017).

[11] *See*, Appendix A.

[12] For example, the London suburb of Surbiton also was designated as a single seat, but the Isle of Wight had an electorate of 95,000 and Surbiton had only 48,000 electors.

12.8 Recognition of Existing or Historical Boundaries

The criterion of recognizing and preserving the core of existing districts is accepted in many nations as a legitimate means of avoiding voter confusion, recognizing established communities of interest, and possibly preserving experience or seniority in the national legislature. In Germany this shaping of new boundaries to look as much as possible like existing ones is seen favorably as a means of maintaining continuity.

In the U.S. the principle of preserving the "core" of existing districts when drawing new ones is considered a legitimate criterion even when it aids incumbents, but is not a justification for any population imbalance. In many nations this is not true.

OSCE standards followed by most European Union members recognize "maintaining historical continuity" as a legitimate criterion for drawing electoral districts.[13] Maintaining the stability of constituency boundaries is deemed by some national legislatures to be as important as readjusting boundaries based on population changes.

Based on my experience, however, the argument that existing electoral district boundaries justify a new election district boundary is primarily a way of urging the status quo to benefit incumbents. No incumbent is willing to propose that the law explicitly provide that protecting incumbents is a legitimate criterion—few if any voters would support such a criterion. Instead, they use, and I think abuse, the argument that the boundary of the district from which they were elected is an "historical" boundary that should be preserved in any redistricting.

12.9 Diaspora, Out-of-Country, or Overseas Voting

Many countries[14] now allow citizens outside the country (i.e. the diaspora) to vote in presidential and national legislative elections. External voting is most common in Europe, but is found in every region of the globe. As of 2006, at least 91 countries allowed their expatriate citizens to vote: 21 African countries, 13 countries in the Americas, 15 Asian countries, 6 Pacific countries and 36 European countries.[15] Out

[13] *See*, Appendix A. and http://aceproject.org/ace-en/topics

[14] Among these nations are Italy, Portugal, Croatia, Turkey, Greece, Algeria, Australia, Austria, Belgium, Botswana, Brazil, Canada, Chad, Chile, Columbia, Costa Rica, France, Gabon, Germany, India, Ireland, Japan, Lesotho, Luxembourg, Mali, Malta, Mauritius, Mozambique, Namibia, Netherlands, New Zealand, Niger, Philippines, Rwanda, Senegal, Singapore, South Africa, Spain, Sweden, Switzerland, Togo, Tunisia, United States, United Kingdom, and Zimbabwe.

[15] This is among nations in the U.N. ACE reports that 115 nations and territories have some provision for "external voting." http://aceproject.org/ace-en/topics

of country voting has become more important and more common as people have become more mobile and as the number of refugees has increased.

In most countries the expatriates must register before the election. There are four questions which each country must answer. Most countries answer them differently.

Who is eligible to vote? The countries vary significantly. Some countries allow all citizen expatriates to vote if they can get to an allowable voting site. Others impose restrictions. For example, in Germany, a citizen who lives abroad may vote in Parliamentary elections if they have resided in Germany for an uninterrupted period for at least 3 months in the past 25 years since their 14th birthday and if they are familiar with German politics and are affected by it. By contrast, a citizen of France, Portugal, South Africa, or the Philippines may vote in parliamentary elections regardless of how long they have lived abroad.[16]

In which elections may they vote? Voting is commonly limited to only national elections, such as for president, the national legislature, or referenda. There are exceptions, such as the United States.

Where can they vote? Some nations permit voting by mail. In others the place of voting may be limited. In at least one nation, Malta, the expatriate must be physically present in the country to vote. Turkey allows qualified persons to vote at designated embassies throughout the world, but the person can only vote in the presidential election and for a party in the PR portion of the country's mixed system, not in the constituency or local elections. Other nations also allow citizens living abroad to vote at designated sites, such as embassies.

Are they entitled to separate representation? Some countries have separate non-geographical constituencies or seats in the national legislature for voters in the diaspora. For example, France has 11 seats in the Chamber of Deputies reserved for French citizens living outside the country. Italy has seats reserved in both of its chambers. Croatia has two seats reserved for Croatian citizens living outside the country. In Macedonia, up to three additional MPs are elected in a single out-of-country constituency.

A decision to allow persons in the diaspora to vote raises several issues. For one, the countries vary as to whether a person obtains citizenship by birth or "blood". This issue is discussed elsewhere. Another issue is the difficulty in knowing the size of this group of persons eligible to vote.[17] If one or more seats are set aside for this

[16]Other examples include: A citizen living abroad may vote in New Zealand if they have lived in the country for at least a year at some point in their lives and have visited within the past 3 years. In Sweden, citizens living abroad may vote, but must renew their registration every 10 years. India disqualifies citizens who have acquired the citizenship of another country. Some countries, such as Brazil and Belgium, have compulsory voting that applies to all citizens, even registered expatriates. http://aceproject.org/ace-en/topics

[17]For example, in the new Italian system there are four foreign zones. There is a discrepancy in the number of votes needed to be elected in the different zones, with Europe electing 2 senators by about two million voters, while the zone of North and Central America with 451,062 and the zone of Africa, Asia, Oceania and Antarctica with 213,561 voters elect one senator. The average quotient for a domestic constituency is 96,171 votes in the lower chamber, ranging from 93,868 in Friuli to 98,252 in Umbria. The average quotient among domestic constituencies for a seat in the Senate is 165,167 votes ranging from 126,324 in Umbria to 204,011 in Toscana.

group, it may mean that these constituencies are significantly smaller or larger than the other constituencies. If these groups consistently vote for certain parties, this may create an advantage for this party. In some parts of the world, such as Central or Eastern Europe, most of the "diaspora" may be just across the country's border and be able to vote twice—once as part of the diaspora of one nation and once as the resident of another nation in which they reside.

In the United States, a person may vote absentee in local and national elections if registered and if permitted by state law, but there are special federal rules applicable to military and other government personnel assigned overseas.

12.10 Territories

Some countries have territories that are part of the country for specific purposes, but lack voting representation in the national legislature. For example, U.S. territories, such as Puerto Rico, Guam, and the American Virgin Islands, are subject to U.S. laws, but do not have a voting member of Congress. The last territories admitted as states with senators and representatives were Alaska and Hawaii in 1959. On the other hand, France has actually designated certain overseas areas, such as French Guiana, Guadeloupe, Martinique, and Reunion, as départements of the country with representation in the national legislature.

12.11 Prohibiting Political Bias

One criterion aimed at limiting political gerrymandering is that "no district boundary should be drawn to advantage or disadvantage any person or group." This criterion has recently appeared within the United States, but it depends on court enforcement, and a violation is likely to be difficult to prove. Nevertheless, inclusion of this prohibition among redistricting criteria may have some prophylactic effect. The most recent, but unfinished, review of constituencies in the U.K. forbids the consideration of "voting patterns and the possible impact on future election results."[18]

On the other hand, these criteria can provide a standard against which the legality of any redistricting plan can be measured. During the past decade, at least ten states in the United States have invalidated legislative or commission redistricting plans because they were partisan gerrymanders or violated state redistricting criteria in an effort to draw districts that satisfied incumbents or political parties. However, such results are possible only if a jurisdiction has specific legal criteria and its courts are willing to enforce those criteria.

[18]*Guide to the 2018 Review of Parliamentary Constituencies,* **Boundary Commission for Northern Ireland (2016)**.

12.12 Conclusion

These neutral criteria for drawing electoral districts are important and generally are well intended and sometimes followed. The relative importance of each criterion can be disputed. Nations may have differing criteria. Overall, these criteria have a positive effect by providing some general guidelines. They are, however, mostly subjective, often in conflict, and too vague to provide an effective restraint on gerrymandering of electoral districts.

The criteria are largely toothless as restraints on firmly held political objectives and actually are often used by members of a national legislature, state legislature or redistricting commission to falsely justify almost any but the most extreme result that serves political goals. One means of testing whether a criterion is actually being used to hide a gerrymander is to see if the criterion proffered as justification for a particular district is being applied uniformly throughout the redistricting proposal. This same test can be applied to any proposed allocation of seats that varies from absolute population or elector equality.

Court enforcement of the criteria is necessary, but, even as a lawyer who has litigated many redistricting cases, I agree that court enforcement of the criteria can be overused and can be political in its own nature, scope, and purpose.

Ultimately, these criteria are only as meaningful as the integrity and objectivity of the persons applying them in the redistricting process. Otherwise they often become merely a ruse for hiding political motives. The issue is public trust.

The legal acceptability of a specific redistricting or reallocation plan essentially involves three basic issues—(1) whether the criteria proffered in support of a specific plan are legitimate public interests as established by law, (2) whether the proffered criteria were systematically applied throughout the plan, and (3) whether the proffered interest justifies the imbalance in population or voters, if any, which it causes.

Chapter 13
The Institution Responsible for Redistricting or Reallocating Seats in the National Legislature

Historically, if a country periodically redrew electoral districts or reallocated seats in the national legislature among fixed districts or multi-member districts, it was the national legislative body that usually exercised that authority indirectly through a legislative committee, with the final authority resting in the national legislature itself. Some nations continue to use this structure.

Many nations, however, have provided for commissions outside the national legislature to periodically review the need for changes in districts and to develop plans for redrawing the nation's electoral districts or to reallocate seats among multi-member districts. This kind of an outside commission, however, is not an independent commission even if their supporters insist on giving them this label. The real power remains with the national legislature itself, which in most cases can toss out the commission's plan altogether, change or amend it, or delay it so that its changes do not affect the reelection of sitting members.

In a few nations, these commissions are authorized to act without the approval of the national legislature and do not include on the commission any politicians or persons who are selected by the politicians or have a personal interest in the outcome of the redistricting or reallocation. These are truly **independent commissions.**

13.1 Is Political Influence Desirable?

The overriding issue for determining the institution responsible for redistricting or reallocating seats in the national legislature is whether a decision about a constituency or allocation should or should reflect the political desires of politicians or political parties. In the view of some observers, any decision about redistricting or reallocation is quintessentially political and should be made by elected politicians because they are familiar with the process and the issues. For this reason, even in

S. Bickerstaff, *Election Systems and Gerrymandering Worldwide*, Studies in Choice and Welfare, https://doi.org/10.1007/978-3-030-30837-7_13

some nations that rely on a redistricting commission, politicians are included on the commission or in the decision-making process.

From my experience, politicians have no knowledge of the appropriate issues in the redistricting or reallocation processes that cannot be learned by intelligent and conscientious non-politicians. No matter how many times a politician has gone through the redistricting or reallocation processes, he or she has to learn the basics again. Relevant data and information is secured from qualified staff which could be available to members of an independent commission. Politicians know politics, but this is a subject that should be excluded or at least minimized. The only way in which to remove political self-interest from processes is to remove the politicians, and others affected by political motives. The processes are better if entirely nonpolitical.

Tensions between these competing views underlie the question of which institution should be responsible for redistricting or reallocating national legislative seats and how any redistricting commission should be structured.

13.2 National Legislatures

In most nations, the national legislature has the final decision about whether redistricting or reallocation of seats takes place and, if so, how or when it is implemented.[1] This puts these issues squarely in the control of the very persons most affected by the decisions—self-interest is obvious. If a plan is developed by a committee of the national legislature, by a commission designated to make recommendations, or a commission with politicians or politically motivated appointees, the final plan is not free of self-serving interest.

Not all members of a national legislature start out with an intention to gerrymander the electoral district in which they were elected, or any other district. Often, however, they react to the situation as it occurs. Many legislators have good intentions, but the fear of political defeat prevails. For many it becomes a matter of survival. Gerrymander or possibly kill your political future! Even the most capable of legislators is affected.

[1]Nations in which the national legislature controls the allocation of seats or the redrawing of electoral districts include: Albania, Algeria, Bahamas, Barbados, Belgium, Belize, Benin, Brazil, Bulgaria, Cape Verde, Cameroon, Canada (Provincial Parliaments, with some using commissions), Chile, Croatia, Cyprus, Czech Republic, Dominica, Dominican Republic, Egypt, Finland, France, Gabon, Germany, Greece, Guinea, Hungary, Indonesia, Iceland, Ireland, Italy, Jamaica, Japan, Jordan, Kiribati, Republic of Korea, Kyrgyzstan, Lebanon, Luxemburg, Latvia, Libya, Macedonia, Madagascar, Malaysia, Marshall Islands, Mauritius, Mali, Micronesia, Myanmar, Namibia, New Caledonia, Nicaragua, Niue, Niger, Palestinian Territories, Panama, Papua New Guinea, Peru, Philippines, Poland, Russian Federation, Saint Lucia, Saint Vincent and the Grenadines, Sweden, Slovenia, Swaziland, Togo, Tuvalu, Uganda, United Kingdom, and United States (apportioning of seats in House of Representatives to states), and Zimbabwe.

13.2.1 Plans Developed by States or Provinces

The United States and Canada apparently are among the few countries in which the boundaries of the districts for election of representatives in the national legislative body are drawn by state or provincial legislatures or a commission designated by those legislative bodies. In the U.S. the state legislatures draw the state's congressional districts or designate an outside commission to do so. Some form of a commission is used in many states, although most of these commissions are not truly independent of the legislature's influence. Some states use commissions to redraw state legislative districts, but leave the redrawing of congressional districts to the state legislature.

An entirely new set of political self-interest concerns emerge when a state or provincial legislature draws national legislative districts. Many of these state or provincial legislators harbor the ambition to someday win election to the national legislature and want these districts to be "friendly" to such hopes.

13.3 Commissions

To some, the answer to limiting or eliminating political influence is as simple as removing redistricting authority from the legislative body and entrusting it to a commission outside the legislature. Many nations worldwide now use such a commission or government agency to redistrict or to reallocate seats in the national legislature. It is apparent, however, that political influence is not so easily avoided.

It is critical to understand that "independence" from political influence does not mean merely that a national legislator does not serve on the commission or that the national legislature cannot amend the commission's plan.

13.3.1 Legislative Control of Commission Action

A commission's "independence" can have many meanings. Some think that a commission is "independent" if it is merely outside the legislative structure. This is wrong.

Germany is an example of where an outside commission is present, but it is appointed by the president and the national legislature retains almost full discretion over what action, if any, to take with regard to a commission's findings. The Electoral Districts Commission (EDC) conducts a review of seat allocations and districts at the beginning of each new Bundestag, but the decision of whether to accept the Commission's recommendations rests almost entirely with the Bundestag itself. In France, the French commission has been ineffective in the opinion of the OSCE/ODHIR.

Others believe that a commission is independent if its plans cannot be changed (amended or rejected) by the legislature even though the commission's product requires legislative approval before becoming effective. The United Kingdom, along with members of its Commonwealth that have adopted the Boundary Commission Model, are examples of nations with such a system. The nation's parliament can postpone the changes and thus protect incumbents from having to seek election in newly redrawn constituencies. Most recently the UK Parliament has done so with the Sixth Review of Constituencies.

A final group of nations mistakenly label a commission as "independent" if it has authority to enact a redistricting or reallocation plan without national legislative approval, but includes politicians, government employees, political appointees, or others susceptible to political loyalties or influence among its members? Consider the example of India. While the reallocation of districts among the states has been postponed in India, the redrawing of the nation's constituencies for election to the national legislative chambers (Lok Sabha and Vidham Sabha) has continued. An outside commission within each state adopts district boundaries, but, importantly, legislators from the affected state are included by law as associate members of the commission. As a result, although the commission is sometimes hailed as an "independent" commission, its plans are often seen as gerrymanders to help the ruling party or coalition and incumbents.[2]

A commission is truly independent of the probability of political bias only if its members lack any self-serving incentive and act strictly in accordance with objective legally approved guidelines, and its plans take effect without any action of the national legislature. Considerations for designing an independent commission are set out at the end of this Chapter.

13.3.2 The U.K. Boundary Commissions

The United Kingdom claims to have pioneered the commission approach. A separate four-person Boundary Commission exists for England, Scotland, Wales and Northern Ireland. These commissions are permanent, are chaired ex officio by the speaker of the House of Commons, and operate for the specific purpose of periodically reviewing and redrawing the boundaries of the nation's constituencies.

These commissions are ostensibly "independent," but have drawn criticism as being influenced by the political parties and members of Parliament to produce plans biased for certain political parties or candidates.[3] Until 20 years ago, the creation of

[2] *See, Changing Patterns of Democracy and Representation in India* by Jugdep S. Chima, 52 **Asian Survey** 239–246 (No. 2, March/April 2012) available @ www.jstor.org

[3] *See, Electoral Distortion Despite Redistricting by Independent Commissions: The British Case, 1950–2005* by Ron Johnson, Charles Pattie, and David Rossiter at page 205 in **Redistricting in Comparative Perspective** by Lisa Handley & Bernard Grofman, eds., Oxford Univ. Press (2008)

voting districts by the Boundary Commissions was ostensibly a largely apolitical process, according to geographer Ron Johnston at the University of Bristol, UK. In the 1990s, supporters of the Labour party, then in opposition, realized that they could influence the creation of parliamentary constituencies by submitting their own maps to the Boundary Commissions for consideration, which opened the door to all parties jockeying for influence. The jockeying continues.

The Parliament itself determines by law the allocation of seats among the four entities that make up the U.K. The Parliament by law sets out the criteria that the boundary commissions are obligated to consider in redrawing electoral districts and may include specific exceptions to these criteria. Most importantly, however, a boundary commission's plan does not take effect until approved by the UK Parliament.

Most of the democracies once ruled by the United Kingdom have followed its lead and adopted commissions.[4] A major difference among these nations is that some,[5] unlike the U.K., have commissions whose plans take effect without approval of the national legislature. Several other democracies have adopted boundary commissions similar to those used in the United Kingdom.

Three problems plague the U.K. boundary commission model. One is that the political parties have successfully manipulated the commissions' outcome by testifying before the commissions and using objective criteria to essentially "bamboozle" them into unwittingly making political decisions about district boundaries. As a result, elections in the U.K. have often produced parliaments in which the make-up in term of party affiliation is inconsistent with the total vote received nationwide by the parties. This result has been criticized as a bias caused by the district boundaries.[6]

A second problem with the Boundary Commission Model in the United Kingdom is that a commission's plan ultimately requires Parliament's approval before it can take effect. Even if a commission's plan avoids being skewed for a group or incumbent's advantage, it is susceptible to such an outcome if it becomes effective only with approval of the national legislature, and thus can be postponed to protect incumbents by maintaining the status quo.

A third problem is that, historically, the commission plans have taken years to develop. Thus, they are largely based on outdated data regarding the number of electors or eligible voters in each constituency. The British Parliament has exacerbated this problem by taking years to act on a commission's plan and often

---

and **PUTTING VOTERS IN THEIR PLACE** by Ron Johnson & Charles Pattie (Oxford Univ. Press 2006).

[4]These include: Australia, New Zealand, and Canada, as well as many of the Caribbean countries (e.g., Bahamas, Barbados, St. Lucia and St. Vincent and the Grenadines) and several Anglophone African countries (e.g., Botswana, Namibia, and Zimbabwe).

[5]These include the commissions in New Zealand, Australia, and Canada.

[6]*Electoral Distortion Despite Redistricting by Independent Commissions: The British Case, 1950–2005* by Ron Johnson, Charles Pattie, and David Rossiter at page 205 in **Redistricting in Comparative Perspective** by Lisa Handley & Bernard Grofman, eds., Oxford Univ. Press (2008).

postponing the date on which some of the redrawn districts become effective. These actions are effectively gerrymanders that benefit incumbents.

As discussed previously in Chap. 8, the latest commissions' review stalled as the Parliament was unable to muster votes for adoption of new constituencies. The boundary commissions were scheduled to report their findings in 2013 but were told by the Parliament to begin over again to report in 2018.

A similar problem arises when a commission's redistricting plan requires approval by the country's chief executive. This occurs in at least two nations, Cameroon and Zimbabwe.

13.3.3 The Size of Commissions

Redistricting commissions tend to be relatively small in size, ranging from three to seven or nine members. Canada, for example, has three-member commissions in each of its provinces; The United Kingdom has four-member commissions; and a number of Caribbean countries have five-member commissions (e.g., Bahamas, Barbados). New Zealand, India, and Germany each have seven-member commissions; Albania has a nine-member commission.

13.3.4 The Make-Up of Commissions

The make-up of these commissions is set by law and varies among countries, with some prohibiting public officials from becoming members[7] while others expressly include political party representatives among the commission's members.[8] In New Zealand, two political appointees, one representing the governing party and one the opposition parties, serve on the commission. The theory behind their presence on the commission is that it permits "political" input and helps prevent political bias in a proposed redistricting plan.[9]

The presence of political party representatives or legislators on a commission is unnecessary. To the extent that it is argued that a political party's representative on a commission is necessary to spot aspects of a plan that has detrimental effects on the party or the legislature, the proper venue for airing such concerns is through

---

[7]These nations include Canada and Botswana.

[8]These nations include the United Kingdom, New Zealand, Barbados, India (as associate members), Papua New Guinea, St. Vincent, and the Bahamas.

[9]*An Independent Commission with Political Input: New Zealand's Electoral Redistribution Practices* by Alan McRobie at page 27 in **Redistricting in Comparative Perspective** by Lisa Handley & Bernard Grofman, eds., Oxford Univ. Press (2008). It appears that the presence of politicians on the commission has not overly biased the commission.

testimony in a public hearing where they can be contested if necessary. There is no need for the politician to be on the commission to submit his or her concern about proposed plans so long as the commission's actions are public and transparent.

Allowing factual statements or presentations in private meetings of the commission's members is contrary to open government and representative democracy. Having politicians, or their designees or employees, on a commission increases the possibility that such statements will occur and that the final redistricting plan will be rife with self-interest, politics, misinformation, and incumbency protection—the essential ingredients for gerrymandering electoral districts.

While the absence of such persons on the commission may improve the chances that a final plan will be politically unbiased, there still exists an opportunity for abuse if the members of the commission are not careful to retain their objectivity. Therefore, commission actions and proffered plans must be subject to public scrutiny before adoption.

Several countries use members of the judiciary on their commissions to increase the perceived wisdom and objectivity of the commissions. Sometimes these judicial officers serve along-side other prescribed members of the commission, but often chair the commissions, as in most of the Canadian provinces and in New Zealand. In the United Kingdom, senior judges serve as Deputy Chairs of the four Boundary Commissions. In at least one country, Turkey, all of the members of the commission for allocating seats in the country's PR system to provinces prior to each parliamentary election are judges. As discussed in the Case-Study of Turkey in Appendix C, the result seems to be working well. Of course, the value of having judges on a commission depends on whether the judiciary in a country is independent of political influence.

13.3.5 Election Commissions

In a few other nations (at least 21), the commission exists as an election commission generally with broader authority than a boundary commission. In some of these countries, the election commission is relatively free from executive and legislative pressure, but in other countries this is less true. In a few nations, such as Mexico, this government agency has a reputation for being independent of political influence. In others, however, these commissions are seen largely as tools of the party in power in the executive and legislative offices. For example, in Iran's presidential election in 2009, the nation's election commission was accused of fraud that helped its boss, the incumbent president, win reelection.[10]

[10] *See* Appendix C, the Case Study of Iran.

13.4 The Good Side of Political Influence on Reallocating Seats or Redistricting

It must be acknowledged that some observers see little or no harm in political considerations affecting redistricting or reallocation decisions. If a little gerrymandering can help a "good" political party or an experienced lawmaker win election, doesn't the nation benefit?

It is wrong to accept the proposition that gerrymandering is acceptable if used for a purpose that some think is "good." No person or group should be able to manipulate the redistricting or reallocation processes for their own self-interest.

13.5 The Bad Side of Political Influence on a Commission

There are at least three reasons for concern over redistricting by a commission that includes politicians or persons appointed by or answerable to politicians.

An obvious concern is that a commission may gerrymander districts to favor specific political parties. In an effort to prevent such partisan gerrymanders, it is common to have commissions balanced in membership between the nation's political parties in a bi-partisan manner. However, if a political party is to be represented on the commission, it often will choose a representative that is strongly partisan and who can be expected to battle for a plan favorable to his or her party when a more objective and public-interest view is needed.

A second concern is that the political representatives may reach a compromise so that the final plan does not favor any particular political party, but gerrymanders districts to protect incumbents from all parties. This is an incumbent gerrymander just as if the incumbents had drawn the plan themselves.

A third concern is that a commission may draw districts in such a manner that they benefit the political parties that are represented on the commission and effectively "lock out" other parties, especially new ones.

Even if political officials are not included on the commission, there is concern that a member of the commission could use the post for his or her own benefit by currying favors from politicians, possibly with the objective of later seeking elected office.

On the other hand, the commission in New Zealand has a good reputation for partisan fairness despite including politicians in its membership. However, the nation's population is relatively small and the commission is known for making minimal changes in district boundaries—a policy that benefits incumbents.

13.6 The U.S. Experience

Although states are responsible for redrawing congressional districts in the U.S., at least 21 of them now use some form of commission outside the legislature for redistricting or under special circumstances, such as to convene if the legislature adjourns without adopting a redistricting plan. These commissions are largely a result of a movement in the United States seeking ways to lessen partisan gridlock or political influence on redistricting; this movement has had only limited success.[11] Some of these commissions lack authority over congressional redistricting.

13.7 Criteria for Independent Commissions

Commentators have pointed to the success of commissions in some countries and implied that such success will necessarily accompany the use of any commission. Too often, however, these commentators do not acknowledge that some commissions, once hailed as models of good practice, have flamed-out under the pressures of redistricting and reallocation.[12]

The following steps are the essential criteria for designing a nonpolitical redistricting or reallocation process:

13.7.1 Designing a Truly Fair and Apolitical Means of Choosing the Members of the Commission

Government or political officials, or members selected by these officials, are often undesirable as commission members because their decisions are politically biased. Even a nation's elections officers may be swayed by politics—the heralded boundary commissions of the UK have been seen as producing politically biased plans.

---

[11]The most popular form of commission in the U.S. (used in 12 states) is the bi-partisan commission, in which an equal number of Republicans and Democrats serve on the commission, and there is an "independent" member or members to break ties. These bipartisan commissions were once seen as a positive reform, but, other than the citizen commission in California, have largely been a failure at reducing political influence and bias. A political party's members on such a commission are generally selected because of their strong partisanship, instead of objectivity, and are expected to vote for the outcome that most favors their party or satisfies incumbents of both parties. In the recent redistricting cycle alone, at least six state supreme courts invalidated redistricting plans drawn by these (then) eleven bipartisan commissions as violating the state's constitution. The only apparent reason for the plans not complying with state law was the bipartisan commission's effort to achieve a plan that pleased the incumbents of both political parties.

[12]In an effort to push back against this trend, some cities and states in the United States have begun to use commissions composed of regular citizens rather than political appointees or government employees. The state of California first approved such a commission by referendum in 2008. Several U.S. cities have also done so, such as Austin [TX] and San Diego [CA]). See, *Making Local Redistricting Less Political: Independent Redistricting Commissions for U.S. Cities* by Steve Bickerstaff, 13 **Election Law Journal** 419 (2014).

13.7.2 Choosing the Right Commissioners

The most important characteristics for members of an independent commission are competency, impartiality and integrity. Many nations include election officials, geographers, demographers, or sociologists by law on their commission. In reality the skills ostensibly obtained from these named professionals can be obtained through competent staff and are unnecessary in the commissioners themselves.

13.7.3 Avoiding Political Influence on the Commission Decisions

One means for achieving this goal is to limit membership on a redistricting commission to competent persons interested in governance but unlikely to be driven by a political agenda. Requirements that a commission member cannot have a political background (e.g. held public office or employment) and that every commission member is barred from running for public office, at least for a prescribed term, after serving on the commission further this objective.

13.7.4 Achieving Racial, Ethnic, Geographic and Religious Diversity Among Members on the Commission

There are many means by which such diversity can be achieved.

13.7.5 Encouraging Public Participation

In many nations, redistricting and reallocation are processes which occur, if at all, without public participation or even public knowledge. This lack of transparency is incongruous with the idea, or possibly fiction, that the decisions are being made in furtherance of the publicly approved criteria.

Of equal or greater importance than mere public participation is the opportunity for the public to respond meaningfully to a commission's proposed process and draft plans, and the ability of the commission to respond to public comments. Such an opportunity must be provided many times through the repeated dissemination of maps, online and by print, as the maps are changed in response to public comment. This is counter to the current law of several countries where the emphasis is on a redistricting being explained to the public, if at all, only after it is adopted.

13.7.6 Imposing Requirements for How Electoral Districts Should Be Drawn, Such As

- A measureable standard for equality in population or eligible voters;
- A definite timeframe in which the commission must review all districts and act to equalize persons or electors among all districts nationwide;
- Where reliable data exists, a requirement (trigger) to redraw specific malapportioned districts between nationwide redistricting;
- A clear recognition of the difference between maximum allowable deviations for extraordinary cases where they are justified and the general obligation to keep the deviation to a minimum among all but these extraordinary cases;
- General guidelines such as contiguity, compactness, and recognition of natural barriers; and
- Specific barriers to political discrimination, such as requiring that no district can be designed to favor or to disfavor a particular candidate or political party, or the ban on consideration of certain data, such as voting history.

13.7.7 Including Provisions for the Protection of Electoral Minorities

See Chap. 11.

13.7.8 Mandating Transparency

Technology has dramatically increased the opportunity for transparency and for public participation in the redistricting process. An essential starting point for achieving transparency in decision-making is to prevent non-public communications about districting changes with the members and staff of the commission. The rules applicable in courts provide an example of how this may be achieved by requiring that all communications about redistricting be in a public hearing or in writing, filed with a designated official, and available to the public.

13.8 Conclusion

The Code of Good Practice clearly prefers the use of redistricting commissions.[13] My research supports this conclusion.

[13]*See,* Appendix A.

The Code also provides that any commission should have a majority of "independent" members and "should include a geographer [and] a sociologist." These guidelines are mistaken. Such members are unnecessary as such expertise can be obtained through competent staff. The code also provides that a commission should have "a balanced representation of the parties and, if necessary, representatives of national minorities." The inclusion of minorities is appropriate. If politicians, or their appointees, are included in the membership of the commission, then a balanced representation of parties is essential.

The important qualifications for the members of a commission are competence, integrity, and objectivity, not specific professional or political experience. If members of a commission are chosen with these characteristics, relevant data can be furnished by expert staff and political views and concerns, as well as testimony on the criteria, can be expressed through public testimony rather than through membership on the commission.

The Code equivocates on the issue of independence for the commission by indicating that the national legislature should take into consideration the views of the commission, not that the commission itself should be independent of the national legislature and authorized to adopt new district lines or seat allocations without legislative action. This is a mistaken view.

A commission's plan must take effect without legislative or executive approval.

Chapter 14
The Role of Courts

Courts worldwide[1] generally have assumed a very limited role in the redistricting process because, in part, many of the applicable laws are vague and brief. The national legislature has considerable discretion, which has led to a visible tension in some countries between courts trying to enforce legal or generally accepted standards of voter equality and national legislatures battling to maintain the status quo or its political decisions.

14.1 Some Nations Bar Court Review

In some nations,[2] the constitution or law expressly bars court review of redistricting or seat allocation plans. In some of these nations the courts have confirmed that under the nation's constitution the authority of courts does not extend to questions about the delimitation of constituencies or the allotment of seats to such constituencies.

An express bar of court review may seem extraordinary, but it is consistent with the overall view that litigation challenging redistricting or the allocation of seats in the national legislature can create confusion, intrude in the province of the public's elected representatives, and interfere with democratic elections. It recognizes that such litigation can itself be used for political purposes and that such litigation, or the threat of such litigation, can instill a redistricting plan with political bias. Moreover,

[1]The analysis in this chapter is helped immensely by the fact that in many countries in which the principal language is not English the constitutional or supreme court of the country provides an English version online of some of its opinions. Only the opinion in the country's principal language is authoritative. The quotes in this chapter are from these online English versions. Many of these opinions online do not have page numbers.

[2]These nations include New Zealand, Pakistan, Nepal, Barbados, Trinidad and Tobago, India, Australia, and Tanzania.

S. Bickerstaff, *Election Systems and Gerrymandering Worldwide*, Studies in Choice and Welfare, https://doi.org/10.1007/978-3-030-30837-7_14

the courts may be corrupt or pro-government. Thus, even in the absence of any express constitutional bar to court review, such litigation is generally avoided except in the most extreme circumstances.

14.1.1 India

Article 329a of the Constitution of India mandates:

> Notwithstanding anything in this Constitution
>
> (a) the validity of any law relating to the delimitation of constituencies or the allotment of seats to such constituencies, made or purporting to be made under article 327 or article 328, shall not be called in question in any court. . . .

In the 1966 opinion in *Meghrai Kothari v. Union of India,*[3] the Supreme Court of India found that this mandate extended to the final plans of the Delimitation Commission and explained:

> There seems to be very good reason behind such a provision. If the orders . . . were not to be treated as final, the effect would be that any voter, if he so wished, could hold up an election indefinitely by questioning the delimitation of the constituencies from court to court. [T]he Act clearly demonstrates the intention of the' Legislature that the orders (of the Commission) . . . were to be treated as law which was not to be questioned in any court.

This bar on court review was confirmed again in 2010 when the Supreme Court of India upheld the postponement of the allocation of seats in the national legislature until after the next census (after 2031) in *J&K National Party v. Union of India.*[4] The Court In that opinion discussed the U.S. decision in *Baker v. Carr*[5] and cited with agreement the dissenting opinion:

> However, Justice Frankfurter and Justice Harlan dissented and held that the nature of controversy is unfit for federal judicial action, and that the existing apportionment was not so unreasonable so as to offend the equal protection clause.

The Court went on to note with approval the opinion of the lower court and the 1993 ruling in *R.C. Poudyal v. Union of India*[6]*:*

> It is true that the right to vote is central to the right of participation in the democratic process. However, there is less consensus amongst theorists on the propriety of judicial activism in the voting area. In India, the Delimitation Laws . . . are immune from the judicial test of their validity and the process of allotment of seats and constituencies is not liable to be called in question in any court by virtue of Article 329 (a) of the Constitution.

---

[3]Meghraj Kothari vs Delimitation Commission (Union of India), 1967 AIR 669, 1967 SCR (1) 400 (September 20, 1966) at Para. 119, pages 383 and 536–537 of the report available @ https://www.advocatekhoj.com and https://www.sci.gov.in

[4]J&K; National Panthers Party vs The Union of India (November 9, 2010) at para. 16 available @ https://www.sci.gov.in and https://indiankanoon.org

[5]369 US 186 (1962).

[6]R.C. Poudyal v. Union of India, 1993 SCR (1) 891 (February 10, 1993).

The Supreme Court noted that the law of Australia also had a bar and concluded:

> The mandate of Article 329A is that any law relating to the delimitation of constituencies or the allotment of seats to such constituencies shall not be called in question in any Court.[7]

14.1.2 Australia and New Zealand

Similarly, the Constitution or law in both Australia and New Zealand[8] provide that their respective redistricting commission's plans are not subject to challenge in court. The Australian law, however, allows challenges based on the nation's Constitution. This has permitted some limited challenges, which are discussed later in this Chapter.

One writer feels that the ban in these countries is more justified because the redistricting and reallocation decisions are made by an ostensibly "non-political" commission; rather than the parliament.[9]

14.1.3 Pakistan

An important legal distinction is whether the ban is embodied in a nation's constitution or statutory law. If the ban is in statutory law and the claim is constitutional, then a different result is possible.

Courts are sometimes unwilling to entirely abdicate their authority to review election issues even when the nation's national legislature has attempted by law to prevent such review. Pakistan is an example of where the nation's courts have made a few narrow forays. In *Arshad Mehmood v. Commissioner/Delimitation Authority* (2014)[10] the Lahore court explained:

> In conclusion, the ouster clause under Section 10A of the Act does not, in the slightest, abridge or curtail the constitutional jurisdiction of this Court to judicially review the orders, notifications and the acts of the executive i.e., the Delimitation Authority and Delimitation Officer in this case. .... Courts usually give due weightage to any administrative urgency of the Executive but this does not mean that the doors leading to courts can be shut down as this would result in curtailing and abridging the judicial power. This is opposed to independence of judiciary and the institutional framework of separation of powers.

---

[7] J&K; National Panthers Party vs The Union of India (November 9, 2010) at para. 27 available @ https://www.sci.gov.in and https://indiankanoon.org

[8] Timmons v. Governor-General, Wellington High Court (April 21, 1983). Discussed at 2 - **New Zealand Law Review** 298 (1984).

[9] *See, The Role of Courts in the Electoral Boundary Delimitation Process* by Lisa Handley in **INTERNATIONAL ELECTION REMEDIES** (Jack Young, ed., American Bar Association (2017).

[10] Arshad Mehmood v. Commmissioner/ Delimination Authority of the State of Gujranwala, 2014 PLD Lahore 221 (Pak) (2014); Sheikh Attiq-ur-Rehman v. Syed Ali Murtaza, 2014 YLR 1215 (2014). *See*, Khan v. Election Commission of Pakistan, 2012 PLD 120, Supreme Court of Pakistan (2012) (Election Contest), all opinions available at www.supremecourt.gov.pk

14.2 Court Deference to Legislative or Commission Decisions

Laws worldwide generally grant so much flexibility to the national legislature or redistricting commission that even when no express bar is present any court challenge is doomed and is avoided.

The United Kingdom is an example. In 1983, four members of the Labour Party brought suit against the English Boundary Commission on the basis that it gave too much weight to political subdivision boundaries and too little weight to making constituencies equal in population. The courts in *R. v. Boundary Commission for England ex parte Foote*[11] rejected the claim on the basis that the plaintiffs had failed to meet their burden of proving that the commission had clearly failed to follow the rules, not merely that an alternative answer was available. No subsequent case has been successful.

14.3 Court Intervention Around the World

There are some nations in which the courts have played a major role. Some courts have spoken strongly about the importance of voter equality. Even in these few instances, however, a country's highest court has always stopped short of imposing a remedy itself and has, instead, allowed the national legislature to address the problem. Sometimes the national legislature has been reluctant to do so. At the same time the courts generally have not tried to enforce their decisions against the legislators or to adopt their own remedy. The same political in-fighting and self-interest that initially caused the illegality of the nation's election system has often blocked its reform.[12]

I have divided these court decisions between those that expressly reject any requirement for absolute voter equality and those that demonstrate the ongoing battle between courts and the national legislature over voter equality.

14.4 Court Rejection of Absolute Voter Equality

14.4.1 Canada

The Canadian courts have expressly rejected the U.S. concept of absolute "voter parity" in favor of a standard of "effective representation". The court in *Reference re Prov. Electoral Boundaries* (1991)[13] explained:

---

[11]Ex parte Foote, [1983] QB 600 (Eng.).

[12]The major exception to this worldwide restraint is, of course, the United States, where courts play a critical role in redistricting. I discuss the U.S. later in this chapter.

[13]Reference re Prov. Electoral Boundaries (Sask) [1991] 2 S.C.R. 158, 183 (Can.).

> [F]actors like geography, community history, community interests, and minority representation may need to be taken into account to ensure that our legislative assemblies effectively represent the diversity of our social mosaic.

The Canadian courts have acted to protect minority communities from division and vote dilution.[14]

14.4.2 Australia

Australia has a statutory ban on court review, but allows an exception for constitutional claims. In 1996 the High Court of Australia in *McGinty v. Western Australia*[15] considered whether the intrinsic meaning of "representative democracy" was voter equality. The Court said:

> The plaintiffs submit that disparities in voting power are inconsistent with the principle of representative democracy as that principle is understood at the present time.
>
> . . . .
>
> "Representative democracy" has been used as a shorthand description of the form of government prescribed by the Commonwealth Constitution in order to explain how the freedom to discuss governments and political matters is implied in the Constitution. As "the people" are to choose their elected representatives, it has been held that the people must be left free to discuss political and economic matters in order to perform their constitutional functions.
>
> . . . .
>
> It is logically impermissible to treat "representative democracy" as though it were contained in the Constitution, to attribute to the term a meaning or content derived from sources extrinsic to the Constitution and then to invalidate a law for inconsistency with the meaning or content so attributed.
>
> . . . .
>
> The principle of "representative democracy" can be given the status of a constitutional imperative, but only in so far as the meaning and content of that principle are implied in the text and structure of the Constitution.

The Court could not find a specific requirement for representative democracy or voter equality in the Constitution of Western Australia or Constitution of Australia. The Court expressly addressed the United States requirements for population equality in historical context and rejected them in favor of the Canadian concept of "effective representation." The Court concluded, "The term 'representative democracy' implies that the franchise be so general in its scope and voting power be so distributed among those who have the franchise that those who are elected to govern can fairly be seen to be representatives of the people who are governed."

---

[14]Raiche v. Canada (Attorney General), [F.C.], 2004 F.C. 679, (2005), 1 F.C.R. 93 (Can.).

[15]McGinty v W Australia, 186 CLR 140 (1996). There are no page or paragraph numbers in the online version of the opinion.

14.4.3 India

As indicated earlier, India has a bar on challenges to delimitation orders. However, the Supreme Court of India has gone further to also expressly reject the concept of voter equality. In *J&K; National Panthers Party vs The Union of India*[16] the Court explained in 2010 that "This Court has already held relying on the Constitution Bench judgment in Poudyal that ensuring uniformity in the value of votes is not a constitutionally mandated imperative of free and fair election under our constitutional dispensation." In the earlier case of *R.C. Poudyal vs Union of India,*[17] in which the Court had upheld the reservation of seats for certain minorities, the Court had held:

> The principle of mathematical proportionality of representation is not a declared basic requirement in each and every part of the territory of India. The systemic deficiencies in the plenitude of the doctrine of full and effective representation has not been understood in the constitutional philosophy as derogating from the democratic principle. The inequalities in representation in the present case are an inheritance and compulsion from the past. Historical considerations have justified a differential treatment. . . . Article 170 incorporates the rule of 'fair and effective representation'. Though the rule 'one person one vote' is a broad principle of democracy, it is more a declaration of a political ideal than a mandate for enforcement with arithmetical accuracy. These are the usual problems that arise in the delimitation of constituencies. In what is called "First- past- the-post" system of elections, the variations in the size and in the voting populations of different constituencies, detract from a strict achievement of this ideal. . . . The concept of political equality underlying a democratic system is a political value. Perfect political equality is only ideological.

14.5 The Battle Over Voter Equality Between the Courts and the Legislature

14.5.1 Croatia

In 2010, Croatia's unicameral national legislature was elected by PR voting in 10 multi-member districts (constituencies), which had not been redrawn or had seats reallocated since adopted 11 years earlier. Each district elected 14 members of the legislature. The Constitutional Court of Croatia[18] was asked to determine whether the election system was unconstitutional as malapportioned.[19] The Court concluded that "both the legality and the general democratic character of the

[16]J&K; National Panthers Party vs The Union of India (November 9, 2010) at para. 27 available @ https://www.sci.gov.in and https://indiankanoon.org

[17]R.C. Poudyal v. Union of India, 1993 SCR (1) 891 (February 10, 1993) at para 126 of the judgment available @ https://www.sci.gov.in and https://indiankanoon.org

[18]The Constitutional Court of Croatia is not part of the judicial system, but a court sui generis,

[19]THE CONSTITUTIONALCOURT OF THE REPUBLIC OF CROATIA No. U-X-6472/2010 Zagreb (December 8, 2010) at para. 6 available @ https://www.usud.hr

elections depend on the equal distribution of the voters in the general constituencies (the equality of votes directly depends on this distribution)" and that under the law, "the constituencies must not differ by more than ±5%" in the number of electors. The Court asked the government to provide it with the number of electors in each district so that a comparison could be made. The government replied that it did not have this data.

Rather than being deterred from its analysis, the Court turned to a comparison of the number of actual voters in each constituency in the most recent election. These numbers varied widely (>25%). The Court reasoned "constituencies that are once determined undergo changes by the nature of things." The Croatian Parliament (Zastupnički Dom) was ordered to make the necessary changes "without delay, but also . . . to determine the competent bodies and the rules for the delimitation procedure, i.e. the procedure for defining and harmonizing constituency territories and boundaries." The Court explained:

> In this context the Constitutional Court notes that delimitation requires predetermined delimitation standards and includes procedural delimitation rules, the most important of which are: rules on the deadlines and competencies for monitoring and proposing delimitation, rules on the supervisory bodies and their supervisory authority in the procedure of planning constituency territories (i.e. in the procedure of "drawing the boundaries" of the constituencies), rules about the participation of the public in delimitation, and rules about the competencies and procedure of supervision over the direct application in the field of the "constituency map" accepted in the Constituency Act.[20]

The Court acknowledged that the Constitution also requires "as possible" the recognition of the territories of the local governments.

Some members of the Croatian National Legislature saw the Court's action as political. The Court's decision (as well as many other decisions) was met with hostility. The national legislature did not act by the time of the next election. In 2015 the OSCE noted that the variation in the number of voters per representative among the 10 domestic constituencies had reached >35% from the quota and that the constituencies remained unchanged from 1999.[21]

Today Croatia has 12 constituencies, but apparently the 10 domestic (intra-country) constituencies and the allocation of seats among those constituencies remains unchanged. The new constituencies include a nationwide constituency for the election of certain minorities and a constituency for Croatians outside the country.

The events in Croatia are an example of the tension that exists worldwide between the courts and the national legislatures over the issue of voter equality. Too often the courts face delay or totally ineffective action by the politicians even in the face of strong language from the courts about the need for greater voter equality.

[20] *Id.*

[21] REPUBLIC OF CROATIA, PARLIAMENTARY ELECTIONS of 8 November 2015, Assessment, Final Report, OSCE/ODHIR (February 19,216).

14.5.2 Germany

In 2008 the Constitutional Court of Germany declared the then-existing version of Germany's mixed member proportional (MMP) system for election to the Bundestag unconstitutional because it operated to over represent some political parties and states and to cause a "negative vote weight effect."[22] The Court explained:

> The formation of the country seating contingents according to the number of voters in accordance with § 6 (1) sentence 1 BWG enables the effect of the negative voting weight and therefore violates the principles of equality and immediacy of choice as well as equal opportunities of the parties. In the system of proportional representation created by the legislator (sic), overhang mandates (Section 6 (5) BWG) are acceptable only to an extent that does not nullify the basic character of the election as proportional representation. The principles of equality of choice and equal opportunities between the parties have been violated in the event of overhang mandates of more than half the strength of the group.

Parts of a revision passed by the national legislature in 2012 were also declared unconstitutional. A second revision passed in 2013 won court approval and is now in effect. For a further explanation, see A Case-Study of Germany in Appendix C.

14.5.3 France

A similar, but interesting scenario played out in France over 2 decades.[23]

The Conseil Constitutionnel is the highest constitutional authority in the nation. It was asked on several occasions to intercede and require the national legislature to reallocate the seats and redraw the constituencies in the national plan adopted in 1986, which had been based on 1982 census results. In 1986, the Conseil warned the national legislature to avoid population deviations in the then proposed legislation except when required by "precise urgent necessities."[24] Following passage, however, the Conseil upheld the legislation saying, "the choices made by the legislators have [not] manifestly violated the constitutional requirements."[25]

The Conseil continued to prod the French legislature to act to reduce deviation. After almost 2 decades without any redistricting or reallocation of seats in the national legislature, the Conseil in 2003 recognized that over half of the existing consistencies deviated 25% or more from the average in each administrative département (fixed district).[26] The Conseil said that it was incumbent on the legislature to act, yet it did

---

[22]BVerfGE 121 (2009) 266–317, Judgment of the Second Senate on 3 July 2008, –2 BvC 1/07, BvC 7/07. available @ https://www.bundesverfassungsgericht.de

[23]See, A Case Study of France in Appendix C.

[24]*Decision No. 86-208 DC, Conseil Constitutionnel [CC]* (July 2, 1986).

[25]Decision No. 86-218 DC, Conseil Constitutionnel [CC] (Nov. 18, 1986).

[26]In REPUBLIC OF FRANCE, PARLIAMENTARY ELECTIONS 10 and 17 June 2012, Final Report, at n.6 on page 4, OSCE/ODIHR (September 12, 2012) the OSCE observed "In its

not do so. In a later advisory opinion, the Conseil suggested that the national legislature should act in time for the 2007 elections, or as soon thereafter as possible. The national legislature again did not act.

After reviewing the elections in 2007, the Conseil in 2008 declared:

> For more than twenty years, the Constitutional Council recalls that "the National Assembly, designated by direct universal suffrage, must be elected on essentially demographic bases" (9). However, the current breakdown of constituencies, which results from Law No. 86-1197 of 24 November 1986, is based on data from the 1982 general census. Since then, two general censuses, carried out in 1990 and 1999, have brought to light disparities in representation that are not compatible with the combined provisions of Article 6 of the Declaration of 1789 and Articles 3 and 24 of the Constitution. Moreover, the very terms of the Act of 24 November 1986, codified in Article L. 125 of the Electoral Code, have become obsolete since the suppression of the general censuses by Article 156 of the Act of 27 February 2002 on the local democracy.
>
> It is therefore incumbent on the legislator to modify this division. In its comments of 7 July 2005, the Council had argued that if remodeling was not done before the next parliamentary elections, which it considered unfortunate, it should be undertaken the day after the elections. This reasoning has based a reservation of interpretation in recital 7 of the decision n ° 2007-547 DC of February 15, 2007. It is now imperative to proceed to this division.[27]

Later in 2008, the Conseil importantly ruled that the statutory guarantee of two seats to each département was unconstitutional.[28] It said:

> [T]he maintenance of a minimum of two deputies for each departement is no longer justified by an imperative of general interest likely to mitigate the scope of the fundamental rule that the National Assembly must be elected on essentially demographic grounds; it follows that the above-mentioned provisions must be declared contrary to the Constitution; is more justified by an imperative of general interest likely to lessen the scope of the fundamental rule according to which the National Assembly must be elected on essentially demographic bases; it follows that the above-mentioned provisions must be declared contrary to the Constitution. . . .

The Conseil noted that 20% in the deviation of the population of a particular constituency from the respective average of all constituencies in the French

---

Observations Related to the Legislative Elections of 2002 and 2007, released on 15 May 2003 and 29 May 2008 respectively, the Constitutional Council stated that it was urgent to proceed with the re-districting of the constituencies in order to respect the constitutional principle of equality of representation." *See,* OBSERVATIONS DU CONSEIL CONSTITUTIONNEL RELATIVES AUX ELECTIONS LEGISLATIVES DE JUIN 2002, Conseil Constitutionnel (May 15, 2003) and OBSERVATIONS DU CONSEIL CONSTITUTIONNEL SUR LES ECHEANCES ELECTORALES DE 2007, Conseil Constitutionnel (July 7, 2008).

[27]Decision No. 2008-24 ELEC of May 29, 2008, Observations of the Conseil Constitutionnel on the parliamentary elections of 10 and 17 June 2007. The Conseil observed, "It was asked to condemn population differences ranging from 75,131 to 125,393 inhabitants in the 3rd and 21st districts of Paris, from 82,974 to 151,565 in the 3rd and 12th districts of Bouches-du-Rhône, from 86,690 to 158,193 in the 6th and 1st constituencies of Yvelines."

[28]Decision no. 2008-573 DC, Conseil Constitutional at Para 23 (January 8, 2009).

départements or overseas territories does not in itself contradict the constitutional principle of equal electoral law if done for reasons of general interest

> . . . [T]he National Assembly, designated by direct universal suffrage, must be elected on essentially demographic bases according to a distribution of seats of deputies and a delimitation of the legislative constituencies respecting at best the equality suffrage; whereas, if the legislator can take into account imperatives of general interest likely to attenuate the scope of this fundamental rule, it can do so only to a limited extent;
>
> . . .
>
> This deviation may create situations where the principle of equal electoral law will be violated or, in the interests of favorable election results, abusive by setting boundaries for constituencies. Therefore, the application of this maximum population deviation is possible only in exceptional cases, with proper justification.[29] This can only be used on a limited and case-by-case basis, on the basis of clear, overriding requirements of general interest (such as those relating to geographical factors), in accordance with the principle of proportionality.[30]

Finally, the national legislature acted in 2010. Its resulting plan has been oft-criticized, but has withstood legal challenge. In 2012, the OSCE/ODHIR concluded, "As the national census was done away with in 2002, the (French) Electoral Code no longer provides for fixed redistricting. Legislation should be amended to provide for periodic reviews of Legislation."[31]

Throughout this period, France's ostensibly "independent" redistricting commission remained ineffective as the national legislature charted its own course.

14.5.4 Italy

The 2017 change of the election system in Italy also resulted from court intervention. On December 4, 2013, the Constitutional Court found the election system adopted in 2005 to be unconstitutional[32] because it provided an unlimited majority bonus, which was meant to assure that a political party had a majority in the national legislature, and provided for nationwide "closed" PR party lists. This 2005 law had been designed to produce a stable national government instead of an unstable coalition government to tackle the difficult problems, especially economic,

---

[29]Emphasis added.

[30]*Id. at* Paras 21 and, 26. This part of the Conseil's opinion was important to the decision of the Lithuanian Constitutional Court in ON THE COMPLIANCE OF ARTICLE 9, PARAGRAPH 1 OF THE REPUBLIC OF LITHUANIA LAW ON THE ELECTION OF THE REPUBLIC OF LITHUANIA (CONVENTION OF 6 NOVEMBER 2012) TO THE CONSTITUTION OF THE REPUBLIC OF LITHUANIA, No. KT27-N16 (October 20, 2015). The English version has no page numbers.

[31]REPUBLIC OF FRANCE, PARLIAMENTARY ELECTIONS 10 and 17 June 2012, Final Report, OSCE/ODIHR (September 12, 2012).

[32]*See, The Italian Constitutional Court Rules on Electoral System* by Giacomo Delledonne and Giovanni Boggero in **the Int'l J. Const. L. Blog** (Feb. 8, 2017) @http://www.iconnectblog.com

confronting the nation, but was unpopular because it resulted in long party lists with no avenue for voters to show a preference for individuals.

The situation became more confused in 2015 when voters rejected a proposal to make the Italian Senate appointed (indirectly elected through the local legislatures). A 2015 law providing for PR elections in the lower chamber using a two round system (TRS) was found to be inadequate. The Constitutional Court deemed the two-round system unconstitutional because it would allow a party to get to the second ballot without meeting any threshold; hence, it would distort the will of the electors by having the same effect of a plurality bonus allocated without any minimum requirement.

Finally, the Court in 2017 spelled out what would be legally acceptable—a new mixed electoral system for both chambers with no majority bonus unless the winning party received at least 40% of the vote, and a PR system allowing preference voting.[33] The Italian Parliament adopted a new system. It was a mixed system (P), with 37% of seats allocated using a FPTP electoral system and 63% using a regional PR method, including the seats allocated to Italians abroad, with one round of voting. Voters were allowed two preference votes (one male, one female) in the election to the lower chamber. The party with the greatest number of votes nationwide were entitled to a majority bonus, but only if it had received at least 40% of the nationwide vote. The first election under the new system occurred in March, 2018.[34]

14.5.5 Mongolia

For its 2012 election, Mongolia had a parallel (P) mixed system. However, in 2016 the nation's highest court ruled that the PR component of the system was unconstitutional because it did not constitute "direct" elections. Rather than resisting the ruling, the country's national legislature immediately enacted a system of 76 single-member electoral districts. The ruling party thought that such a system would lead to a two-party system. The winning candidate had to receive at least 28% of the valid vote to be elected; if not, another election would be held. Voter turnout had to be at least 50% in a constituency for the result to be valid. The ruling party lost 29 of its 34 seats.

14.5.6 Republic of Korea (South Korea)

In 2014, the Constitutional Court of the Republic of Korea held that the population disparities among the Assembly constituencies (approximately 2-1) were resulting in

[33] *See,* Chap. 7 and Judgment No. 17, Italian Constitutional Court (2017).

[34] A further discussion of the Italian decision and quotes from the Court's opinion are found in Chap. 7.

unequal representation. The Court mandated that the constituencies must be redrawn for the 2016 elections, with the number of persons in any given constituency not exceeding ±33% from the average number of constituents in all districts. A deadline of 31 December 2015 was set for the redistricting to take place.

This deadline was missed. The National Election Commission was forced to allow registered candidates to campaign without a set map of constituencies. The crisis was ultimately resolved in February 2016 with an agreement between the two major parties that allowed a new electoral map to be passed that raised the single-member districts from 246 to 253 (a benefit to incumbents), while decreasing the number of PR seats from 54 to 47.[35]

14.5.7 Japan

Japan has a mixed system (P). In its latest incarnation, the lower house consists of 289 members elected in single-member constituencies and 176 elected by PR voting in multi-member districts called "blocs" to which seats are allocated.

In terms of the single-member constituencies, the Constitution requires that counties (a nominal administrative unit) and small cities not be split and that each prefecture receive at least one representative. It also requires that the ratio between the most populous and least populous constituencies not exceed 2-1 (Japan uses the American Method of calculating disparity). These often conflicting requirements created a dilemma. In a series of decisions (1972, 1980, 1983, 1990, 1992, 2006, 2009, 2011, and 2017) the Supreme Court of Japan declared the districts in the upper or lower chambers malapportioned.[36] In each instance, the Court did not invalidate the prior election. It left the nation's legislature (Diet) to overcome the imbalance through redistricting or the reallocation of seats. The last legislative action was in 2017 to get the deviation below two to one. A further reform is ostensibly planned to be implemented after the 2020 census figures are available and is not expected to take effect before 2022.

[35] *See, NEC allows campaigning without new electoral map*, **Korea Joongang News** (Dec 31, 2015) available at http://koreajoongangdaily.joins.com; **JUDICIAL REVIEW IN NEW DEMOCRACIES: CONSTITUTIONAL COURTS IN ASIAN CASES** by Tom Ginsberg, Cambridge Press (2003).

[36] *High court rules vote weight gap in Japan's 2017 general election was unconstitutional*, **Japan Times** (FEB 8, 2018); *The Politics of Redistricting in Japan: A Contradiction between Equal Population and Respect for Local Government Boundaries* by Tashimasha Moriwaki at page 107 in **Redistricting in Comparative Perspective** by Lisa Handley & Bernard Grofman, eds., Oxford Univ. Press (2008).

14.5.8 Northern Ireland

The 1959 legislative elections in Northern Ireland came during a period of renewed violence. The electoral districts in the Dáil Éireann Parliament were alleged to be gerrymandered to favor the Unionists over the Catholics. In 1961 the High Court struck down the 1959 Electoral Amendment Act as unconstitutional in *O'Donovan v. Attorney General* (1961).[37] Irish politician John O'Donovan had challenged the 1959 Act on the basis that there were "grave inequalities" among the constituencies with "no relevant circumstances to justify" them. The High Court agreed and suggested that the ratio of representation to population across constituencies should differ by no more than 5%.

The Court relied on the "so far as it is possible" ("sa mhéid gur féidir é") condition of the Constitution and concluded that a 5% variation was the limit without exceptional circumstances. The Court also condemned the legislature for failing to act within the 12 years specified in the Constitution. The decision is said to have led to the adoption of a redistricting commission.

14.5.9 Eastern Europe

Hungary, Ukraine, Lithuania, Croatia, and most of the nations in Eastern Europe adopted democratic constitutions hastily after the collapse of the Soviet Union and without much experience with the democratic form of government.[38] As a result, their constitutional provisions regarding redistricting were brief and vague. However, both the Ukraine and Lithuania authorize the courts to review redistricting plans developed by the country's Election Commission, which is responsible for redistricting.

14.5.10 Hungary

In 2005, the Constitutional Court of Hungary[39] found that nation's electoral law was invalid because it failed to specify when redistricting should occur and because the electoral districts deviated by as much as 3-1 in electors. The Court mandated that the national legislature act before 2007 to address the concerns, but the legislature

[37]O'Donovan v. Attorney General, Irish Reports 114 (1961). See, In the Matter of Article 26 of the Constitution and in the Matter of the ELECTORAL (AMENDMENT) BILL, (July 14, 1961).

[38]*See, Districting and Redistricting in Central Europe* by Marina Popescu and Gabor Toka in **REDISTRICTING IN COMPARATINE PERSPECTIVE** (Oxford, 2008).

[39]Constitutional Court of Hungary, Opinion. #22/2005 (January 17, 2005).

failed to do so. The Court ruled again in 2010 that the disparities in population made the system unconstitutional.[40]

An English summary[41] of the Court's 2010 opinion said:

> Therefore, the Constitutional Court stated, Parliament had neglected its duty as legislator and created an unconstitutional situation. In addition, the Court set out a constitutional requirement to the legislator that the number of people entitled to vote in individual voting districts should differ to the least extent possible, and only for an adequate constitutional reason. The legislator must also aim at the slightest possible difference in defining the mandates to be won on regional electoral lists. The mandates will have to be adjusted according to the number of voters registered in a directory. The legislator must try to ensure that the principle of equality is manifest both in the case of voting districts and that of regional lists.

Confronted with gridlock on the issue of redistricting, the Hungarian national legislature in 2012 changed to a mixed (P) voting system. The new Elections Act stipulates that the average deviation in number of registered voters must not exceed 15% countrywide unless justified by "geographical, ethnic, historical, religious and other local characteristics," and was in no case to not exceed 20%. The OSCE/ ODIHR concluded that this was an improvement.[42]

14.5.11 Iceland

The Supreme Court of Iceland declared the 2010 election to the Islandic Constitutional Assembly null and void on January 25, 2011. The decision did not involve voter equality or the fairness of the election system, but it was a further indication of the willingness of the Iceland Court to intervene in elections.

Iceland adopted a change to six multi-member constituencies in 2002 to balance the weight of different districts of the country since under the previous system of constituencies a vote cast in the sparsely populated areas around the country counted much more than a vote cast in the Capital Region.

In November 2012, the Icelandic Parliament asked the Council of Europe's Commission for Democracy through Law (Venice Commission) to provide an opinion on the draft of a new Constitution which included a provision that the votes of electors everywhere in the country shall have equal weight. However, the constitutional proposal was rejected by the Parliament in March 2013. This imbalance between districts has been reduced, but still exists.

---

[40]Constitutional Court of Hungary, Opinion #193/2010 (2010).

[41]http://www.codices.coe.int

[42]JOINT OPINION ON THE ACT ON THE ELECTIONS OF MEMBERS OF PARLIAMENT OF HUNGARY, OSCE/ODIHR and European Parliament (2012).

14.5.12 *Lithuania*

In October 2015, the Constitutional Court of Lithuania[43] declared the country's electoral districts to be unconstitutional, with the largest constituency being 50% larger than the smallest. The Court said:

> Whichever system of the election of the members of the Seimas (exclusively proportional, or exclusively majoritarian, or a mixed system of elections in which the proportional and majoritarian systems of elections are combined) is chosen by the legislature, the legal regulation established by means of a law must ensure that these elections are conducted in compliance with the principles of democratic, free, and fair elections, as consolidated in the Constitution.
>
> ....
>
> The Constitution of the Republic of Lithuania . . . entails a duty to the legislator, taking into account all circumstances relevant to the formation of constituencies of significance (inter alia, the electoral migration, other demographic factors, and the integrity of constituencies), to establish such legal regulation, according to which constituencies should be formed in such a way as to ensure that the number of voters is as even as possible distributed in the constituencies. This is an important precondition for ensuring the equivalence of the votes of all voters and the equal importance of the votes of all voters in determining the results of voting. The legislator, in exercising this duty arising from the Constitution and determining the corresponding legal regulation, cannot create preconditions to deny, distort or unduly restrict equal suffrage.

The Court went on to say, "Summing up the reviewed practice of foreign state constitutional justice institutions, it needs to be noted that constituencies must be formed in accordance with the right to equal electoral rights: constituencies must be made up of the same number of inhabitants or electors as possible, and the differences in this number must be constitutionally justified."[44]

In December 2015, the Election Commission redrew the nation's 71 single member seats in response to the Court's ruling.

14.5.13 *Others*

Courts also reportedly intervened in the redistricting or reallocation processes in the countries of Indonesia and the Czech Republic. I was unable to verify these court decisions or the nature of the court's ruling.

---

[43]THE CONSTITUTIONAL COURT OF THE REPUBLIC OF LITHUANIA, ON THE COMPLIANCE OF ARTICLE 9, PARAGRAPH 1 OF THE REPUBLIC OF LITHUANIA LAW ON THE ELECTION OF THE REPUBLIC OF LITHUANIA (CONVENTION OF 6 NOVEMBER 2012) TO THE CONSTITUTION OF THE REPUBLIC OF LITHUANIA, No. KT27-N16 (October 20, 2015) available @ www.lrkt.lt/en. The English version of the opinion has no page numbers.

[44]Emphasis added.

14.5.14 United States

The biggest exception to court restraint in regard to redistricting issues is the United States. Since the United States has no single federal redistricting plan, the court action involving congressional districts, as well as state and local legislative districts, takes place in the individual states. Both state and federal courts in the U.S. states routinely intervene in the redistricting process. After each decennial census, litigants rush to court to attack the newly adopted redistricting plans. Dozens of cases are filed, with many decided within a year. Many of the rules governing redistricting in the U.S. have been set by these courts through interpretation of state or federal law. Some observers view such significant court involvement as having a positive effect. Others see it as overkill.

The most important differences in the U.S., however, are not the mere presence of frequent court intervention, but that the cases are on a very fast track and that, if the state legislature or local government does not promptly remedy an unlawful redistricting plan, the court will do so.[45]

It is the obligation, with rare "exigent" exceptions, of the U.S. courts to see that every election occurs using a constitutional redistricting plan. Congressional elections, and many state or local elections, occur at least every 2 years. As a result, if the state legislature or local government does not redistrict immediately after each decennial census to accommodate population changes, or adopts a redistricting plan that is unlawful, such as containing an excessive population deviation or discriminating against any racial or ethnic group, and fails to cure the flaw in time for the next primary or general election, a state or federal court will probably adopt a "temporary" plan, usually within months of when the lawsuit is filed, to correct these flaws in time for the first election of the decade.

The state or local government often challenges these "temporary" plans and appeals the court's decision in an effort to allow the government's plan to be used. These efforts to "stay" the court's plan generally are unsuccessful because the government is asking permission to have persons vote and live under a plan that has been held illegal. U.S. courts are reluctant to allow this to occur.

These obligations on U.S. courts effectively enforce the requirement for periodic redistricting and all legal requirements for how the districts must be drawn in the United States. In most states (like the adage that "nothing is as permanent as that which is temporary"), the court's "temporary" plan, or a slight modification thereof, often continues to be used for elections throughout the remainder of the decade because once a person becomes an incumbent under the court plan he or she is likely to oppose change. Therefore, it is important to the government that the original plan be upheld and remains in place for any upcoming election.

---

[45] *See, Gerrymandering from the Bench? The Electoral Consequences of Judicial Redistricting* by James B. Cottrill and Terri J. Peretti, **Election Law Journal** (2012), published online (Sep 3, 2013) @ https://doi.org

14.6 The Limits of Court Intervention

In each of these nations, other than the U.S., the courts have deferred to the legislatures or commissions to find a remedy. They stopped short of prescribing their own redistricting or reallocation plans even when the legislature did not act immediately. The result has been that in many nations, the national legislature resisted change and persons voted or members of the national legislatures continued to serve under plans that had been found unconstitutional. Although the reluctance to enter the "political thicket" of redistricting may have disappeared in redistricting cases in the U.S., it, or a similar policy of deference to the legislature's role, remains very much a part of jurisprudence worldwide.

Court intervention in matters affecting redistricting and reallocation is an exception around the world and, when it has occurred, the national legislature has often been slow to cooperate. This gap between court rulings and legislative action rises above the usual conflict between the branches of government because it directly affects a legislator's political and personal self-interest, not just policy.

14.7 America's Failure: Partisan Gerrymandering

Even in the United States, however, the U.S. Supreme Court has avoided invalidating any redistricting plan merely because it is gerrymandered for personal or political purposes (i.e. a partisan gerrymander).

The U.S. courts have relied on the U.S. Constitution and The Voting Rights Act as the reasons for invalidating plans found malapportioned or racially discriminatory.[46] In those same cases, however, the Court has rejected claims that the plans were unconstitutional partisan gerrymanders.

In its first foray into the question of political gerrymandering in 1973 the United States Supreme Court reasoned that it would be "idle" to hold that "any political consideration taken into account in fashioning a reapportionment plan is sufficient to invalidate it" because districting "inevitably has and is intended to have substantial political consequences."[47]

The issue is straightforward—if redistricting is and always has been a quintessentially political process, how and why should courts interject themselves as referees? How would a court measure when that political process has clearly gone beyond what is "customary" and what is "unconstitutional?" Would not the courts themselves become entangled and dragged down to the basest level of biased political decision-making by determining winners and losers in the ongoing partisan battles unless they had such a clear standard?

[46]See, e.g., League of United Latin American Citizens v. Perry, 548 U. S. 399 [2006].

[47]Gaffney v. Cummings, 412 U. S. 735, 752 (1973).

In 1986, a majority of the U.S. Supreme Court (*Davis v. Bandemer*) agreed that partisan gerrymandering could violate the U.S. Constitution, but the Justices could not agree on a standard to apply to determine "when political gerrymandering has gone too far." During the intervening 33 years not a single federal case has finally held a redistricting plan invalid because it was a partisan gerrymander.

The pendency of cases before the Supreme Court in 2018–2019 raised the potential of a ruling reaffirming that partisan gerrymandering was justiciable and establishing a standard to use in future litigation.

On June 27, 2019, the U.S. Supreme Court by 5-to-4 vote in *Rucho v Common Cause* held that partisan gerrymandering was a "political question" that was not justiciable in federal court—thus bringing an end to this elusive right. In an opinion written by Chief Justice Roberts, the Court explained that "The practice was known in the Colonies prior to Independence, and the Framers were familiar with it at the time of the drafting and ratification of the Constitution" and that election matters had been assigned by the Constitution to the states. Chief Justice Roberts noted "Partisan gerrymandering claims invariably sound in a desire for proportional representation" and "it is not even clear what fairness looks like in this context. There is a large measure of 'unfairness' in any winner-take-all system." He concluded.

Federal judges have no license to reallocate political power between the two major political parties, with no plausible grant of authority in the Constitution, and no legal standards to limit and direct their decisions.

In a harsh dissent written by Justice Kagan on behalf of four justices, the Justice began by claiming that, "For the first time ever, this Court refuses to remedy a constitutional violation because it thinks the task beyond judicial capabilities" and "partisan gerrymanders here debased and dishonored our democracy, turning upside-down the core American idea that all governmental power derives from the people." Justice Kagan accused the Court majority of ignoring these harms, being complacent, and with the idea "that if we have lived with partisan gerrymanders so long, we will survive."

This ruling in *Rucho* applies only to U.S. federal courts. During the past decade, at least ten states have invalidated legislative or commission redistricting plans because they were partisan gerrymanders or violated state redistricting criteria in an effort to draw districts that satisfied incumbents or political parties.

In June of 2018 the U.S. Supreme Court ruled in two cases involving partisan gerrymandering. Many had hoped that the Court would finally find partisan gerrymandering fully justiciable in federal courts, and establish clear standards that could be applied to find at least the most egregious examples of legislative gerrymandering invalid. The Court sidestepped these issues.

The Court's decision was not a surprise to any lawyer who has actually litigated redistricting cases. I have seen many political scientists' theories about how to measure the amount of partisanship in a redistricting plan. For each theory, another political scientist has a contrary theory. Two political scientists can look at identical data and reach opposing or contradictory conclusions, often on the basis of who is paying their fee. As a lawyer who has presented or cross-examined numerous "expert witnesses" in different types of cases, it is a nightmare to think about important election policy issues being decided by dueling expert witnesses.

While as a practitioner I lament the spectacle of dueling experts deciding the future of representative democracy, I have a far greater fear of the harm that partisanship and political self-interest is doing to our representative democracies. It is regrettable that the U.S. Supreme Court has failed to provide the same leadership on the issue of partisan gerrymandering as it provided 55 years ago on the issue of voter equality.

14.8 Conclusion

One of the notable surprises to me from this review of court decisions is how powerfully worded courts have been in supporting voter equality in some of the newer democracies. At the same time I was surprised at how legislatures in some of the older democracies seemed to take the issue of voter equality lightly and how often the national legislatures attempted to maintain the status quo even in the face of very explicit court rulings demanding change. Maintaining the status quo in such circumstances is merely a gerrymander to benefit the self-interest of incumbents and the controlling political party at the expense of voting equality and the public interest.

It is also notable that many of these courts recognized that any deviation from voter equality requires "general interest" justification, which does not include election advantages, and that limits on deviation are only for exceptional cases. Even though the decisions in Canada, Australia, and New Zealand reject the rigid "one person, one vote" standard of the U.S., they allow major deviations only in the context of legitimate public interests such as natural features and local community boundaries. In other words, the principle of voter equality is an important principle to courts in many countries even when the legislature's political self-interest prevents it from acting.

The story of court involvement and legislative reaction is different in every country, but the tension between courts and national legislatures comes across clearly in many nations. Too often the legislature's intransigence stymies or at least delays any remedy for a court's concerns. Gerrymandering abounds.

While I believe that it is correct to observe that courts usually do not interfere with a legislature's redistricting or reallocation decisions, it also must be noted that a few courts have had the courage to do so. All courts face the difficulty of enforcement in the face of a hostile or recalcitrant national legislature.

The absence of court intervention or effective court intervention is the biggest reason why a nation's legal standards and requirements for redistricting of electoral districts or the reallocation of seats among multi-member districts are frequently ignored. There are many pressures for keeping the status quo, not the least of which is to protect incumbents.

While court intervention is critical to prevent the worst of political gerrymandering from taking full effect, the only reliable means of actually removing political gerrymandering and its threat to representative democracy is by assuring that political self-interest is not allowed to determine how seats in the legislature are allocated or electoral districts are drawn. Courts are a necessary but not a satisfactory answer.

Chapter 15
Conclusion

Gerrymandering electoral districts is an existential threat to representative democracy. An elected representative, who cares as much or more about his or her political future than about the welfare of the nation or constituents, is acting contrary to the premise of representative democracy. Nevertheless, it has become acceptable worldwide to think of redistricting and reallocation of seats in a legislative body as quintessentially political processes even though, by doing so, we are making the concept of representative democracy a sham—where a politician' self-interest trumps the public good.

This book's investigation of the international practices of districting, redistricting, and gerrymandering leads me to the following conclusions.

15.1 Gerrymandering Is a Worldwide Problem

When gerrymandering electoral districts is mentioned, it is the bizarre shape of some congressional electoral districts in the United States that usually is the focus. However, as discussed in Chaps. 5 and 14, this bizarre shape is a direct result of the legal obligation in the United States to make all congressional districts in a state's plan absolutely equal in population. To achieve this result while also creating districts that advantage or disadvantage certain groups or individuals, some districts in a plan are purposefully drawn to include or exclude pockets of persons based on the race or ethnicity of the persons or how those persons have voted in the past. These districts are often bizarre in appearance. Certainly, the U.S. has many such congressional districts.

The same result of advantaging or disadvantaging groups, parties, or individuals can be achieved more easily in other nations in which the allocation of seats is not automatic, or there is a lax standard of equality in persons or electors per representative among districts. An allocation or redistricting that intentionally discriminates

S. Bickerstaff, *Election Systems and Gerrymandering Worldwide*, Studies in Choice and Welfare, https://doi.org/10.1007/978-3-030-30837-7_15

under such conditions is a gerrymander regardless whether it results in malapportionment or bizarre district shapes.

15.2 How to Identify a Gerrymander

Any effort to prevent gerrymanders or to search for gerrymanders in a plan for allocating seats in the national legislature or for redrawing single-member or multi-member electoral district boundaries must be systematic and fact-intensive. Gerrymanders are seldom obvious, especially in nations with lax requirements for equal voting power. A possible analysis should:

1. Determine the election system in question and the applicable law within the nation in regard to the timing and standards for the allocation of seats or drawing of electoral districts;
2. Determine the opportunities in the election system for gerrymandering, such as in the allocation of seats, drawing of single-member or multi-member district boundaries, timeliness, and the basis, such as electors or total population, used in that country for measuring equality among the districts;
3. Determine whether the redistricting or reallocation is timely;
4. Calculate the number of electors or persons for each single-member or multi-member district in the plan;
5. Calculate the number of persons and electors per representative for each single-member and multi-member district in the plan;
6. Determine the racial, ethnic, or religious make-up of each district if this information is available;
7. Determine the ideal number of persons or electors per representative (quota) for the nation as a whole and for each fixed or special multi-member district;
8. Compare the ideal number per representative with the actual number in each district and identify those districts that vary significantly, such as more than $\pm 5\%$, from the ideal;
9. Determine if any single-member or multi-member district is oddly shaped. Shape alone is not a sufficient indicator of gerrymandering, but it should not be ignored;
10. Determine the reason given by the legislature or commission for any single-member or multi-member district that is oddly shaped or significantly above or below the ideal number of persons or electors for the nation or the multi-member district to which the seats have been allocated, and whether this reason complies with the nation's laws;
11. Determine whether the reason given by the legislature or commission for a specific questionable district or allocation has been applied uniformly within the plan; and
12. Where data permits, analyze whether the plan needlessly divides or packs persons or electors from any racial, ethnic, or religious minority.

The issue is not only the legality or illegality of a particular reallocation or redistricting plan, but whether the plan provides for fair elections and an equal opportunity for voter representation. If the legislature or commission cannot justify any variance from equal voting power for all of its persons or electors or any variance from the neutral factors established by law, then it is not a true representative democracy. Any significant variance should be rare and justified by neutral criteria applied uniformly nationwide.

15.3 Equal Voting Power Is Denied Voters Worldwide

The principle that every voter should possess a equal opportunity to affect national policy by electing a representative of their choice to the national legislature is generally accepted, but inconsistently implemented worldwide. Although international standards suggest that no constituency should vary from the "average or quota" by more than 10%, national standards are consistently higher. Many nations, including developed countries, have a history of failing to timely redistrict or reallocate seats in the national legislature even when those higher deviations are exceeded. All of this amounts to gerrymandering.

15.4 Many Nations Fail to Follow their Own Rules

A nation's self-imposed legal rules for redistricting or the reallocation of seats in a national legislature are often not followed because there is no institution to reliably enforce them.

Courts outside the U.S. mostly remain entirely out of the "political thicket" of redistricting, or have given the national legislature or redistricting commission great discretion about how to balance the conflicting criteria and the practicalities of the situation. A rationale for this deference is that the members of the legislature are experienced in redistricting matters and are directly elected by the voters; thus are representatives of the people on redistricting just as on other policy matters. This rationale makes no sense when these members of the legislature are themselves elected under an unfair gerrymandered system and are self-interested in maintaining or enhancing that system.

This limit on the role of the courts is generally accepted because: (1) few observers want to repeat in their country the redistricting litigation morass seen in the United States; (2) many see litigation as merely another means of bringing politics into the process; and (3) some distrust the courts as biased or even corrupt. As someone who has litigated redistricting cases in the U.S. for 40 years, I value the courts as a means of searching for truth and enforcing legal standards. I disagree with this limit on the role of courts and think that the limit essentially deprives people of the rights that they correctly expect from representative democracy.

15.5 The Election Structure in Most Countries Is Biased toward Rural Areas

A bias favoring rural areas continues to prevail worldwide. In country after country the urban districts are overpopulated and the rural districts are underpopulated. The greatest disparities are a result of historical policy decisions, such as guaranteeing each state or province a prescribed number of seats in the national legislature regardless of the state or province's number of persons or eligible voters, or geography, such as an island. These reasons are problematic, but at least they have a basis, sometimes disputed, in policy. In many countries, however, the disparities are systemic and have little or no clear basis other than that the rural areas have hung on to their historical dominance in national legislatures despite the faster growth in urban centers. This imbalance between urban and rural areas was one of the major reasons for the birth of the "one person, one vote" doctrine in the U.S.

15.6 No Discretion in the Allocation of Seats

The best process for preventing gerrymandering in the allocation of seats among states, provinces, administrative units, or predetermined multi-member districts is to remove the need for any subjective decision-making. The process should be automatic according to a legally prescribed timeline and formula, calculated by an objective agency or commission, and without any ability of the national legislature or any commission to delay or change it. The current system in the U.S. provides a good example of such a process, but this system evolved from an earlier one that was abused by Congress.

15.7 Proportional Representation Is Only an Election System Option, Not an Answer to Gerrymandering

Some see proportional representation systems as an answer to gerrymandering, but this is more dogma than reality.

Only a handful of nations rely solely on nationwide PR elections. Virtually all nations with any PR elections have a geographical component to their election systems because legislative PR elections overemphasize the importance of the political party at the expense of the individual voter's right to choose his or her representative and the representative's accountability to constituents. Even many of the nations that use solely a nationwide PR system to elect representatives in the national legislature have open party lists, independent candidates, or even primaries as means of allowing voters some freedom to elect the person of their choice, instead of leaving the decision wholly to the parties.

Unfortunately, this geographical component also allows gerrymandering in the allocation of seats if the process is subject to political control or influence.

15.8 Redistricting Commissions Alone Are Not the Answer

Allowing a national legislature to draw electoral district boundaries or to reallocate seats in a national legislature invites decisions that are intended to favor or disfavor a particular candidate or political party—generally incumbents or the government. It is desirable to eliminate this self-interest.

Many political scientists, however, hail a commission as the solution while remaining blind to the realities of what is necessary to truly make that commission "independent" of legislative influence and control. The presence of such a commission in a nation often gives a false sense of fairness. It is naïve for anyone to think that a political group that is fighting hard through elections to control a country will not try to directly or indirectly influence the critical redistricting and reallocation decisions that ultimately may determine the success or failure of its efforts.

Persons who favor use of a redistricting or boundary commission are often blind to how such commissions may yield to political pressures, or knowingly or unknowingly bend the criteria for political reasons, or see their work delayed or blocked by a national legislature. A commission is only as dedicated to "neutral criteria" as its members are "independent" of political influence, partisan objectives, and self-serving motives. To be an effective constraint on political influence, a commission must be designed with this objective in mind, with its work required to be open, transparent, final, and its plans carefully monitored for political bias. It is not enough to simply bar politicians from serving on a commission.

My review of processes worldwide shows that both legislatures and commissions are susceptible to political bias. A commission without politicians is a step forward, but a truly independent commission is one structured as described in Chap. 13 to act without any reliance on legislative action at all, and with members of the commission chosen for objectivity and without any means of benefiting from the outcome. Such a commission offers the best potential for an unbiased redistricting process and an end to gerrymandering.

15.9 Conclusion

Drawing electoral districts and allocating seats among multi-member districts are zero-sum processes. No plan pleases absolutely everyone. Under such circumstances, making the process fair, the criteria clear, and the decision-maker responsive to public comment is critical to winning trust from a skeptical public and to the future of representative democracy. This observation is accurate whether the issue is allocation of seats in Iran or drawing congressional districts in Texas.

Appendix A: International Standards

There are few international standards for redistricting. A usable source, however, is the Code of Good Practice in Electoral Matters (Code of Good Practice) adopted in 2002 by the European Commission for Democracy through Law, or Venice Commission. This Commission was created in 1990 as an advisory body of the Council of Europe. It was created after the fall of the Berlin Wall to advise on constitutional matters and to assist in the development of democratic systems and institutions in the recently independent nations of Eastern Europe. Section 2.2, Equal Voting Power, of this Code is reproduced below along with the Organization for Security and Cooperation in Europe (OSCE) policy statement on equal voting power and the United Nation's guidance on redistricting and reallocation of seats.

In this book, I have contrasted this view of "good practice" with international realities.

The European Commission for Democracy through Law, or Venice Commission, in 2002, adopted a Code of Good Practice in Electoral Matters. Section 2.2 reads as follows:

A.1 Code of Good Practice in Electoral Matters

A.1.1 Equal Voting Power

Seats must be evenly distributed between constituencies.

This must at least apply to elections to lower houses of parliament and regional and local elections;

It entails a clear and balanced distribution of seats among constituencies on the basis of one of the following allocation criteria: population, number of resident nationals (including minors), number of registered voters, and the number of people actually voting. An appropriate combination of these criteria may be envisaged;

S. Bickerstaff, *Election Systems and Gerrymandering Worldwide*, Studies in Choice and Welfare, https://doi.org/10.1007/978-3-030-30837-7

The geographical criterion and administrative, or even historical, boundaries may be taken into consideration;

The permissible departure from the norm should not be more than 10%, and certainly should not exceed 15% except in special circumstances (protection of a concentrated minority, sparsely populated administrative entity);

In order to guarantee equal voting power, the distribution of seats must be reviewed at least every 10 years, preferably outside election periods;

With multi-member constituencies, seats should be redistributed preferably without redefining constituency boundaries, which should, where possible, coincide with administrative boundaries;

When constituency boundaries are redefined—which must be in a single-member system—it must be done:

Impartially;
Without detriment to national minorities;
Taking account of the opinion of a committee, a majority of whose members are independent; this committee should preferably include a geographer, a sociologist, a balanced representation of the parties and, if necessary, representatives of national minorities.

A.2 Organization for Security and Cooperation in Europe (OSCE) Guidelines

According to OSCE commitments, all votes should carry the same weight to ensure equal representation. This means that each elected representative should represent a similar number of registered electors. For example, in a majority voting system, the size of the electorate should not vary by more than approximately 10% from constituency to constituency. Under the proportional representation system, the size of the electorate may vary, but the number of representatives for each district should be proportional to the size of the electorate. The election law should provide detailed and uniform criteria for the drawing of electoral-district boundaries, specifying considerations such as the number of voting population per district and geographic, administrative, and historical continuity of boundaries. The boundaries should be drawn in a transparent manner, under the principle of political neutrality, ideally by a non-partisan commission of experts. A domestic observer group should assess whether election districts have been drawn in a transparent manner to ensure as far as possible that all votes carry the same weight or whether they have been drawn in "a selective, discriminatory, and biased manner."

A.3 UN (Center for Human Rights): Human Rights and Elections: A Handbook on the Legal, Technical, and Human Rights Aspects of Elections, Annex II Para. V.b

When voting is conducted on the basis of electoral districts, the said districts shall be established on an equitable basis such as would make the result most accurately and completely reflect the will of all the voters.

Appendix B: International Election Systems

The following lists are compiled largely from the Comparative list of the ACE, the Electoral Knowledge Network (2012) at http://aceproject.org; International Institute for Democracy and Electoral Assistance (IDEA) at http://www.idea.int/resources/databases; Lisa Handley, "Appendix C: Criteria Considered in the Delimitation Process," Delimitation Equity Project: Resource Guide, IFES Center for Transitional and Post-Conflict Governance and USAID, 2006, Chap. 2; and my own research. The organizations' work is invaluable, but it is incomplete and sometimes inconsistent or outdated. I have verified most of the information and expanded the lists to include some countries not in the original lists or deleted some, but I have not independently verified the accuracy of every part of every list.[1]

[1]Please note this appendix uses the following abbreviations: PR—proportional representation, voting with each party entitled to representation according to its share of the vote; FPTP—first-past-the-post, plurality voting with a single winner; TRS—two round system, usually majority voting with a single winner; MMP—mixed member proportional, with a mix of FPTP and PR elections; P—parallel system (also called Mixed Member Majoritarian [MMM]), with a mix of FPTP and PR elections; STV—single transferable vote, with ranked or preferential voting in a MMD designed to achieve proportional representation; SNTV—single non-transferable vote, designed to produce plurality winners in multi-member districts; AV—alternative vote (also called instant run-off voting) with ranked or preferential voting among multiple candidate designed to achieve one winner with a majority; Blk—block voting (also called multiple non-transferable vote), designed for electing several representatives from the same party in a multimember electoral district; SMD—single-member district; MMD—Multi-member district.

S. Bickerstaff, *Election Systems and Gerrymandering Worldwide*, Studies in Choice and Welfare, https://doi.org/10.1007/978-3-030-30837-7

B.1 Bicameral or Unicameral National Legislature

B.1.1 Bicameral Legislatures with Upper House Not Directly Elected (Usually Selected by States or Provinces [Indirectly Elected] or Appointed by Head of State or Monarch)

Afghanistan, Austria, Bahamas, Barbados, Belarus, Belize, Bermuda, Bhutan (Monarch appoints 11 members), Bosnia & Herzegovina, Botswana, Cambodia, Cameroon, Canada, The Democratic Republic of the Congo, Republic of the Congo (Brazzaville)(appointment by monarch), Ethiopia, France, Gabon, Germany, Grenada, Indonesia, Ireland, Jamaica, Jordan, Kazakhstan, Lesotho, Malaysia, Myanmar, Morocco (appointed by Monarch), Namibia, Nepal, Netherlands, Pakistan, Rwanda, Russian Federation, Saint Lucia, South Africa, Sudan, Swaziland (appointed by Monarch), Thailand (appointed ½ by lower chamber and ½ by government), Tajikistan, Trinidad and Tobago, Saint Lucia, Uzbekistan, United Kingdom (appointed by Monarch and hereditary), and Yemen.

B.1.2 Bicameral Legislatures with Some Members of Upper House Directly Elected

Australia (STV), Belgium (PR), Bolivia (PR), Brazil (3 elected by majority for each of 26 states and Federal District), Chile (PR), Colombia (PR), Czech Republic (TRS), Dominican Republic (FPTP), Haiti (3 elected by majority [TRS] in each of 10 administrative département), India (STV), Indonesia (SNTV), Italy (P), Japan (P), Jordan (SMD), Kazakhstan (FPTP, with 9 appointed), Liberia [2 elected in FPTP from each of 15 counties for 9 year terms], Mexico (P), Nigeria (FPTP), Palau (In MMDs; there are no political Parties), Paraguay (PR), Philippines (nationwide through majority at-large voting), Poland (FPTP), Romania (PR), Spain (FPTP), Switzerland (FPTP), United States (FPTP), Uruguay (PR nationwide), and Zimbabwe (PR, with addition of eighteen tribal chiefs and two disabled persons).

B.1.3 Unicameral Legislatures

Andorra, Anguilla, Albania, Algeria, Aruba, Azerbaijan, Armenia, Bangladesh, Benin, Botswana, Bulgaria, Burkina Faso, Cameroon, Cape Verde, Central African Republic, Cook Islands, Costa Rica, Cote d'Ivoire, Cyprus (North), Cyprus, Croatia, Denmark, Djibouti, Dominica, El Salvador, Ecuador, Estonia, Egypt, Eritrea, Equatorial Guinea, Falkland Islands (Maldives), Finland, Fiji, Georgia, Guernsey, Ghana, Greenland, Gambia, Guinea, Guinea-Bissau, Greece, Guatemala, Guyana,

Honduras, Hong Kong, Hungary, Iceland, Iran, Iraq, Israel, Jersey, Kenya, Kosovo, Republic of Korea, Kosovo, Kyrgyzstan, Laos, Latvia, Lebanon, Lithuania, Libya, Luxembourg, Macedonia, Macau, Mali, Malta, Malawi, Marshall Islands, Mauritius, Monaco, Mongolia, Montenegro, Monserrat, Micronesia, Republic of Moldova, Mozambique, Nauru, New Zealand, New Caledonia, Nicaragua, Niue, Norway, Papua New Guinea, Palestinian Territories, Panama, Peru, Portugal, San Marino, Saint Helena, St. Kitts and Nevis, St. Vincent and Grenadines, Samoa, Senegal, Serbia, Seychelles, Sierra Leone, Singapore, Slovakia, Slovenia, Sri Lanka, Suriname, Sweden, Taiwan, Tanzania, Togo, Tonga, Tunisia, Turkey, Uganda, Ukraine, Vanuatu, Venezucla, Virgin Islands (British), Virgin Islands (U.S.), Wallis and Fortuna, Zambia, and Zanzibar.

B.2 Method of Election of Members to Lower House or Unicameral National Legislature

B.2.1 Fixed Multi-Member Districts Generally with FPTP, TRS, or AV Elections (FPTP Unless Shown Otherwise) Within the District (Sometimes with Exceptions for Specific Areas or Groups)

American Samoa, Anguilla, Australia (AV), Azerbaijan, Bahamas, Bahrain (TRS), Bangladesh, Barbados, Belarus (TRS), Belize, Bermuda, Botswana, Canada, Republic of Congo (Brazzaville) (TRS), Cook Islands, Cote d'Ivoire (Ivory Coast), Cuba (TRS), Dominica (nine appointed), Egypt, Eritrea, Ethiopia, France (TRS), French Polynesia (TRS), Gabon (TRS, nine MMD), Gambia, Ghana, Grenada, Haiti (TRS), Iran (TRS), India, Jamaica, Japan, Kenya (12 appointed), Kiribati (TRS), Laos, Liberia, Maldives, Mali (TRS), Malta, Myanmar (25% appointed by military), Malaysia, Malta, Marshall Islands, Malawi, Monserrat, Mozambique, Micronesia, New Caledonia (TRS), Nigeria, Niue, Northern Mariana Islands, Oman, Pakistan (with PR for seats set aside for women and non-Muslims), Papua New Guinea (AV), Samoa, St. Kitts and Nevis, St. Lucia, St. Vincent and the Grenadines (six appointed), Seychelles, Sierra Leone, Singapore (nine appointed by parties), Solomon Islands, Swaziland, Tanzania (with 75 seats set aside for women chosen by PR; and ten members appointed by President), Tokelau (TRS, protectorate of New Zealand), Turkmenistan (TRS), Uganda, United Kingdom, United States, Uzbekistan (TRS), Vanuatu (SNTV), British Virgin Islands, U.S. Virgin Islands, Wallis and Fortuna (TRS), Viet Nam (TRS), Yemen, Zambia, and Zimbabwe.

B.2.2 Fixed or Special Multi-Member Districts Generally with Proportional Representation Elections Within the District (Sometimes with Exceptions for Specific Areas or Groups, or Post-Election Distribution of Seats to Districts for Political Parties Based on National Vote)

Albania (changed to PR in 2008), Angola, Albania, Argentina (DSV), Algeria, Aruba, Austria, Belgium, Benin, Bosnia & Herzegovina, Bhutan, Brazil, Bulgaria, Burkina Faso, Cape Verde, Cambodia, Chile (changed to PR in 2017), Columbia, Costa Rica (DSV), Croatia, Cyprus (North and South), Czech Republic, Denmark, Dominican Republic, El Salvador, Equatorial Guinea, Estonia, Finland, Faroe Islands, Greece, Greenland, Guatemala, Guyana, Hong Kong, Honduras, Iceland, Indonesia (some provinces divided into MMDs), Iraq, Ireland (STV), Kosovo, Latvia, Liechtenstein (Two MMD constituencies), Luxembourg (Four MMD constituencies), Malta (STV), Mauritius (BV), Macedonia, Mongolia, Moldova, Morocco, Montenegro, Mozambique, Namibia, Nicaragua, Norway, Palestine, Peru, Poland, Portugal, Palestinian Territories (BV), Romania (changed to PR in 2015), Rwanda, San Marino, Slovenia, South Africa, South Sudan, Spain, Sri Lanka, Sweden, Sudan, Switzerland, Tunisia, Turkey (MMD in three largest cities), and Uruguay (DSV).

B.2.3 Mixed System: Partly Single-Member Districts Within Fixed Districts and Partly PR with Parallel System [P] or Mixed Member Proportional [MMP]) Within Special Multi-Member Districts or Nationwide (Sometimes with Exceptions for Specific Areas or Groups, or Post-Election Distribution of Seats to Districts for Political Parties Based on National Vote)

Andorra (P), Armenia (P), Antigua and Barbados (P), Bolivia (MMP), Cameroon (P), Chad (P), Democratic Republic of Congo (Kinshasa) (P), Djibouti (P), Ecuador (P), Georgia (P), Germany (MMP), Guatemala (P), Guinea (P), Hungary (P, changed from MMP in 2012), Italy (P, changed in 2018), Japan (P), Jordan (P, with seats reserved for women, Christians, and Chechens/Circassians), Republic of Korea (P, South Korea), Lesotho (MMP), Lithuania (P), Libya (P), Madagascar (P), Mauritania (P), Mexico (P), Monaco (P), Nepal (P), New Zealand (MMP), Niger (P), Panama (P), Pakistan (P), Philippines (P), Puerto Rico (P), Russian Federation (P beginning in 2016), Romania (Changed from MMP to FPTP in 2006 and then to PR in 2015), Senegal (P), South Sudan (P), Taiwan (P), Tajikistan (P), Tanzania

(P), Thailand (P), Ukraine (P), Venezuela ((changed from MMP to P in 2010), and Zanzibar (MMP).

B.2.4 The Nation as One District (Single Constituency)

Lower Chamber or Unicameral National Legislature

Fiji (PR), Italy (Changed to Parallel System in 2018), Iraq, Israel (PR), Kazakhstan (PR), Kyrgyzstan (PR), Netherlands (PR), Serbia (PR), Slovakia (PR), Namibia (PR), and Russian Federation (PR nationwide from 2007 to 2015; changed to Parallel system (P) in 2016).

Upper Chamber

Colombia (including indigenous seats), Palau, Paraguay, Philippines, and Uruguay.

B.2.5 Block Vote (BLK)

Falkland Islands, Guernsey, Jersey, Kuwait, Lebanon, Mauritius, Pitcairn Islands, St. Helena, Syria, and Tuvalu.

B.3 Base for Drawing Districts and Determining Voting Equality Among Districts

These lists are incomplete because I had difficulty going beyond the website lists of countries that used population or electors for redistricting or for the reallocation of seats. The data generally was inconsistent or not located to verify nations not on the published lists. The difference between the standards would not normally make a difference in redistricting or reallocation unless there is a disproportionate percentage of noncitizen or youth in an area. Please note that at least two nations, Canada and Australia, allocate seats on the basis of population but draw districts on the basis of electors.

B.3.1 Total Population

Botswana, Bulgaria, Cameroon, Canada, Czech Republic, Dominica, Dominican Republic, Finland, France, India, Indonesia, Ireland, Iraq, Italy, Japan, Kenya, Republic of Korea, Lithuania, Liberia, Mauritius, Mexico, New Zealand, Nigeria, Pakistan, Palestinian Territories, Panama, Papua New Guinea, Poland, Spain, Sudan, Saint Lucia, Saint Vincent & the Grenadines, Seychelles, Uganda, United States, and Yemen.

B.3.2 Eligible or Registered Voters (Electors) (Citizens of Voting Age; Some Nations Mandate Registration and Voting)

Albania, Armenia, Australia, Bahamas, Bangladesh, Barbados, Belize, Croatia, Finland, France, Iceland, Jamaica, Kyrgyzstan, Lesotho, Macedonia, Malaysia, Namibia, Singapore, Ukraine, United Kingdom, Uganda, Uruguay, and Zimbabwe.

B.3.3 Citizen Population (All Citizens, Including those Too Young to Vote)

Belgium, Germany, Nepal, Norway, Sweden, and Turkey.

B.3.4 Voters in Previous Election

Belarus and Tanzania.

B.4 Legal Standard Set by Law for Voter Equality

Albania (± 5%), Armenia (± 15%), Australia (± 15% at creation), Belarus (± 10%), Canada (± 25%), Croatia (± 5%), Germany (± 25%), Hungary (± 20%), Italy (± 20%), Lithuania (± 25%), Macedonia (± 3%), New Zealand (± 5%), Papua New Guinea (±20%), Singapore (± 30%), Ukraine (± 10%), United Kingdom (± 5%

with exceptions; pending), United States (court imposed de minimus), Yemen (± 5%), and Zimbabwe (±20%).

The following democracies have no explicit standard for voter equality:

Bahamas, Bangladesh, Barbados, Botswana, Bulgaria, Cameroon, Czech Republic, Dominica, Dominican Republic, France, Hungary, Iceland, India, Indonesia, Ireland, Italy, Jamaica, Kenya, Republic of Korea (South Korea), Lesotho, Malaysia, Mauritius, Mexico, Namibia, Nepal, Nigeria, Pakistan, Palestinian Territories, Panama, Poland, Saint Lucia, Saint Vincent and the Grenadines, Sweden, Tanzania, Turkey, and Uruguay.

B.5 Legal Prompts for Redistricting or Reallocation of Seats or Review of Deviation

(∗ marks nations in which there is no prompt or the prompt is essentially "as needed." This list was compiled largely through a questionnaire sent in the early 2000s by ACE.)

Albania (5 yrs.), Armenia (4 yrs.), Australia (7 yrs.), Bahamas (5 yrs.), Bangladesh∗, Barbados∗, Belarus∗, Belgium (10 yrs.), Belize∗, Botswana (5–10 yrs.), Bulgaria∗, Cameroon∗. Canada (10 yrs.), Croatia∗, Czech Republic∗, Finland∗, France∗ (12–14 yrs. Repealed 2002), Germany (5 yrs.), Hungary∗, Iceland∗, India (10 yrs., redistricting only), Indonesia∗, Ireland (12 yrs.), Jamaica (10 yrs.), Japan (10 yrs.), Kenya (10 yrs.), Republic of Korea∗, Kyrgyzstan∗, Lesotho (10 yrs.), Lithuania (4 yrs.), Macedonia∗, Malaysia (8 yrs.), Mauritius (10 yrs.), Mexico (10 yrs.), Nepal (10 yrs.), New Zealand (5 yrs.), Nigeria 10 yrs.), Pakistan (10 yrs.), Palestine Territories∗, Papua New Guinea (10 yrs.), Panama∗, Poland∗, Saint Lucia (3–7 yrs.), Saint Vincent and the Grenadines (8 yrs.), Scychelles∗, Singapore∗, Sweden∗, Tanzania (10 yrs.), Turkey (5 yrs.), Uganda∗, Ukraine∗, United Kingdom (8–12 yrs.), United States (10 yrs.), Yemen∗, and Zimbabwe (5 yrs.).

B.6 Redistricting Criteria

B.6.1 Population Equality

Virtually every democracy claims that voter equality is an explicit or implicit criterion for redrawing electoral districts or reallocating seats in the national legislature. The standard for equality varies widely among nations.

B.6.2 Compact or Contiguous Districts

Albania, Armenia, Barbados, Botswana, Belarus, Dominican Republic, France (contiguity), India, Indonesia (contiguity), Italy, Jamaica (contiguity), and Pakistan.

B.6.3 Districts that Respect Administrative Boundaries

Albania, Bangladesh, Barbados, Botswana, Cameroon, Canada, Croatia, Czech Republic, Dominica, Dominican Republic, France, Germany, Hungary, India, Indonesia, Italy, Japan, Kenya, Republic of Korea, Kyrgyzstan, Lithuania, Malaysia, Mauritius, Mexico, Namibia Pakistan, Panama, Poland, Saint Lucia, Saint Vincent and the Grenadines, Seychelles, Tanzania, Turkey, Uganda, Ukraine, United Kingdom, United States (some states), and Yemen.

B.7 Final Authority for Approving or Reviewing Redistricting or Reallocation Plan for Election to National Legislature

B.7.1 National Legislature (in Many of these Countries the National Legislature Acts Through Legislation Requiring the Executive's Approval)

Albania, Algeria, Bahamas, Barbados, Belgium, Belize, Benin, Brazil, Bulgaria, Cape Verde, Cameroon, Canada (Provincial Parliaments, with commissions), Chile, Croatia, Cyprus, Czech Republic, Dominica, Egypt, Finland, France, Gabon, Germany, Greece, Guinea, Hungary (legislature selects members of commission), Indonesia, Iceland, Ireland, Italy, Jamaica, Japan, Jordan, Kiribati, Republic of Korea, Lebanon, Luxemburg, Latvia, Libya, Macedonia, Madagascar, Malaysia, Marshall Islands, Mauritius, Mali, Micronesia, Myanmar, New Caledonia, Nicaragua, Niue, Niger, Palestinian Territories, Panama, Papua New Guinea, Peru, Philippines, Poland, Russian Federation, Saint Lucia, Saint Vincent and the Grenadines, Sweden, Slovenia, Swaziland, Togo, Tuvalu, Uganda, United Kingdom, United States (apportioning of seats in House of Representatives to states), Ukraine, and Zimbabwe.

B.7.2 State Legislatures or Provinces

United States (for drawing single-member districts; some states now use a commission), Canada (each province or territory has a commission).

B.7.3 Commissions

Some are permanent government bodies with additional electoral responsibilities). (Many nations with commissions, such as the U.K. boundary commissions, are included above under national legislature because a commission's plan goes to the national legislature for review and adoption, and, depending on the nation's law, may be delayed, amended, or rejected.)

Armenia, Australia, Bangladesh, Botswana, Dominican Republic, India (with legislators as associate members), Indonesia, Kenya, Lesotho, Lithuania, Mexico, Nepal, New Zealand, Nigeria, Pakistan, Seychelles, Singapore, Tanzania, Turkey, and Yemen.

Appendix C: Case Studies

C.1 A Case Study of the United States

In 1783, the 13 American colonies won their independence from Britain through the Treaty of Paris. The colonies cooperated as a matter of necessity during the war with Britain and afterward through a loose confederation. They were very different in geographical size, population and culture. Some depended primarily on seafaring, some on farming, and some on slavery. Some were constrained by natural barriers, such as the Atlantic Ocean, or other colonies and were unable to grow in size; others claimed vast land to the west into which they expected to expand. Under the Articles of Confederation, there was no president or federal judicial system. The former colonies were denominated "states" in this confederation, but essentially remained separate sovereigns.

In 1787, representatives of the states met in a convention ostensibly for the purpose of amending the Articles of Confederation. Instead, this convention adopted an entirely different structure and document—a constitution that proposed to join the colonies together in a union under a federal government that had a president, federal judicial system and meaningful powers. The Constitution was ratified by 1790, and the "United States of America" as we know it was created.

The Constitution was possible only because of political compromises among the state representatives at the convention. Some of these compromises directly affected elections and the issue of voting power in the United States, including:

- Each state retained control over the "Times, Places and Manner of holding Elections" for U.S Senators and Representatives;
- The U.S. Senate consisted of two senators from each state despite the differences in the number of persons among the states;
- The U.S. House of Representatives consisted of members elected by the people of each state. Each state was to be apportioned members in the House of Representatives "according to their respective numbers" as determined by an "enumeration" (census) conducted "within every. .. Term of ten years";

S. Bickerstaff, *Election Systems and Gerrymandering Worldwide*, Studies in Choice and Welfare, https://doi.org/10.1007/978-3-030-30837-7

- For purposes of apportionment of and representation in the House of Representatives, only 3/5 of the persons other than free persons were counted; and
- Each state was to have at least one member in the House of Representatives.

The XIII, XIV, and XV amendments (1865, 1868, and 1870) to the Constitution eliminated slavery and changed the apportionment of the House of Representatives to all persons "excluding Indians not taxed." The XVII amendment (1913) required that the two senators from each state must be directly elected, instead of being appointed by a state's legislature. The XIX amendment (1920) prohibited states from denying or abridging the right to vote on account of a person's sex. Otherwise the original constitutional provisions on elections remain essentially unchanged.

C.2 A Case Study of Iran

According to last national census (2011), Iran's population was 75.15 million. It is now approximately 83 million. A common misconception in America is that Iran is not a democracy. Iran's first constitution was adopted in 1905. The first competitive elections were held in 1906, but were effectively suspended under Reza Shah Pahlavi. A new constitution was approved by national referendum after the 1979 revolution and provides, for example, in Article Six that:

> In the Islamic Republic of Iran, the affairs of the country must be administered on the basis of public opinion expressed by the means of elections, including the election of the President, the representatives of the Islamic Consultative Assembly, and the members of councils, or by means of referenda in matters specified in other articles of this Constitution.[2]

Today, city and village councils, the nation's president, and members of the national unicameral parliament (the Islamic Consultative Assembly [Majlis]) are directly elected (mayors are elected by the city or village council). Even the members of the "Assembly of Experts" that selects the Supreme Leader are directly elected. Suffrage is essentially universal for Iranians age eighteen or above and ballots are secret. Women vote and hold elective office. The first Supreme Leader, Ruhollah Khomeini, explained, "In the world there is no democracy better than Iran's democracy. Such a thing has never been seen before."

The members of the national legislature, Majlis (currently 290), are directly elected for a term of 4 years from a mix of single and multi-member electoral districts (196 constituencies) that exist within general districts usually consisting of a province or combination of provinces. For example, the province of Tehran and surrounding environs are divided into six electoral districts from which 38 representatives (30 from the city of Tehran) are elected. Five of the 290 seats in the Majlis are reserved for certain religious minorities, including Armenian Christians, Zoroastrians, and Jews.

---

[2](Translated at [http://en.mfa.ir] and [http://www.president.ir/en])

Iran has even made an attempt to achieve a rough equality of population per representative, but, as in most western democracies, this effort has fallen victim to changing demographics and politics. Based on the 2011 census, the provinces are very unequal in the average number of persons and voters per constituency. For example, Tehran with a population of 12,183,391 has 38 seats in the national legislature for an average of 320,615 persons per representative. By comparison, the Iranian province of Eastern Azerbaijan has a population of 3,724,620 with 19 seats in the national legislature, or an average of 196,032 persons per representative, while the province of Razavi Khorasan has the same number of seats (19), but for a population of 5,994,402 or an average per representative of 315,495 persons). The average constituency size in Semnan province is only 157,804. A significant, but somewhat smaller, disparity exists among the constituencies based on eligible voters.

This wide disparity in population and voters in each constituency exists nationwide and is a result of the apparent failure to reallocate seats since at least 1985. I was unable to determine whether the failure to reallocate seats is intended to benefit any specific faction, such as hardliners, or if the districts are gerrymandered. It is apparent, however, that the rural areas benefit most from the current allocation of seats.

Presidential and Majlis elections are conducted under a structure that is commonly called a two-round system (TRS) and may be found in other nations, such as France, which has only single-member parliamentary constituencies. In Iran, each elector has a single vote in presidential elections. An absolute majority (50%) is necessary to win the Presidency. In Majlis elections, however, each elector has as many votes as there are seats at stake in the district and may vote them as a block. After the first round of voting the candidates who have received the highest number of votes (at least 25%) are elected up to the number of seats at stake in the district. If too few candidates meet the required minimum level of support, the unsuccessful candidates, up to twice as many as there are seats left to be filled, participate in a second round to fill the remaining seats.

Iran has a dynamic civil polity that has not been conducive to the formation of official political parties. Instead, potential voters are split among many diverse political organizations. However, the leading candidates are unofficially labeled as either reformists/moderates, who champion international rapprochement and greater individual freedom within Iran, or hard-liners/Principlists, who distrust foreigners and see themselves as defenders of a strict Islamic code and the 1979 revolution. Candidates from both of these factions operate within the existing system.

There are persons who oppose the existing system, but the number and identity of these persons are generally unknown because for a person to become a candidate he or she must agree to adhere to the nation's Constitution and to remain loyal to Islamic ideals. These opponents of the existing system are frequently alleged to be "foreign agents" bribed or otherwise influenced by foreign powers interested in a regime change in Iran.

Elections in Iran are vigorously contested, with televised debates, negative ads, misleading political promises, worries about the economy, street rallies, allegations that an opponent is corrupt, and many of the other characteristics we regrettably have come to expect in democratic elections. Government officials are required to remain neutral. Some critics say that these elections are only for show. If so, they definitely are a good imitation of democratic elections.

Iranian presidents generally came from the reformer/moderate political group in the 1990s and early 2000s and gave the U.S. many opportunities to improve U. S./Iranian relations and to stabilize the Middle East. This policy changed when the U.S. publically and foolishly labeled Iran as a member of the "Axis of Evil" in 2002. This statement probably was seen as political rhetoric in America, but it had significant repercussions within Iran—undermining the reformer/moderate leaders and strengthening the hard-liners' argument that the U.S. was not trustworthy. America's threats and apparent intransigence contributed to the election of a hard-liner, Mahmoud Ahmadinejad, as President of Iran in 2005.

Ahmadinejad's administration ended the opportunity for improved relations with the U.S. and almost drove the U.S. and Iran to war. He denied existence of the Holocaust and was fond of vocalizing anti-American and anti-Israeli rhetoric and threats. Even more alarming, however, were his steps to accelerate Iran's nuclear and missile programs and to increase Iranian support of Hezbollah and the Palestinians. As a former associate member of the Islamic Revolutionary Guard, Ahmadinejad expanded the role and power of that organization.

Ahmadinejad's harsh rhetoric was not limited to foreign nations. In his winning reelection campaign in 2009, Ahmadinejad described his reformer/moderate critics, including former President Akbar Hashemi Rafsanjani, as corrupt and "acting like Hitler." Iranian law limited Ahmadinejad to two consecutive terms as president. He abided by this proscription and did not seek reelection in 2013.

The current reformer/moderate president, Hassan Rouhani, was elected in 2013 largely because of a failing economy and his pledge of rapprochement with the world. The nuclear agreement was the culmination of this pledge. Rouhani was reelected in 2017 after framing the vote as a choice between his support for greater civil liberties and the hard-liners' "extremism", such as the continued arrest of reformist leaders and activists. Rouhani is barred from seeking reelection in 2021.

On the other hand, Iran's government is unlike any western democracy. Iran's Constitution establishes the country as an Islamic Republic. Day-to-day affairs are handled within the elected government structure, but all decisions are subject ultimately to scrutiny to determine if they comply with the religious underpinnings of the 1979 Islamic revolution. Article Four of the Constitution explains:

> All civil, penal, financial, economic, administrative, cultural, military, political, and other laws and regulations must be based on Islamic criteria. This principle applies absolutely and generally to all articles of the Constitution as well as to all other laws and regulations, and the Fatwa - of the Guardian Council are judges in this matter.[3]

Three unusual aspects of the nation's Islamic governance structure stand out—The Supreme Leader, the Guardian Council, and the presence of a State Religion.

[3](Translated at [http://en.mfa.ir] and [http://www.president.ir/en])

For many Americans, the term Supreme Leader conjures up the image of an absolute ruler like Stalin, Gadhafi, Kim Jong-un, or Saddam Hussein. For the Supreme Leader in Iran, however, there is none of the self-gratification or ruthless quest for personal or familial power that you find in these absolute rulers. In reality, the Supreme Leader of Iran is more akin to the sovereign in a constitutional monarchy, but without a hereditary title and with an overriding responsibility—the preservation of the Islamic Republic and the ideology of the 1979 Revolution.

The Constitution requires that the Supreme Leader be a high ranking cleric selected by the Assembly of Experts, a group of 88 Islamic theologians elected for 8-year terms. The Supreme Leader has no term of office. The Assembly of Experts theoretically can remove him, but the power has never been used. As a result, only two men, Ruhollah Khomeini and his successor, Ali Hosseini Khamenei, have served as Supreme Leader since the 1979 revolution.

Like kings and queens in some western countries Iran's Supreme Leader has no direct role in the making of law and policy, but, unlike many of his western counterparts, he has enormous influence through his position as religious leader and his power to appoint many government officials. For example, the Islamic Revolutionary Guard and the military report directly to him rather than to the President, and the Supreme Leader appoints the head of the judiciary and half of the Guardian Council.

Although often described by American politicians and media as a "hard-liner," each of the nation's two supreme leaders appears to have tried to straddle the gap between moderates and hard-liners—thus meeting the Supreme Leader's prime obligation by keeping most Iranians satisfied with the Islamic Republic. For example, the nuclear agreement in 2015 would not have happened over the objection of the hard-liners without the support of the current Supreme Leader, Ali Hosseini Khamenei. The final agreement was approved by 161–59 (with 13 abstentions) in the Majlis and by an undisclosed majority in a divided Guardian Council.

The Guardian Council consists of 12 jurists, half (6) appointed by the Supreme Leader and half (6) by the Majlis from a list provided by the head of the judiciary. The Council members serve 6-year staggered terms. The Council is sometimes compared to a constitutional court or a second chamber of a parliament in other countries because it considers whether laws passed by the Majlis comply with the Constitution. The Council is authorized to interpret the Constitution. Past conflicts between the Majlis and the Council led to the creation of an ad hoc body, the Expediency Council, which is appointed by the Supreme Leader, to mediate between the two bodies.

More unusual is the Guardian Council's role of screening potential candidates for the Presidency, Majlis, and Assembly of Experts.[4] The Council, aided by various state agencies, determines who can stand for election. In one sense such a screening

[4]A committee of the Majlis vets candidates for local offices.

is necessary to remove unserious candidates as the candidates nominate themselves.[5] On the other hand, such vetting of potential candidates is clearly susceptible to abuse. The extent to which such abuse occurs is unclear. There are criteria established by law, but critics claim that these criteria are vague and that the Council is controlled by hard-liners and discriminate in favor of hard-liner candidates by disapproving many reformer/moderate candidates. This accusation, however, is undercut by the reality that over at least the past 20 years the Council has approved a roughly equivalent number of reformer/moderate and hardliner candidates to run for the presidency.

Two of the last three presidents of Iran have come from among the reformists, most current local elected officials are characterized as reformists, and the Council in 2017 rejected the application of hard-liner, and former president Ahmadinejad to run for president against Rouhani. Nevertheless, no candidate will be approved by the Council unless he or she shows allegiance to the revolution.

In the formative stages of America, one subject of near consensus was that the government should not be able to establish a national religion. This requirement for the separation of church and state was embodied in the First Amendment to the U.S. Constitution to the effect that the government shall "make no law respecting an establishment of religion...." Iran takes the opposite approach.

The Islamic Republic of Iran is founded on the theocratic principle that all aspects of the government must adhere to Islamic doctrine and that much of the leadership of the country is explicitly entrusted to Muslim clerics. At the same time, Article Fourteen of the Iranian Constitution provides that "the government of the Islamic Republic of Iran and all Muslims are duty-bound to treat non-Muslims in conformity with ethical norms and the principles of Islamic justice and equity, and to respect their human rights." Individuals are free to worship in religions other than Islam, but the role of these non-Muslims in governance is strictly limited.

Like many persons worldwide I watched with interest and sympathy as protesters in 2009 took to the streets of Iran in support of reformer/moderate candidate, Mur Hossein Mousavi, and with accusations that hard-liner candidate, Mahmoud Ahmadinejad, won reelection as president only through voter fraud or intentional miscounting by election authorities under his control as President. However, as an attorney who has participated in several post-election legal battles, I know that exaggerated claims of voting fraud are common among losing candidates and their supporters. Therefore, I watched closely to see how the government reacted and whether the fraud could be shown.

The Supreme Leader, Ali Hosseini Khamenei, initially urged Iranians to honor Ahmadinejad's apparent victory, but, after protests worsened, he assured Iranians that all allegations of fraud would be reviewed by the Guardian Council. The Council considered the allegations and undertook a televised recount of a randomly selected 10% of the votes. It found no fraud. Documents actually filed with the

[5]For example, 680 persons applied to run for president in 2009; 1213 applied in 2013, with eight approved.

Council challenged only a small fraction of the allegedly illegal votes being claimed in the media and necessary to overturn the election. No evidence of fraud or widespread miscounting was released publicly or, presumably, submitted to the Council. Ultimately the Council upheld Ahmadinejad's reelection with 62.9% of the vote.

I cannot say with certainty whether voting fraud or voter suppression occurred as international observers were banned. Certainly Ahmadinejad had both the motive and, as president, the opportunity to engage in such tactics. However, the steps taken post-election by the Supreme Leader and Guardian Council are similar to ones that might be expected in a western democracy to determine the legitimate outcome of a disputed election.

It is interesting to note that although he won reelection, Ahmadinejad lost the good will of the Supreme Leader. The Constitution limited Ahmadinejad to two consecutive terms so he was not a candidate in 2013 when Rouhani won. The Supreme Leader advised Ahmadinejad not to run for president in 2017. The reasons are unclear, but the Supreme Leader had seen the protests after the 2009 election as a potential threat to the Islamic Republic and was displeased with the negative image that Ahmadinejad presented worldwide. Ahmadinejad disregarded the Supreme Leader's advice against running and announced his candidacy. The Guardian Council, however, rejected his application to become a candidate in 2017.

Many aspects of the Iranian political scene are changing. The number of women in elective office is increasing. The influence of clerics in the Majlis continues to wane. In fact, after the 2016 election, there were actually more women (6%) than clerics (down from almost 50% in 1980) in the Majlis and an increasing number of members with advanced educational degrees. A similar shift away from the election of hard-liner/Principlists was evident at the local level.

Some members of the Islamic Republican Guard have been arrested for corruption—possibly indicating a lessening of that organization's independence and power.[6] The role of women in politics, however, remains controversial, with an ongoing dispute about whether a woman can be qualified to be a "theologian" eligible for election to the Assembly of Experts or selection as the Supreme Leader. Such disputes are actually a positive sign insofar as it suggests that views are evolving.

Muslim clerics continue to exercise ultimate control through the Guardian Council and the Supreme Leader. It is wrong, however, to assume that all Muslim clerics today oppose reform or change, or that change does not happen. This apparent movement toward a more open society is fragile. It can end if hard-liners regain or extend their dominance in the next presidential election (2021) when Rouhani is barred by the constitution from seeking a third term.

[6]This was the trend before Donald Trump became President and withdrew from the nuclear agreement. U.S. actions and anti-Iran rhetoric have strengthened the hard-liners and the Islamic Republican Guard.

Recent actions by U.S. President Donald Trump have upset this trend toward reform. Hard-liners have been boosted by the U.S. announcement that it would not abide by the nuclear agreement, by the imposition of economic sanctions, and most recently by the build-up of U.S. military forces in the region. Hard-liners have essentially claimed that they warned Iranians, including the Supreme Leader, that the Americans could not be trusted. The ultimate outcome of the U.S. actions is still unknown and seems aimed at causing "regime change" in Iran, possibly back to an authoritarian regime such as existed under the Shah or exists today in Saudi Arabia.

Some Western sources, such as Freedom House, either deny that Iran is a democracy or insist that it ranks near the bottom of countries in terms of personal freedom. Other critics suggest that Iran's actions in Syria and aid to the Palestinians, through Hezbollah, show its aggressive nature. By contrast, the International Foundation for Election Systems (IFES) says "Iran's constitution establishes the nation as

Fig. C.1 Provinces of Iran Map. The map is reprinted with permission from Perry-Castañeda Library Map Collection at the University of Texas (The 31 provinces of Iran are divided into 196 separate electoral districts from which 285 members of the national legislature (Majlis) are elected. Five of the 290 seats in the Majlis are reserved for certain religious minorities, including Armenian Christians, Zoroastrians, and Jews)

both a democracy and a theocracy, blending the liberal notion of popular sovereignty with oversight by the Guardian Council to ensure political candidates; laws and regulations adhere to Islamic practices."[7] Admittedly, Iran does not fit the definition of a democracy as commonly understood by Americans, but our definition should not be the only accepted definition.[8]

Iran is a nation where elections are held and elections matter. Iran still has too few female candidates, too much influence from Muslim clerics (Mullahs), too much secrecy, too much power held by the Islamic Revolutionary Guard, and too much control by the unelected Supreme Leader and Guardian Council to meet the U.S. ideal of democracy. However, in comparison with its autocratic Arab neigh bors, such as Saudi Arabia, Iran is a bastion of democracy (Fig. C.1).

C.3 A Case Study of Germany

According to the German media leader, *Der Spiegel*, "Germany's voting system is complicated, to the point that not even most Germans completely understand it."[9] I will try to explain it.

Germany is a federal republic consisting of 16 states (Länder). According to the first census since reunification, Germany's population was 80,219,695 on May 9, 2011, making it the 16th most populous country in the world.

The national legislature is bicameral. The "upper chamber", or Bundesrat, consists of 69 members chosen by the governments of the 16 German states. These members have no term and serve at the pleasure of the state government. If the state government changes, it is probable that the state's members in the Bundesrat will change. The number of votes given to each state varies based on a rule of digressive proportionality according to population. Each state is allocated 3–6 votes in the Bundesrat. Each state must vote as a bloc.

The "lower chamber", or Bundestag, consists of members directly elected for 4-year terms. Two hundred and ninety-nine members are elected from constituencies allocated to the states. These members are elected by plurality FPTP from single-member electoral districts (Wahikreisen). Other members are elected based on a nationwide proportional representation system in which each party receiving at least

---

[7] *Duality by Design* by Yasmin Alem (**IFES**) at *Foreword (2011)* available at [https://www.ifes.org/publications/duality-design-iranian-electoral-system]

[8] Is it so difficult for us to imagine that Muslims, inspired by the notion of electing their leaders, can design a democracy for their own culture?

[9] *Der Spiegel Online* at https://www.spiegel.de/international/germany/german-election-system-explained. The article further observed "One person, one vote – if only it were that easy. Germany's voting system is exceedingly difficult to understand, stemming from the country's combination of parliamentary democracy, in which parties are supreme, and a desire to allow voters to choose a local candidate. Throw in the need for states to be fairly represented in parliament and what you get is both one of the fairest and most complicated systems around."

5% of the vote nationwide receives seats in the Bundestag in proportion to the party's vote nationwide.

This Mixed Member Proportional system ([MMP] also called the "Additional Member" system) was supposed to work by reducing the number of seats won by a party in the nationwide election by the seats won in the direct single-member district elections. A few other nations, such as New Zealand (changed to MMP system in 1993), Hungary (changed from MMP to Parallel System [P] in 2011), Lesotho, Venezuela (changed from MMP to Parallel [P] system in 2015), Zanzibar, and Bolivia, followed the German model.

In some cases, however, a party's candidates under MMP won more district elections than seats to which the party was entitled according to the proportion of the vote it received nationwide. Parties legally refused to give up the single-member district seats that they had won. This led to excess seats in the Bundestag—a phenomenon known as overhang mandates or Überhangmandate. After the 2009 election there were 24 such overhang mandate seats in the Bundestag. This system operated to over-represent some political parties and states and to cause a "negative vote weight effect" in which a vote for a party could actually have a negative effect.

In 2008 the Constitutional Court of Germany declared this system for election to the Bundestag unconstitutional for a variety of reasons. Parts of a revision passed by the national legislature in 2012 were also declared unconstitutional. A second revision passed in 2013 won court approval and is now in effect. The basic solution was to add to the size of the Bundestag.

The new election system for the Bundestag is the same as the old one in some ways. It continues to combine the members elected from the 299 single-member districts with those elected as a result of a closed list proportional representation system. In an election, each voter has two votes—one for a candidate for the single-member district in which the voter resides and another for a party for proportional representation. The two votes appear on the same ballot. A voter need not select a candidate on the district election list that is in the same party which the voter selects on the second list. If a party earns additional seats based on its percentage of votes in the nationwide proportional election, these members are selected state-by-state from a closed party list. Under the 2013 revision, however, if a party wins more direct district election seats than it is entitled under the proportional system, it keeps the seats, but the other parties are compensated with additional seats so that ratio of votes received nationwide to seats in the Bundestag is consistent with the national vote and is "fair." This means that the size of the Bundestag can grow—although the number of single-member constituencies remains at 299 seats. The Bundestag had 631 members after the 2013 election. Some observers predict it can grow to over 800 members under the new system.

Officially, Germany has a specific process by which seats in the national legislature are supposed to be reallocated among the states and districts redrawn according to population changes. An Electoral Districts Commission (EDC) is created and appointed by the president at the beginning of each national legislative term. The Commission reports on population changes and on potential redistricting and reallocation proposals. It has 15 months to finish its report. The national legislature receives the report and decides whether to approve the changes. As might be expected, the legislature has a history of rejecting the EDC recommendations and leaving the status quo in place. For example, as of 2000 the allocation of districts had not changed since 1980 in the western Länder, and since 1990 in the eastern Länder despite population changes.

ACE and OSCE concluded,

> However, Länder governments – particularly if they are due to lose a seat – do not relish a change in constituency boundaries. Members of Parliament are also likely to object to changes in constituency lines: new constituency boundaries could make it more difficult for incumbent legislators to win and could lead to the loss of a party seat. Therefore, Parliament often simply accepts only those changes that are mandated by law, retaining the status quo as much as possible.[10]

The national legislature not only rejected reallocation recommendations in 1983, 1987, and 1990, but also rejected the EDC constituency delimitation plan for a united Germany in 1994. In 1995, the Bundestag voted to reduce its size, effective in 2002. This major reform reduced the number of single-member constituencies to the current 299 and caused several Länder to lose constituencies. The number of constituencies and the allocation of constituencies among Länder have remained unchanged since 2002. A proposal in 2004 to reduce two states by one seat and to increase two others because of population changes was rejected. Such inaction (some observers say merely "late") in reallocating seats among the states has created a significant disparity among the states in terms of the average constituency of each state.

In 2012 the average single-member constituency size nationwide was 268,293 persons, but Berlin with a population of 3.56 million had 12 constituencies (average 296,666); while Lower Saxony with a population of 7.79 million had 30 constituencies (average 259,666); and Thuringia with 2.181 million had nine constituencies (average 242,333).

The Bundestag has been somewhat more receptive to redrawing individual constituencies than to reallocating seats among states when changes are mandated by law to correct serious malapportionment within a state. Until the reform in 2002, single-member districts were to be designed to be no more than 25% from the "average" within a state and redistricting was to occur if the deviation reached >32% from the average within a state. In the 2002 reform, the percentage for allowable deviation in the drawing of districts was reduced from 25% to 15% from the average and the mandate for redistricting was reduced from >32% to >25% from the average. Some changes in constituency boundaries have occurred in Germany,[11] but according to OSCE/ODIHR the tendency continues for the Bundestag to act only if a change is necessitated by the law and then to keep the status quo to the extent possible in the other constituencies.

---

[10]Boundary Delimitation Annex, Case Study, Germany, *Delimiting Districts in a Mixed Member Proportional System,* at Conclusion (2012), **ACE** available at https://aceproject.org/ace-en/topics/bd/annex/bdy/bdy_de

[11]For example, changes occurred in 2008 and 2013, when 32 out of 299 constituencies were redistricted.

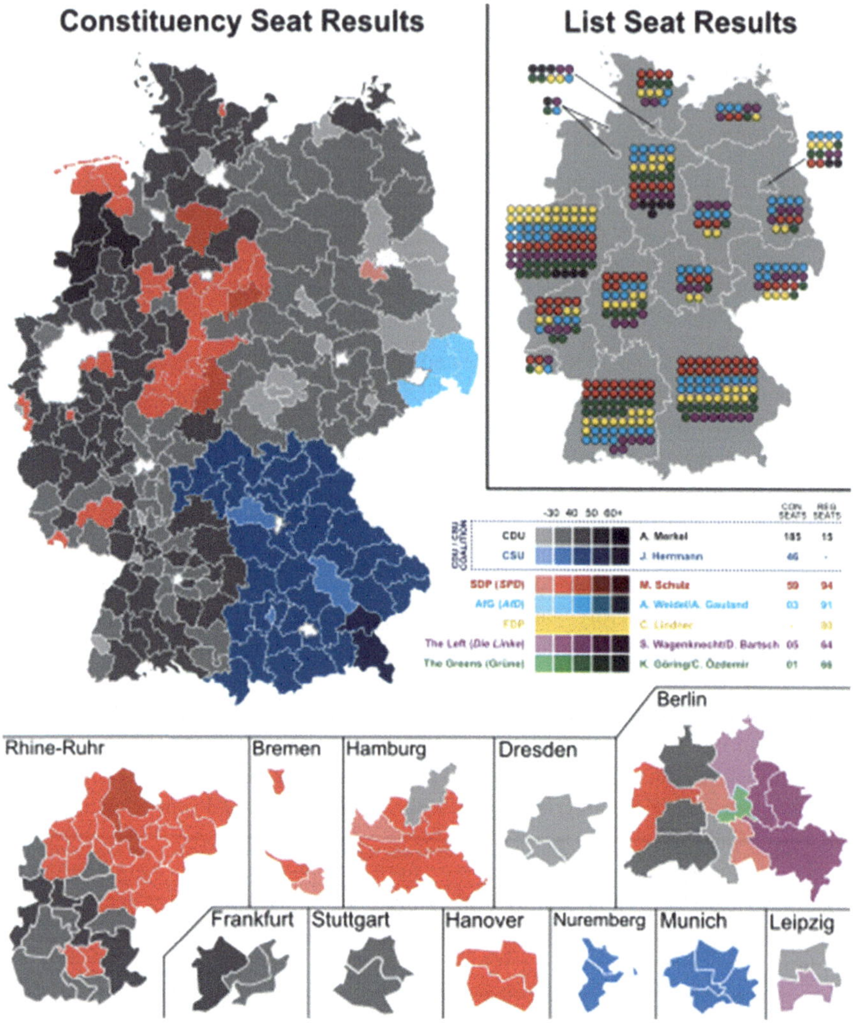

Fig. C.2 Electoral Districts in Germany. The map is courtesy of Dr. Adam Carr @ http://psephos.adam-carr.net

As one academic observer explained, "As for redistricting boundaries within a state: Districts of an incumbent who has represented the district over the last twenty or so years (and who has worked his or her way to the upper echelons within parliament) are hard to touch. Losing a village from the district? Adjoining a new community? Most incumbents hate such an idea. If they are big shots, they occasionally succeed to prevent any changes until they retire."[12] (Fig. C.2).

[12]This quote is from a personal e-mail sent to the author by a German professor familiar with the German redistricting process. I have chosen to keep the professor anonymous.

German courts acknowledge a "continuity principle" to maintain district boundaries and that threatening discontinuity would be counter-productive. For districting cases in Germany this is the sixth principle which courts treat to be on a constitutional level (although not to be found in the Grundgesetz nor in any state constitution). The others are that the election must be universal, direct, free, equal, and secret.

C.4 A Case Study of Turkey

Turkey's unicameral national legislature consists of 550 members elected for 4 year terms from 85 multi-member constituencies in 81 provinces. The members are determined from closed party lists and independent candidates in each province/constituency. Parties are entitled to representation in the national legislature from a province/constituency only if the party receives at least 10% of the vote nationwide and meets other requirements intended to assure that the party has a national presence. This national legislative threshold, however, does not apply to candidates running as independents in the individual districts.

The high threshold for representation of a party in the national legislature and the large number of competing parties combine to benefit the largest parties. Out of the 20 parties competing in 2015 elections, only four actually won seats by exceeding the 10% national threshold. Those four parties essentially split the votes and seats of the smaller parties. This can lead to a substantial advantage for the largest party (AKP). For example, in 2002 the AKP received only 34% of the vote, but ended up with almost 2/3 of the seats in the national legislature as the other 66% of the national vote was split among other parties, most of which received no seats because they failed to reach the threshold.[13]

Turkey annually determines the population of each province using an "Address Based Population Registration System." A permanent and independent electoral council, the Supreme Electoral Board (SBE), reviews these numbers and every 5 years determines the number of seats allocated to each province/constituency. This board is composed of 11 judges[14] elected by the Supreme Court and Council of State for 6-year terms and is tasked with overall authority for elections.[15] According to the OSCE, it enjoys a high level of public confidence.

The number of seats allocated to each province changes according to its population. More populous provinces naturally get more seats, but in preparation for the

[13]In 2002, only two parties met the 10% threshold. Nine independent candidates also won.

[14]The Council consists of seven members and four substitutes.

[15]All members are senior judges, six elected by the Plenary Assembly of the Court of Cassation and five members elected by the Plenary Assembly of the Council of State from among its members. The Chairman and the Vice Chairman are elected by the SBE members. It is responsible for the fair and orderly conduct of the elections, including investigating and deciding any allegations of election irregularities and verifying the election returns.

2015 election, eight provinces/constituencies had their number of seats adjusted from 2011 by the SBE.

According to 2015 numbers a disparity exists between the average constituency size in the major urban areas of Istanbul, Ankara, and Izmir and those in the rural provinces, but these urban areas have a total of 146 seats in the national legislature with an average constituency size only about 15% above the national average.

Every province, however small, has at least two members in the national legislature. This requirement creates an extreme disparity between the average constituency size in the least populous province, Tunceli, at 28,800 and the most populous province, which is in Istanbul, at 166,000. A spot check of the provinces nationwide, however, shows that the average constituency size among the provinces, except in the smallest provinces, appeared to be within ± 15% of the nationwide average (143,165).

Given the on-going and often violent dispute between the Turkish government (controlled by the Justice and Development Party [AKP]) and the Kurdish minority, I focused on how the electoral system has affected the Kurds. The Kurds poll strongly in the southeastern corner of the country, but have been unable historically to meet the high national presence that are legally necessary for seats based on proportional representation. In 2007, however, the Kurdish Democratic Society Party (DTP) circumvented these requirements by fielding independent candidates, who then aligned as a parliamentary bloc once elected—a strategy that enabled Kurdish candidates to win 26 seats. Subsequently the DTP was ordered dissolved for its allegedly anti-government activities. In 2011, the pro-Kurdish Peace and Democracy party (BDP) again got around the barriers to proportional representation by fielding 61 independent candidates—36 were elected (one later was disqualified).

In 2015, the pro-Kurdish forces joined with various groups, including some on the far-left or representing various ethnic minorities, and tried to meet the national threshold. This party, the People's Democratic Party (HDP), exceeded the 10% threshold in both the June general election and the specially-called November national legislative elections. It won 80 seats in June, but saw its strength in the national legislature reduced to only 59 members after the November elections.

Nevertheless, the province, Van, at the core of the pro-Kurdish area has eight members of the national legislature and a constituency average (137,049) that is actually less than the Konya Province, with 14 members and a constituency average of 152,182, that is a center of support for the ruling Justice and Development Party (AKP). A spot check of the allocation of seats to other provinces that strongly supported either the HDP or AKP in 2015 showed a similar result. I also failed to find any article or report alleging that the allocation of seats discriminates against pro-Kurdish voters, or that the electoral districts in the three most populous provinces are gerrymandered. I concluded that the reallocation process was timely and fair. There were, however, accusations of voting irregularities in the November, 2015 election that restored AKP's majority in the national legislature, but I made no attempt to judge these accusations (Fig. C.3).

One result of Turkey's high threshold in an election featuring many political parties is that a large proportion of the electorate cast their votes for parties which are

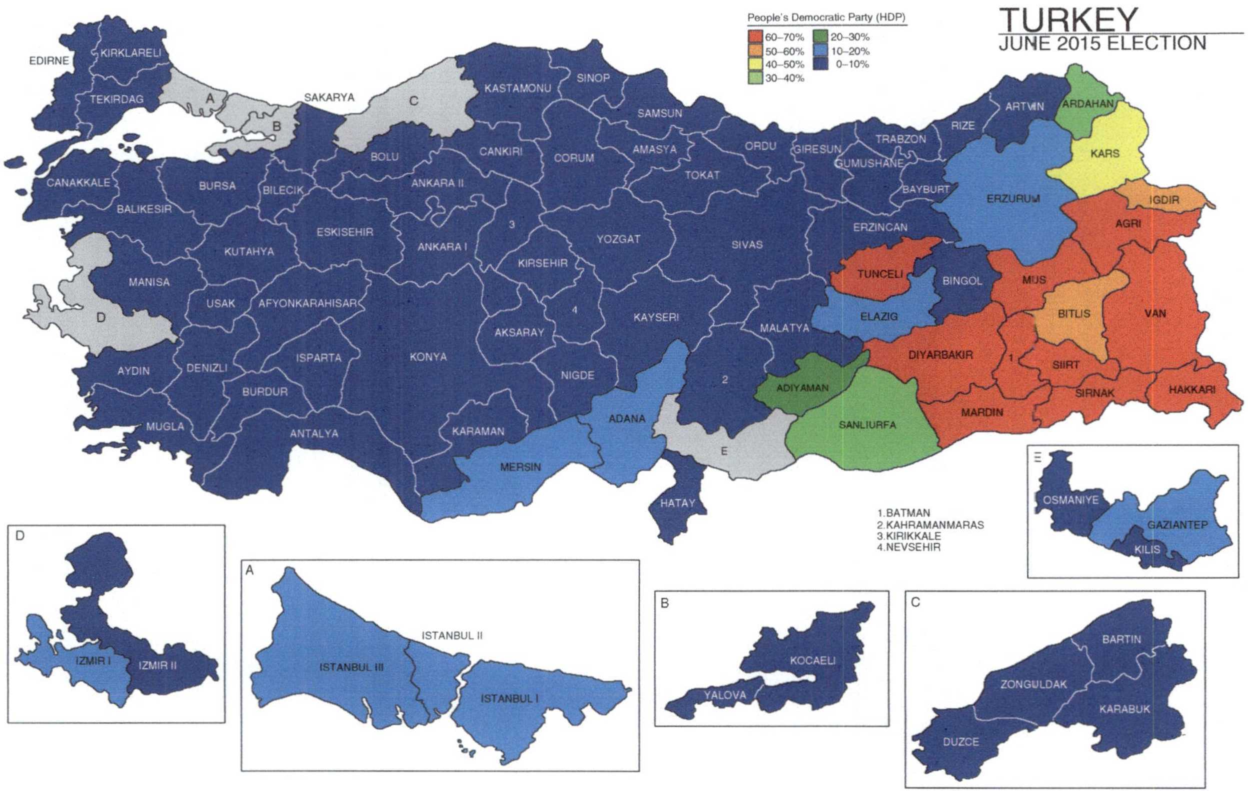

Fig. C.3 Electoral Districts in Turkey. The map is courtesy of Dr. Adam Carr at @ http://psephos.adam-carr.net (The results of the June, 2015 parliamentary election show the strong regional support for the pro-Kurdish, HDP party, in the southeast corner of the country. The largest Kurdish population is actually in Istanbul where it won 11 of 88 available seats in June, 2015 elections)

not represented in the Parliament. Such a requirement defeats the purpose of proportional representation.

C.5 A Case Study of France

France has used many different electoral systems throughout its history for electing national representatives. Many of these changes were allegedly made at the time to limit the voting power of one group or another, such as the Communists in the 1950s. In the words of one writer, "[T]he record shows that at every juncture of history the politicians have manipulated the system to better serve their partisan ends."

The current system was adopted in 1986 and provides for a bicameral national legislature. The upper chamber (Sénat) has 348 members, who serve 6-year terms; 328 members are appointed (indirectly elected) by an electoral college consisting of elected representatives from each of 96 départements in metropolitan France, eight of which are elected from other dependencies, and 12 of which are elected by the French Assembly of French Citizens Abroad.

The lower chamber (National Assembly or Assemblée Nationale) consists of 577 deputies. The seats are allocated among the nation's administrative départements, including 539 representing Metropolitan France, 27 representing the overseas département and overseas collectivities, and 11 representing French residents overseas. Each département is guaranteed one seat (reduced from two by the Conseil Constitutionnel). The representatives are then elected from single-member districts drawn within the départements by the national legislature.

France has a two round election system ((TRS). To be elected in the first round a candidate for the Chamber of Deputies must receive the absolute majority of votes cast by at least a quarter of the registered voters. If necessary, a second round is held between the candidates who obtained a number of votes equal to at least 12.5% of the registered voters; a relative majority is sufficient to win. Out-of-country voters can vote in parliamentary elections by mail and the legislation provides the option of Internet voting. Due to concerns over foreign cyber threats and technical issues, the government decided to suspend the option of Internet voting in 2017 for citizens abroad for parliamentary elections.

The allocation of seats among the départements and the drawing of single-member districts within the départements are controlled by the national legislature. French law provided that the districts are to be redrawn as necessary every 12–14 years, but this requirement was repealed in 2002. Until 2010 the most recent reallocation of seats and redistricting occurred in 1986, based on the 1982 census. Both the 1986 reallocation of seats and redistricting were challenged as unfair. The Conseil Constitutionnel (the nation's highest constitutional authority) avoided the issue of partisan gerrymandering, but warned the national legislature to avoid population deviations in the then proposed legislation except when required by "precise urgent necessities." After passage, however, the Conseil upheld the legislation saying "the choices made by the legislators have [not] manifestly violated the constitutional requirements."

The population disparities among constituencies became worse over time as the country's population continued to grow and to shift. This imbalance in the allocation of seats favored the smaller départements and the redistricting within the départements was seen as favoring the Conservative Party. For example, one writer said that the population varied from 34,374 in Lozere #1 to 188,200 in Val d'Oise #2 among the single-member districts nationwide, and as high as 143% within one département. After almost two decades without any redistricting or reallocation, over half of the nation's single-member districts deviated 25% or more from the average in each administrative unit. The Conseil advised that it was incumbent on the legislature to act in time for the 2005 election. The national legislature did not act.

Perhaps the best explanation for the national legislature's inaction is given in the 2005 statement of then Prime Minister Dominque de Villepin, "We are not going to engage ourselves in a project so demanding of time and energy when all of our efforts must be concentrated on jobs. A spokesperson for the government further explained, "We would risk destabilizing deputies." A deputy elaborated, "With redistricting, when we have almost four hundred deputies, there are sure to be corpses." From one writer's perspective, the result was "catastrophic." He also charged that the government had been "loathe" to present more recent data on the population of the districts.[16] This opinion is consistent with the Parliament's 2002 repeal of the law requiring a national census.

In July 2008, the government launched a formal effort to redistrict the constituencies, with Prime Minister François Fillon consulting the representatives of political parties in Parliament, and presenting a bill to the Cabinet. The changing of constituencies was planned by order of the Interior Ministry and the plan itself was designed by an ad hoc committee composed of one person appointed by the French President, one person appointed by the President of the National Assembly, one person appointed by the President of the Senate, and three judges. All had to first be approved by the Committees of Laws (Commissions des Lois) of the National Assembly and Senate. The national legislature acted in 2010. Its resulting plan has been oft-criticized, but has withstood legal challenge.

In the 2010 legislation, the constituencies of the lower house were reallocated in time for the 2012 elections. Some constituencies were eliminated and some new ones created, including eleven new seats for French citizens abroad. The total number of constituencies remained at 577 deputies (539 in Metropolitan France [Europe], 27 in départements and territories overseas, and 11 for citizens abroad). The redistricting of the constituencies also was controversial because the population deviation among constituencies remained very high (i.e. 1:2 [100%] down from 1:3.6 [260%]). In

[16]All of the quotations in this paragraph appear *in Redistricting in France under Changing Electoral Rules* by Michel Balinski at pages 173 and 185 in **Redistricting in Comparative Perspective** by Lisa Handley & Bernard Grofman, eds., Oxford Univ. Press (2008), citing *Villepin enterre le redécoupage électoral*, **Le Figaro** (June 17, 2005) and *Le gouvernement renonce au redécoupage électoral*, **Le Monde** (June 17, 2005).

effect, the reallocation of seats was seen by some as increasing the number of seats in areas held by the governing center-right coalition led by Union for a Popular Movement at the expense of the areas dominated by the Socialist-led coalition. It also was criticized as overpopulating the electoral districts largely in Paris with a significant minority, generally Muslim, population.

In 2016 approximately 67 million people lived in the French Republic, including all the overseas départements and territories. 64.5 million lived in Metropolitan France (Europe), whereas >2.5 million lived in the French overseas départements and territories. The average constituency size for Metropolitan France was 119,600. Guaranteed a seat[17] and with a population of only 75,784 in 2016, the département of Lozère is the least populated. By contrast, the département of Paris, with a population of 2,240,000 and 18 deputies, had an average population of 124,445 for its constituencies. Overall, France's degree of population deviation is significant and is generally considered one of the highest levels of malapportionment in Europe.

There is no centralized voter register and eligible voters are entered into voter registers at the local level based on their residence registration. There are approximately 46.2 million registered voters, including some 1.4 million registered abroad.

According to the OSCE, the 2010 redistricting was gerrymandered by the controlling Conservative Party. The OSCE also points out that the French Parliament in 2002 did away with the national census and statutory obligation to reallocate seats and to redistrict every 10–12 years. Both actions are considered by the OSCE as steps that further the opportunity to gerrymander districts.[18]

Some writers, however, urge that the malapportionment among districts in France does not necessarily reflect political bias or change the national power struggle among parties. They also claim that the redistricting is much less unfair if analyzed on the basis of registered voters instead of population. Others point to the election in 2017 of Emmanuel Macron as President of France and his party, La République En Marche! (REM), winning a majority of seats in the National Assembly as showing that the nation's malapportionment does not equate to political bias.

History in France and elsewhere is filled with examples of where a gerrymander is unsuccessful. Also, the objectives of gerrymandering are not only to enhance a party's power, but are often to preserve the status quo and to protect incumbents. France has depended on an opaque and untimely redistricting process, malapportionment, and reluctant court intervention to avoid or to minimalize changes to the allocation and shape of its electoral districts. This too is gerrymandering even if it is unsuccessful and fails to achieve the desired political bias (Fig. C.4).

[17]The French Conseil Constitutionnel had earlier eliminated the law's mandate that each département have at least two seats.

[18]REPUBLIC OF FRANCE, PARLIAMENTARY ELECTIONS 10 and 17 June 2012, Final Report at pages 4–5, **OSCE/ODIHR** (September 12, 2012).

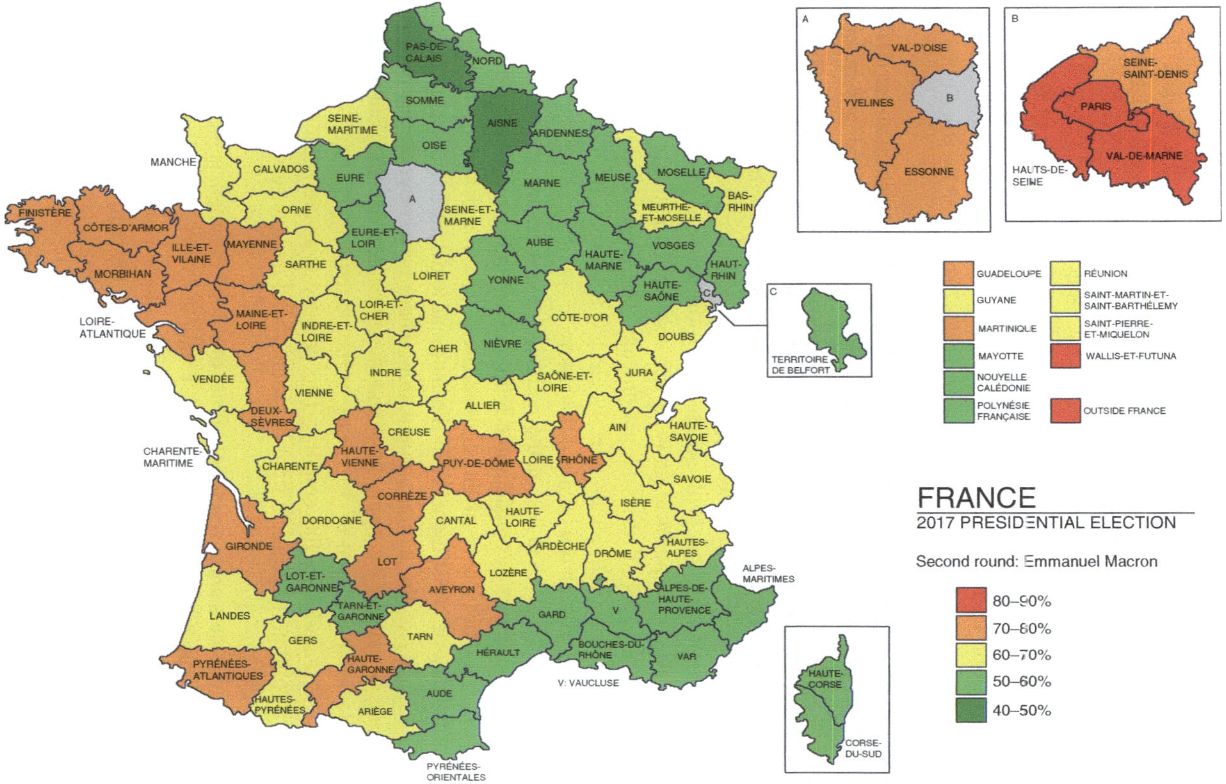

Fig. C.4 Electoral Districts of France. The map is courtesy of Dr. Adam Carr at @ http://psephos.adam-carr.net (Emmanuel Macron won the election. Please note the constituencies outside Metropolitan France)

C.6 A Case Study of Indonesia

Study of Indonesia as a democracy really only began in 2008 with the fall of Suharto's New Order. As the third most populous democracy in the world with 235,500,000 inhabitants (89% Islamic) and great racial, ethnic, ideological, geographic, linguistic, social, and religious diversity, it provides an excellent laboratory for the study of democratic transitions.

Change to an effective democracy has been slow. Direct election of the President only began in 2004. In that same year, direct election of all members of the lower house of the national legislature began as the 208 non-elected seats were eliminated. Indonesia's transition to democracy has been slow, but generally has won plaudits along with its ambitious plan of decentralization and is considered by some to be the best example of democracy in Southeast Asia.

Indonesia is essentially bicameral because it combines a lower chamber (DPR) with a Regional Representatives Council (DPD) that lacks general law-making authority. The lower chamber of the national legislature, or People's Representative Council (DPR) (Dewan Perwakilan Rakyat), has 560 members elected from 77 multi-member constituencies most of which range in size from 3–10 seats. Each of the 33 provinces is guaranteed three seats. Election in the DPR is by open list proportional representation, with an ability by the voter to cast a vote for an individual candidate. For a political party to win seats in the national legislature, it must achieve at least 3.5% of the vote nationwide. The Regional Representatives Council consists of four individuals directly elected from each province. None of these persons can be affiliated with a political party.

The seats in the lower chamber of the national legislature are allocated by the national legislature. There is considerable lobbying around the allocation of seats and constituencies. Thirty-nine of the constituencies (55%) are located in Java—giving it a majority of constituencies in the national legislature. Furthermore, the island has a majority of the nation's population. There is, however, a further bias toward keeping a balance between Java and the remainder of the country. The provinces in Java have a total of 306 seats in the national legislature—compared to 254 for the remainder of the country. The country is overwhelmingly (89%) Islamic, with a continuing political fight between liberal and conservative members of that faith.

On polling day, voters are given four ballots (five if the president is included), one each for the national People's Representative Council (DPR) and Regional Representative Council (DPD) and one each for the voter's local provincial and regency/municipality Regional Representative Councils. Each of the parties is identified with a party number and symbol. Under the symbols, that party's candidates are listed. Voters can vote for just the party or one or more of the candidates, or both, by punching a hole in the ballot with the tool provided. This characteristic means that the contest is often between candidates, not parties. Candidates for the DPD stand on an individual basis, so voters simply need to punch a hole alongside the candidate's picture, ballot number, or name.

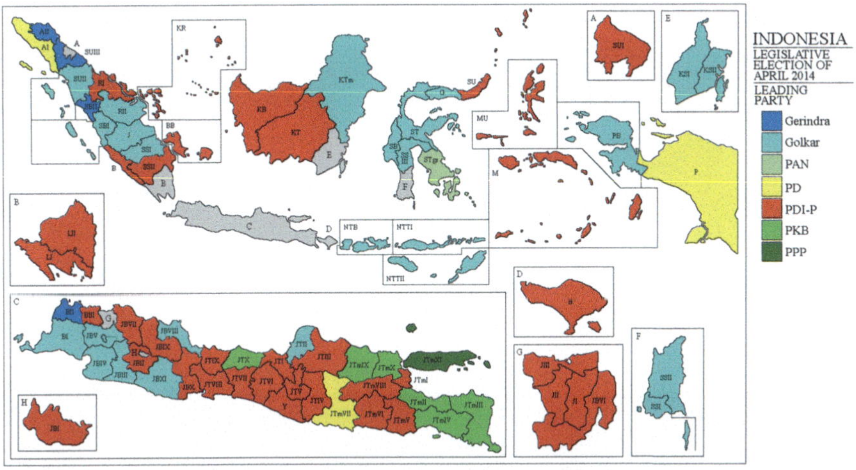

Fig. C.5 Electoral Districts of Indonesia. The map is courtesy of Dr. Adam Carr at http://psephos.adam-carr.net (The map shows the 77 multi-member electoral districts spread among the 33 provinces of Indonesia)

The average constituency size among the provinces varies from about 250,000–500,000, with the national average at 420,538. It is probable that much of this disparity is a result of the guarantee of three seats for each province and the distortion caused by the constraints of a nation being composed of separate islands. This disparity is somewhat offset by a policy of giving greater autonomy to certain of the islands and provinces.

Elections were held in Indonesia on April 17, 2019. For the first time in Indonesian history, the president, vice president, and members of the People's Consultative Assembly (MPR), were elected on the same day. Sixteen parties participated in the elections, with 192 million eligible voters, including voters in Indonesia and 2,049,791 voting abroad. There were 810,329 polling stations in Indonesia and 620 polling stations outside the country. Approximately 8000 candidates ran for the legislative seats. As might be expected in such a large election, there was considerable confusion, with many allegations of duplicate names on the voter lists. Some polling stations had to conduct follow-up voting because of logistical problems. Election results remain incomplete a month after the election (Fig. C.5).

C.7 A Case Study of Uruguay

Officially known as the Oriental Republic of Uruguay (Republica Oriental del Uruguay), Uruguay is situated on the east coast of Latin America bordered on its north by Brazil and on its west by Argentina. It is the second smallest nation in terms of geography in Latin America. There are about 3.5 million inhabitants (Fig. C.6).

Fig. C.6 Electoral Districts of Uruguay. The map is courtesy of Dr. Adam Carr at http://psephos.adam-carr.net (This map shows the 19 départements of Uruguay among which the seats in the lower chamber of its national legislature are allocated)

I selected Uruguay for a case study because it usually escapes world attention and because it has a somewhat unique election system.

Uruguay returned to civilian control in 1985 after the military had seized control with a coup in 1973. Today, it has possibly the best reputation in Latin America for governmental stability, peace, and lack of corruption. Its population growth is less than most of the remainder of Latin America and its median age is higher than the world average.

The President of Uruguay is elected using the two-round system (TRS), with a run-off held if no candidate receives 50% of the vote in the first round. The national legislature is bicameral. The 30 members of the Senate are elected by proportional representation in a single nationwide constituency. The 99 members of the Chamber of Representatives are elected by proportional representation in 19 multi-member constituencies based on the départements.

Both chambers are elected using a form of PR voting called the double simultaneous vote system (DSV), or *ley de lemas*. It is among the most complicated in the world. The system combines primaries and a general election in one event. This system was first established by the Elections Law of 1925, was suspended during the military's rule, but was reinstated with the return of civilian rule in 1985.

Under the system, a political party is a *Lema*. Factions within each party are *sub-lemas*. Each *sub-lema* of each party is allowed to run a rival list of candidates in the election without the party's approval. Their list may include candidates for a few or for all offices at stake. All votes for a party's *sub-lemas* are tabulated for the party to determine its vote total. Often each party has various lists of candidates, among whom prior agreements had been made to unify or transfer votes. As a result, there have been complaints that voters never know for whom they are ultimately voting in the congressional races.

The nation's Electoral Court oversees the elections. The winning candidates for the party are those on the *sub-lema* with the most votes. However, these candidates could win the office (e.g. governor, local council) or seats in the national legislature only if its party wins.

Casting a ballot for a specific lower chamber list results in voting for a specific upper chamber list. The 99 seats in the lower chamber are distributed among the parties using the order of d'Hondt quotas with lemas ceasing to participate in the distribution once they have received the number of seats merited.

Initially this system included the presidency, but Uruguay separated this office (and vice-president) from the DSV system in 1999 while keeping the system for other elective offices including for members of the lower chamber of its bicameral national legislature.

Uruguay has regularly apportioned seats every 5 years for at least the past 60 years. Until 1989 seats were apportioned to départements based on the total votes cast in each département in the immediately preceding election plus any new enrollments on the National Civic Registry in the Département since that election. This was changed to electors (some sources say population) in each département.

Uruguay has regularly redistributed legislative seats at least every 5 years since 1954. For example, the département of Montevideo had a high of 48 seats in 1984 and a low of 40 seats in 1954 and 2014. By contrast, the département of Canelones, which is contiguous to Montevideo, has grown steadily from 10 seats in 1954 to 14 in 2014.

C.8 A Case Study of Lesotho

Lesotho is a nation enclosed within South Africa. It officially is the Kingdom of Lesotho, with a constitutional monarchy, a bicameral legislature, and approximately 2 million inhabitants. Like many of its African neighbors, it has had a difficult time

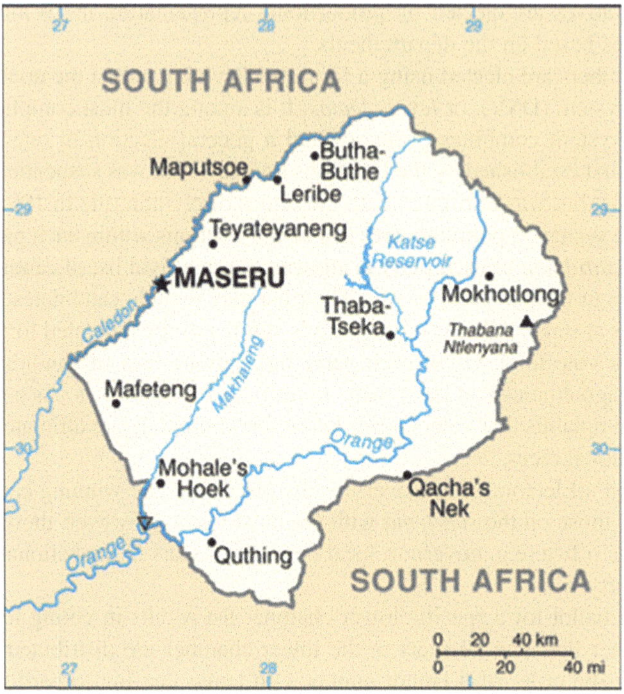

Fig. C.7 The location of Lesotho. The map is from Wikipedia (*A map of Lesotho showing it wholly within South Africa)*

adjusting to democratic government. It also provides, however, an example of how international organizations can be involved in an effort to bring peaceful change (Fig. C.7).

The nation originally was called Basutoland. It became a British protectorate in 1868. In 1966, Basutoland gained its independence from Britain and officially became a constitutional monarchy as the Kingdom of Lesotho. The king was largely a ceremonial post with the first democratic elections scheduled for 1970.

The country was soon torn by rebellion as the newly formed political parties refused to accept election outcomes. Military juntas seized power in 1986 and again in 1991, with democratic government temporarily returned in 1993. The King himself led a coup in 1994. Member states of the Southern African Development Community (SADC) engaged in negotiations to reinstate the civilian government. Elections were held in 1998, but the opposition parties refused to accept the outcome. Armed conflict followed.

Faced with this turmoil, an Interim Political Authority (IPA) was charged in 1998 with reviewing the electoral structure in the country. The IPA followed the German model (MMP) in devising an electoral system that would ensure that the opposition would be represented in the National Assembly, which is the nation's lower chamber. The new system retained the then existing 80 directly elected Assembly seats, but added 40 seats to be filled on a PR basis. Elections were held under this new mixed system beginning in May 2002.

Today, the Senate (upper chamber) has 33 members—22 hereditary chiefs and 11 individuals appointed by the King on the advice of the Council of State. The 120 members of the National Assembly (lower chamber) are elected using the mixed-member proportional (MMP) representation system, with voters casting a single vote. Eighty members are elected from single-member constituencies by first-past-the-post voting, with the remaining 40 elected from a single nationwide constituency in a closed list. They are essentially "leveling" seats. The votes from every constituency are totaled, with votes cast for independent candidates ignored, to give a nationwide total for each party. A quota is then calculated using each party's vote share. The number of seats won in constituencies is deducted in order to give the number of the 40 PR seats that a party is due. If the total number of seats due to be awarded is less than 120, the highest remainder method is used to distribute the remaining PR seats.

A vote of no confidence was passed in the Lesotho parliament on March 1, 2017, after which King Letsie III accepted the Prime Minister's advice to dissolve the National Assembly and to hold snap elections. Elections were set for June 3, 2017. A lawsuit to stop the elections failed.

Fearing further chaos the Christian Council of Lesotho, with support from some international and regional organizations, including the European Union (EU), United Nations Development Programme (UNDP) and the Southern African Development Community (SADC), moved to have registered political parties publicly commit to an inclusive process of implementing a package of reforms recommended by both national and international organizations for Lesotho's long-term peace and political stability. Twenty-five of the 30 registered political parties, including all of the major parties, signed this pledge.

The June, 2017 elections went forward. Women and youth comprise the majority of Lesotho's population, with women and youth constituting 56% and 45% of registered voters respectively. According to official counts, 1,253,421 citizens were registered for the election, of which 697,172 were women and 560,040 were youth. However, only eight women were elected in the single-member constituencies, while the only woman political party leader lost the election in her constituency. Fifteen women won seats through the PR process. Turnout was only 42%. These results continue to be low (Fig. C.8).

The single-member districts are drawn by a commission, the Independent Electoral Commission (IEC), which has general election oversight authority. The commission is not truly independent as it is appointed by the King, but its current chairman is a judge.

A Commonwealth Observer Group described the 2017 election as "peaceful" and "inclusive."

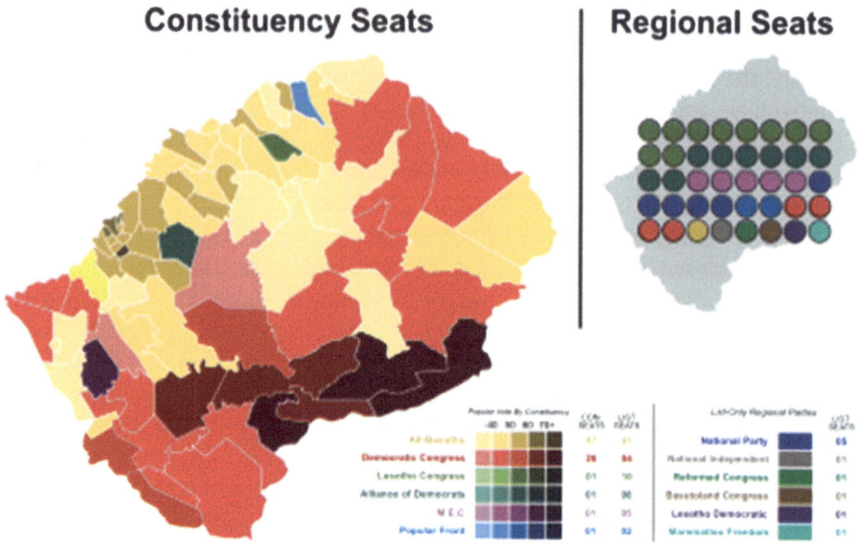

Fig. C.8 Electoral Districts of Lesotho. The map is courtesy of Dr. Adam Carr at http://psephos.adam-carr.net

C.9 A Case Study of Texas 2003: An Example of Masterly Gerrymandering

One of the most infamous gerrymandering incidents in the United States occurred in Texas in 2003. The following map shows the final congressional plan adopted by the Republican-controlled state legislature (and later modified by a federal court). The individual units are Texas counties. The state has 254 counties (Fig. C.9).

Texas Republicans were largely shut out of state office for over 100 years. By 2002, however, Republicans had finally gained full control of the Texas Legislature from the Democrats. Republican Congressman Tom Delay journeyed to Texas in 2003 to lead an effort to have that Legislature redraw the state's congressional districts to favor the Republicans. Fearful of violating the Voting Rights Act, Delay avoided redrawing the congressional districts held by Blacks or Latinos and focused on defeating all 10 of the nonhispanic white Democratic incumbent congressmen. The Democratic members of the state legislature successfully delayed passage of the redistricting by leaving the borders of the State of Texas and thereby breaking the quorum necessary for adoption of the bill.

The legislative battle caught attention around the world as it continued for months.

Eventually, however, the bill passed and only three of the ten incumbent white Democratic congressmen survived. One of these survivors was defeated 2 years later.

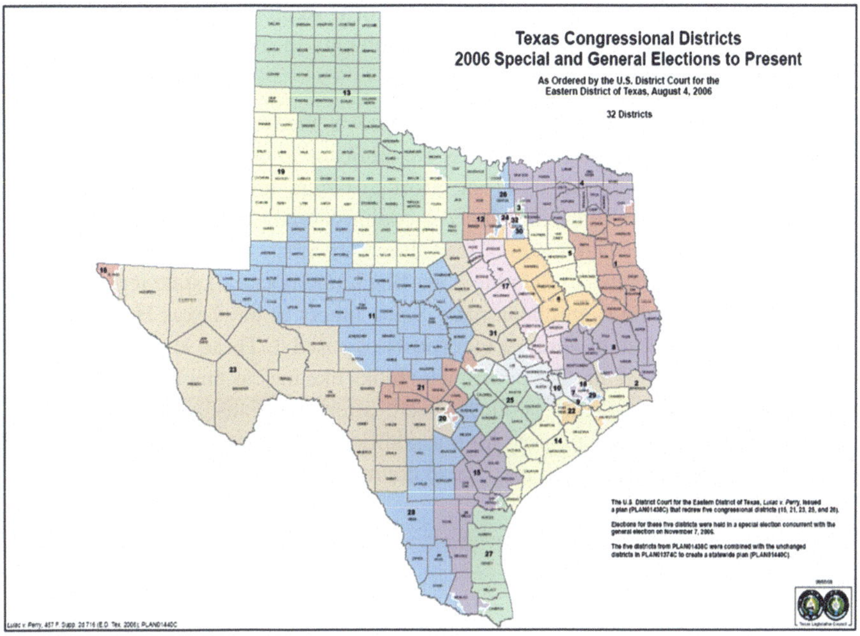

Fig. C.9 Texas Congressional Districts in 2004. This map is courtesy of the Texas Legislative Council

The 2003 congressional redistricting in Texas is a masterly example of gerrymandering. The tactic of using voter inequality was legally unavailable. The redistricting also had to go beyond the usual strategies of cracking and packing because these Democratic incumbents were winning with the vote of persons who generally voted Republican in other races in the same election. Therefore, each district was designed specifically to defeat the particular Democratic incumbent by separating him from his current constituents. In general, this was done by redrawing the district boundaries:

1. To separate the residence or resident county or region of the incumbent from the remainder of his current district;
2. To destroy the community of the current district by fragmenting the remainder among other congressional districts so there would be no single district with most of the voters from the incumbent's current district—thereby making it impossible for the targeted Democratic incumbent to move back into a district composed largely of voters from his current district;
3. To place the residence or resident county of the incumbent in a district in which the overwhelming majority of the voters were not his current constituents and, in most districts, were at the far end of the district from his residence; and

4. To place the residence or resident county of a Republican incumbent and an overwhelming number of his current constituents in the district containing the Democratic incumbent.

Another interesting aspect of the redistricting was the reaction of Black members of the Texas Legislature to this effort by Republicans to eliminate the nonhispanic white Democratic congressmen. In an effort to obtain minority support for their redistricting effort, Republicans included a congressional district that would probably elect an additional Black congressman. Black members of the Texas Legislature were split in their response to the plan. One Black (Democratic) state representative openly championed the Republican plan. Some others in the Texas House silently did so. The two Black state senators vigorously opposed it. These senators explained to me that "I do not need another person who looks like me" as much as I "need votes at the table." To them, the Republicans were offering a Faustian bargian—i.e. to trade ten friendly votes in Congress for one additional Black congressman. As one of the Black senators explained to me, "I can count."[19]

[19]The quotes in the paragraph are from Senator Rodney Ellis. *See,* **LINES IN THE SAND: CONGRESSIONAL REDISTRICTING IN TEXAS AND THE DOWNFALL OF TOM DELAY** by Steve Bickerstaff (Univ. of Texas Press 2007). Senator Ellis retired in 2018.

Bibliography

Books

APPORTIONMENT METHODS AND THEIR APPLICATIONS by Friedrich Pukelsheim, (Springer International Publishing 2014); **PROPORTIONAL REPRESENTATION** (Second Edition 2018).

ASSESSMENT MISSION REPORTS (Electoral Institute for Sustainable Democracy in Africa [EISA], 2012).

BEHIND THE BALLOT BOX: A Citizen's Guide to Voting Systems by Douglas J. Amy, Greenwood Publishing Group (2000).

CODE OF GOOD PRACTICE IN ELECTORAL MATTERS (Adopted by the Venice Commission 2002) available at http://www.venice.coe.int.

DELIMITATION EQUITY PROJECT: RESOURCE GUIDE, IFES CENTER FOR TRANSITIONAL AND POST-CONFLICT GOVERNANCE AND USAID, by Lisa Handley, (IFES, 2006).

DRAWING A NEW CONSTITUENCY MAP FOR THE UNITED KINGDOM: The Parliamentary Voting System and Constituencies Bill 2010 by Michel Balinski, Ron Johnston, Iain McLean, Peyton Young, Angela Cummine (A report prepared for the British Academy, London, 2010).

ELECTORAL MANAGEMENT BODIES AS INSTITUTIONS OF GOVERNANCE by Rafael López-Pintor (United Nations Development Program [UNDP] 2000).

ELECTION OBLIGATIONS and STANDARDS by The Carter Center, (available online at https://www.cartercenter.org/cc-OES-handbook).

EMBODYING DEMOCRACY: Electoral System Design in Post-Communist Europe by Sarah Birch, Frances Millard, Marina Popescu and Kieran Williams (Palgrave Machmillan 2003).

ESTABLISHING THE RULES OF THE GAME: Election Laws in Democracies by Louis Massicotte, André Blais and Antoine Yoshinaka, (Univ. of Toronto Press 2004).

S. Bickerstaff, *Election Systems and Gerrymandering Worldwide*, Studies in Choice and Welfare, https://doi.org/10.1007/978-3-030-30837-7

FIXING THE BOUNDARIES: DEFINING AND REDEFINING SINGLE-MEMBER ELECTORAL DISTRICTS by Ian McLean & David Butler, eds., (Dartmouth Pub. Co. 1996).

HANDBOOK FOR DOMESTIC ELECTION OBSERVERS by OSCE/ODHIR (2003) available at http://www.osce.org).

INTERNATIONAL ELECTION PRINCIPLES by Jack Young, ed., (American Bar Association 2015).

INTERNATIONAL ELECTION REMEDIES by Jack Young, ed., (American Bar Association 2017).

LINES IN THE SAND: CONGRESSIONAL REDISTRICTING IN TEXAS AND THE DOWNFALL OF TOM DELAY by Steve Bickerstaff (Univ. of Texas Press 2007).

THE OXFORD HANDBOOK OF ELECTORAL SYSTEMS by Erik S. Herron, Robert J. Pekkanen, and Matthew S. Shugart, eds., (Oxford Univ. Press 2018).

PUTTING VOTERS IN THEIR PLACE by Ron Johnson & Charles Pattie (Oxford Univ. Press 2006).

PROBLEMS OF DEMOCRATISATION IN INDONESIA by Edward Aspinall & Marcus Mietzner eds., (2010).

REDISTRICTING IN A COMPARATIVE PERSPECTIVE by Lisa Handley & Bernard Grofman, eds., (Oxford Univ. Press 2008).

COMMISIONED RIDINGS DESIGNING CANADA'S ELECTION DISTRICTS by John C. Courtney, (McGill-Queen's Univ. Press 2001).

TREACHEROUS ALLIANCE; The Secret Dealings of Israel, Iran, and the U.S. by Trita Parsi (Yale Univ. Press 2007).

U.S. DEP'T OF COMMERCE: 2010 CENSUS OF POPULATION AND HOUSING (2012).

2015 WESTERN AUSTRALIAN REDISTRIBUTION, ANALYSIS OF NEW ELECTORAL BOUNDARIES by Antony Green (2015).

Court Decisions

I found that the citation style varied among countries and even over time in the same country. I apologize for any discrepancies, but hope that there is sufficient information given on each opinion so that it can be located. The website of the Supreme or Constitutional Court in many of these countries provides English versions of some opinions, but not all opinions are translated to English.

United States

Bush v. Martin, 224 F Supp. 499 (S.D. Tex. 1963), aff'd per curium, 376 U.S. 222 (1964).

Reynold v. Sims, 377 U.S. 533, 562 (1964).
White v. Weiser, 412 U.S. 783 (1973).
Karcher v. Daggett, 462 U.S. 725 (1983).
Thornberg v. Gingles, 478 U.S. 30 (1986).
Bush v. Vera, 517 U.S. 952 (1996).
Shaw v. Reno, 509 U.S. 630 (1993).
League of United Latin American Citizens v. Perry, 548 U.S. 399 (2006).
Shelby County v. Holder, 570 U.S. 2 (2013).
Evenwel v. Abbott, 578 U.S. 1 (April 4, 2016).
Rucho v Common Cause (June 27, 2019).
Dept. of Commerce v New York (June 27, 2019).

Croatia (@ https://www.usud.hr/en)

THE CONSTITUTIONAL COURT OF THE REPUBLIC OF CROATIA No. U-X-6472/2010 Zagreb (December 8, 2010).

India (@ https://www.sci.gov.in)

Meghrai Kothari v. Delimitation Commission (Union of India), 1967 SCR (1) 400 (September 20, 1966).
R.C. Poudyal v. Union of India, 1993 SCR (1) 891 (February 10 1993).
J&K National Panthers Party v. Union of India, 2010 SCR ___ (November 9, 2010).

Germany (@ https://www.bundesverfassungsgericht.de)

BVerfGE 121 (2009) 266-317, Judgment of the Second Senate on 3 July 2008, - 2 BvC 1/07, BvC 7/07.
BVerfGE 131 (2013) 316-376, Judgment of the Second Senate on 25 July 2012. -2 BvF 3/11.
Constituencies for German Federal Elections: Legal Requirements and Their Observance by Sebastian Goderbauer and Martin Wicke (2018) available at https://www.or.rwth-aachen.de.
Political Districting Problem: Literature Review and Discussion with regard to Federal Elections in Germany by Sebastian Goderbauer and Jeff Winandy (2018) available at https://www.or.rwth-aachen.de.

Central and Eastern Europe

Marina Popescu and Gabor Toka, *Districting and Redistricting in Eastern Europe: Regulations and Practices* at page 260 in **REDISTRICTING IN COMPARATIVE PERSPECTIVE**, supra.

England

Ex parte Foote, [1983] QB 600 (Eng.).

Australia

McGinty v W Australia, 186 CLR 140 (1996).

Canada

Reference re Prov. Electoral Boundaries (Sask) [1991] 2 S.C.R. 158, 183 (Can.).

Raiche v. Canada (Attorney General), [F.C.], 2004 F.C. 679, (2005), 1 F.C.R. 93 (Can.) (finding in favor of preserving a Francophone community since it lacked effective representation when split).

Italy (@ https://www.cortecostituzionale.it)

Judgment No. 1/2014, Italian Constitutional Court (2013).

Judgment No. 17, Italian Constitutional Court (2017).

France (@ https://www.conseil-constitutionnel.fr/en)

Decision No. 86-208DC, Conseil Constitutionnel [CC] (July 2, 1986).

Decision No. 86-218DC, Conseil Constitutionnel [CC] (Nov. 18, 1986).

Decision no. 2010-602 DC, Conseil Constitutionnel [CC] February 18, 2010.

OBSERVATIONS DU CONSEIL CONSTITUTIONNEL RELATIVES AUX ELECTIONS LEGISLATIVES DE JUIN 2002, Conseil Constitutionnel (May 15, 2003).

Decision No. 2005-518 DC, Conseil Constitutionnel (July 13, 2005).
Decision No. 2007-547 DC, Conseil Constitutionnel (February 15, 2007).
Decision No. 2008-24 ELEC of May 29, 2008, Observations of the Conseil Constitutionnel on the parliamentary elections of 10 and 17 June 2007 @https://www.legifrance.gouv.fr
Decision no. 2008-573 DC, Conseil Constitutional (January 8, 2009).
CONSEIL CONSTITUTIONNEL OBSERVATIONS DU CONSEIL CONSTITUTIONNEL SUR LES ECHEANCES ELECTORATES DE 2012, Conseil Constitutional (July 11, 2013).

New Zealand

Timmons v. Governor-General, Wellington High Court (April 21, 1983). Discussed at 2 **New Zealand Law Review** 298 (1984).

Pakistan (@ www.supremecourt.gov.pk.)

Arshad Mehmood v. Commmissioner/Delimination Authority of the State of Gujranwala, 2014 PLD Lahore 221 (Pak) (2014).
Khan v. Election Commission of Pakistan, 2012 PLD 120, Supreme Court of Pakistan. (2012) (Election Contest), available
Sheikh Attiq-ur-Rehman v. Syed Ali Murtaza, 2014 YLR 1215 (2014).

Lithuania (www.lrkt.lt/en)

THE CONSTITUTIONAL COURT OF THE REPUBLIC OF LITHUANIA, ON THE COMPLIANCE OF ARTICLE 9, PARAGRAPH 1 OF THE REPUBLIC OF LITHUANIA LAW ON THE ELECTION OF THE REPUBLIC OF LITHUANIA (CONVENTION OF 6 NOVEMBER 2012) TO THE CONSTITUTION OF THE REPUBLIC OF LITHUANIA, No. KT27-N16 (October 20, 2015).

Hungary (@https://hunconcourt.hu)

Constitutional Court of Hungary, Opinion #22/2005 (January 17, 2005).
Constitutional Court of Hungary, Opinion #193/2010 (December 8, 2010).

Maps

Maps of electoral districts in Germany, France, Finland, Mexico, Iran, Turkey, Lesotho, Bulgaria, Sweden, Indonesia, and the Maori districts in New Zealand are reprinted with the permission of Dr. Adam Carr @ http://psephos.adam-carr.net. I am particularly grateful to Dr. Carr. His wonderful website is a tribute to hard-work and ingenuity.

A map of the provinces of the Islamic Republic of Iran is reprinted with permission from the library of the University of Texas.

Maps of Texas congressional districts are reprinted with permission of the Texas Legislative Council and are available @ www.tlc.state.tx.us.

Maps of Illinois congressional districts are reprinted with permission of the Illinois Board of Elections.

Maps of the North Carolina congressional districts are reprinted with permission of the North Carolina Board of Elections.

Maps of the 2017 U.S. congressional districts, the congressional districts in North Carolina at issue in Shaw v Reno, and the 1991 congressional districts in Houston are reprinted with permission of Bickerstaff, Heath, Delgado, Acosta LLP.

A map of Lesotho showing it wholly within South Africa is from Wikipedia.

Major Websites

These websites are the best sources for current information on elections in specific nations worldwide. In general, the organization behind each website serves a different purpose although their organizational purposes overlap. Some give online information on only a few nations. Others give information on more countries, but the information is brief and sometimes misleading. I recommend that if you are interested in elections in a particular nation that you check and compare the information available on several websites, including the nation's election commission or agency website.

www.osce.org/odihr/elections.—Organization for Security and Co-operation for Europe / Office for Democratic Institutions and Human Rights (OSCE/ ODIHR); The OSCE observes elections in 57 (mostly European) nations when invited by the country conducting the election. This website has reports on these elections, which cover issues such as voter registration, campaign finance, voting fraud, election systems, specific elections, etc.

www.aceproject.org.—The Electoral Knowledge Network, Administration And Cost of Elections [ACE] Project—ACE claims to be the largest source of election data online. It is a valuable source on the types of election systems, election laws, boundary delimitation, etc. The Network is also supported by 10 Regional Electoral Resource Centers worldwide. Note especially Lisa Handley, Delimitation Equity

Project: Resource Guide, IFES Center for Transitional and Post-Conflict Governance and USAID, (2006);

www.idea.int.—International Institute for Democracy and Electoral Assistance (IDEA)—IDEA is dedicated to advancing political democracy by assisting governments. The website provides access to reports, handbooks, guides, policy papers, etc. on issues affecting Democracy, including elections.

www.electionpassport.com.—This website was a surprise. It provides election information on 110 countries by region of the world. It is especially useful for small countries and regions of the world that may be overlooked by other websites.

http://psephos.adam-carr.net.—This website contains both election results and, in some instances, colorful depictions of those results on country-wide maps.

www.un.org/undpa/en/elections.—U.N. Electoral Assistance Division (EAD) under the Department of Political Affairs.

www.ifes.org.—International Foundation for Electoral Systems (IFES). IFES provides election assistance in areas such as election management, laws, and political finance to nations worldwide. The website contains short explanations on events in different countries.

www.electionguide.org.—Democracy Assistance and Election News, (IDEA). This website provides basic general data on national elections in 240 nations, territories, and dependent areas, including the country's election system, election turnout and results.

www.loc.gov—U.S. Library of Congress. The website provides basic election system data on all countries.

www.ohchr.org—U.N. High Commissioner for Human Rights. The office assesses the compliance of U.N. members with the International Covenant on Civil and Political Rights (CCPR). This website provides periodic human rights assessments and information for each of the member countries of the U.N.

www.cia.gov—The U.S. Central Intelligence Agency (CIA), World Factbook—The website provides basic election system data on all countries.

www.state.gov—The U.S. Department of State—The website provides basic information on the election system in all countries.

www.cartercenter.org.—The Carter Center—The website provides information primarily on international Election Obligations and Standards. It also has assessment reports on elections in some countries, especially in underdeveloped countries and new democracies.

www.globalelectionsdatabase.com.—This website presents election result data at the national and constituency levels, including the number of registered voters, turnout, etc. for about 36 nations and maps.

www.electionresources.org.—This website provides election information, histories, and results for over 50 countries. The election results are generally current, but some of the election histories have not been updated.

www.freedomhouse.org.—The Freedom House has existed for over 65 years. It is funded by grants from the U.S. government. Its interests go beyond elections, but the website includes some basic election information and short articles on over 150 nations.

welections.wordpress.com—This blog covers only a few countries, but provides generally well-written summaries of election matters in those countries, especially France. Since 2015, this blog has been largely dormant with intermittent posts on elections of particular interest. It is still worth checking.

www.ipu.org—The inter-parliamentary union (ipu) is an organization of parliaments worldwide. This website is particularly useful for short essays and some reports on current issues such as women in government and refugee problems worldwide.

www.polgeonow.com—Political Geography Now—This website includes maps and articles on the latest news pertaining to geopolitical changes to the world's countries, borders, and capitals, as well as territorial control in conflict zones and disputed territories.

www.eisa.org.za—The Electoral Institute for Sustainable Democracy in Africa (EISA)—This website provides election information and reports for most of the countries in Africa. EISA also publishes the biannual Journal of African Elections, with abstracts of the journal's articles available on the website.

http://eed.nsd.uib.no—Norwegian Centre for Research Data (NSD). The website provides access to the European Election Database, which covers election results in all European nations.

www.journalofdemocracy.org.—This is the website for the Journal of Democracy. It has essays available online.

www.utexas.edu/laeda—Latin American Electoral Data (LAED). This website provides access to election results in most nations in Latin America.

http://www.africanews.com—African News—This website provides data on African nations and on their elections.

www.countriesquest.com.—This website has a list of articles about different countries organized by continent. Only a few of the articles concern elections.

https://asiafoundation.org.—The Asian Foundation—This website provides short articles on current issues, including elections, arising among countries in Asia.

https://sadc.int—Southern African Development Community (SADC)—SADC is a Regional Economic Organization consisting of fifteen (15) Member States. These are Angola, Botswana, Democratic Republic of Congo, Lesotho, Madagascar, Malawi, Mauritius, Mozambique, Namibia, Seychelles, South Africa, Swaziland, Tanzania, Zambia and Zimbabwe.

https://anfrel.org.—The Asian Network for Free Elections (ANFREL)—ANFREL is a regional network in Asia working on the promotion of democratic elections. This website chronicles some of the organization's election observations.

www.as-coa.org.—Americas Society Council of the Americas—The website provides short articles on current issues, including elections, arising in Latin America, including South America, Central America, and the Caribbean.

www.merip.org.—Middle East Research and Information Project—This website provides access to articles and op-eds on Middle East politics, culture and society, including elections.

https://tulospalvelu.vaalit.fi/E-2015/en/lasktila.html—Finland Ministry of Justice—This website *provides* information on Finnish Elections and data on eligible voters, turnout, etc. in Finnish elections.

www.opendemocracy.net—Open Democracy—This website provides reporting through brief articles and analysis of social and political issues, including elections, from around the world.

http://iacis.ru/eng—Parliamentary Assembly of the Commonwealth of Independent States—The CIS was formed after the breakup of the Soviet Union. Its members include: Armenia, Azerbaijan, Belarus, Estonia (Withdrew), Georgia (Withdrew), Kazakhstan, Kyrgyzstan, Latvia (Withdrew), Lithuania (Withdrew), Moldova, Russia, Tajikistan, Turkmenistan (Withdrew), Ukraine (Withdrew), and Uzbekistan. The overarching mission is law-making and alignment of national laws among members. It also monitors elections among its member countries through the International Institute for Monitoring Democratic and Parliamentary Process and Suffrage in the CIS (IPA CIS IIMDP).

Articles

These are a few of the specific articles that I found useful. The first articles are arranged alphabetically by country or region. The more general articles are listed last.

Albania

REPUBLIC OF ALBANIA, PARLIAMENTARY ELECTIONS 2013, Final Report, **OSCE/ODHIR** (2013).

Australia

Redistribution in Australia: The Importance of One Vote, One Value by Red Medew at page 97 in **Redistricting in Comparative Perspective** by Lisa Handley & Bernard Grofman, eds., Oxford Univ. Press (2008).

Austria

REPUBLIC OF AUSTRIA, EARLY PARLIAMENTARY ELECTIONS 2017, Final Report, **OSCE/ODHIR** (October 15, 1917).

Canada

Understanding Electoral Reform: Electoral Reform and Direct Democracy in Canada: When Citizens Become Involved by Lawrence LeDuc, 34 **West European Politics** 551-567 (Issue 3, 2011), published online (April 11, 2011).

From Gerrymanders to Independence: District Boundary Readjustments in Canada by John C. Courtney in **Redistricting in Comparative Perspective** by Lisa Handley & Bernard Grofman, eds., Oxford Univ. Press (2008).

The Electoral Boundary Revolution in Canada by R. K. Carty, 15 **American Review of Canadian Studies** 273 (Issue 3, 1985), published online: November 10, 2009.

To End Gerrymandering: The Canadian Model for Reforming the Congressional Redistricting Process in the United States by Anthony J. Gaughan, 41 **Capital University Law Review** 999 (2013).

Political Scientists and Electoral Reforms in Europe and Canada: What They Know, What They Do by Camille Bedock, Damien Bol, and Thomas Ehrhard, 16 **ELECTION LAW JOURNAL** 335 (2017).

Central and Eastern Europe

Districting and Redistricting in Eastern and Central Europe: Regulations and Practices by Marina Popescu and Gabor Toka at page 251 in **Redistricting in Comparative Perspective** by Lisa Handley & Bernard Grofman, eds., Oxford Univ. Press (2008).

REPUBLIC OF CROATIA, PARLIAMENTARY ELECTIONS of 8 November 2015, Assessment, Final Report, **OSCE/ODHIR** (February 19,216).

New Borders and Anomalies in the Balkans: Croatia's Diaspora Constituency by Tihana Bartulac-Blanc, **National Endowment for Democracy** (2007) available at www.ned.org.

HDZ wins election in six constituencies, **EBL News** (Croatia) (September 12, 2016).

CZECH REPUBLIC PARLIAMENTARY ELECTIONS 20-21 October 2017

*PRESIDENTIAL ELECTION January 2018, Mission Report, **OSCE/ODHIR*** (June 5-7, 2017).

Access to Electoral Rights, Czech Republic by Pavel Kandalec, **EUDO Citizenship Observatory** (June 2013).

East Asia

East Asia and the Receding Tide of the Third Wave of Democracy by Larry Diamond (Keynote Speech), **International Conference on Democracy in East Asia and Taiwan,** Global Perspective (2011) available at ldiamond@SStanford.edu.

The daunting state of Southeast Asian democracy by Huong Le Thu, **Australian Strategic Policy Institute** (May 8, 2018).

South-East Asia: lots of elections, not so much democracy by Banyan, **Economist** (May 26 2018).

Southeast Asia Struggles With Democracy, **Voice of America** (2009).

Democracy in Southeast Asia: Achievements, Challenges and Prospects, Electoral Integrity, a **Kofi Annan Foundation Initiative** (Kuala Lumpur, Malaysia September 2-3, 2017).

Constitutional Courts in New Democracies: Understanding Variation in East Asia by Tom Ginsburg, 2 **Global Jurist Advances** Issue 1 (2002).

Estonia

ESTONIA PARLIAMENTARY ELECTIONS March 3 2019, Needs Assessment Mission Report, **OSCE/ODHIR** (November 20, 2018).

Fiji

A New Electoral System for Fiji in 2014: Options for Legitimate Representation by Norm Miller, **Pacific Islands Brief** (No. 3, 2013, Pacific Islands Development Program).

Top 10 things you need to know about Fiji's new electoral system by Thomas Carnegie, **Pacific Scoop** (August 31, 2014).

France

REPUBLIC OF FRANCE, PARLIAMENTARY ELECTIONS 10 and 17 June 2012, Final Report, **OSCE/ODIHR** (September 12, 2012).

REPUBLIC OF FRANCE, PESIDENTIAL AND PARLIAMENTARY ELECTIONS NEEDS ASSESSMENT 2017, **OSCE/ODHIR** (2017).

Elections by Bernard Maligner, **Observatory of [French] Constitutional Jurisprudence** (N ° 30 - JANUARY 2011).

Redistricting in France under Changing Electoral Rules by Michel Balinski at page 173 in **Redistricting in Comparative Perspective** by Lisa Handley & Bernard Grofman, eds., Oxford Univ. Press (2008).

Partisan bias and redistricting in France by Nicolas Sauger and Bernard Grofman, 44 **Electoral Studies 388** (December 2016).

Germany

FEDERAL REPUBLIC OF GERMANY ELECTIONS TO THE FEDERAL PARLIAMENT (BUNDESTAG), Election Assessment Mission Report, **OSCE/ODIHR** (September 2009).

FEDERAL PARLIAMENT (BUNDESTAG), FEDERAL REPUBLIC OF GERMANY ELECTIONS TO THE Final Report**, OSCE/0DIHR** (September 22, 2013).

FEDERAL REPUBLIC OF GERMANY ELECTIONS TO THE FEDERAL PARLIAMENT (BUNDESTAG), Final Report, **OSCE/ODIR** (November 27, 2017).

Annex, Case Study, Germany, Delimiting Districts in a Mixed Member Proportional System, at *Conclusion,* **ACE** available at https://aceproject.org/ace-en/topics/bd/annex/bdy/bdy_de.

The German Election System Explained on **Der Spiegel Online** (2013) at https://www.spiegel.de/international/germany/german-election-system-explained.

The Electoral System of Germany, **The Library of Congress**.

Immigration and Socio-Spatial Segregation—Opportunities and Risks of Ethnic Self-Organization by Rauf Ceylan 46 **German Journal of Urban Studies** no. 2 (2007).

Hungary

JOINT OPINION ON THE ACT ON THE ELECTIONS OF MEMBERS OF PARLIAMENT OF HUNGARY, **COMMISSION FOR DEMOCRACY THROUGH LAW (VENICE COMMISSION) AND OSCE OFFICE FOR DEMOCRATIC INSTITUTIONS AND HUMAN RIGHTS (OSCE/ODIHR)** (June, 2012).

HUNGARY, PARLIAMENTARY ELECTIONS, Limited Election Observation Mission, Final Report, **OSCE/ODIHR** (8 April 2018).

Iceland

ICELAND PARLIAMENTARY ELECTIONS 27 April 2013, Final Report, **OSCE/ODIHR** (June 24, 2013).

ICELAND, EARLY PARLIAMENTARY ELECTIONS 28 October 2017, **OSCE/ODIHR** (March 2018).

India

The Paradox of Political Representation (in India) by Yogendra Yadav (2008) available @ www.india-seminar.com.

Delimitation in India by Alistair McMillan at page 75 in **Redistricting in Comparative Perspective** by Lisa Handley & Bernard Grofman, eds., Oxford Univ. Press (2008).

Changing Patterns of Democracy and Representation in India by Jugdep S. Chima, 52 **Asian Survey** 239-246 (No. 2, March/April 2012) available @ www.jstor.org.

Lok Sabha Election 2019: Delimitation ensures roughly equal number of voters in each constituency; all you need to know in by ,

India FP Research Apr 08, 2019 16:18:22 IST

Iran

Duality by Design by Yasmin Alem (2011), (**IFES**), available at [https://www.ifes.org/publications/duality-design-iranian-electoral-system].

Ireland

Electoral Redistricting in Ireland by John Coakley at page 155 in **Redistricting in Comparative Perspective** by Lisa Handley & Bernard Grofman, eds., Oxford Univ. Press (2008).

Italy

THE ITALIAN REPUBLIC PARLIAMENTARY ELECTIONS 4 March 2018, Final Report, **OSCE/ODIHR** (June, 2018).

The Italian Constitutional Court judgement on the 'Italicum' electoral law: another new reform for Italy? by Roberta Damiani, **The Constitution Unit [UCL]** (July 2018).

Tricks and Treats: The 2005 Italian Electoral Law and Its Consequences by Gianfranco Pasquino, 12 **South European Society and Politics** 79-93 (2009).

Japan

The Politics of Redistricting in Japan: A Contradiction between Equal Population and Respect for Local Government Boundaries by Tashimasha Moriwaki at page 107 in **Redistricting in Comparative Perspective** by Lisa Handley & Bernard Grofman, eds., Oxford Univ. Press (2008).

High court rules vote weight gap in Japan's 2017 general election was unconstitutional, **Japan Times** (February 8, 2018).

Editorial: Supreme Court ruling on vote value disparity a call to greater efforts, **The Mainichi** (Japan's National Daily Since 1922) (September, 2017).

South Korea

NEC allows campaigning without new electoral map, **Korea Joongang News** (Dec 31, 2015) available at http://koreajoongangdaily.joins.com.

Kyrgyzistan

KYRGYZ REPUBLIC, Election Observation Mission Report, and Final Election Report, **OSCE/ODIHR** (2015).

Latvia

REPUBLIC OF LATVIA, PARLIAMENTARY ELECTIONS 6 OCTOBER 2018, Final Report, **OSCE/ODHIR** (January 2019).

Lesotho

Lesotho Election of 2017, **Commonwealth Observer Group** (2017).

Lebanon

A complex new election law, sectarianism, Palestinian refugees, and the 'selfie prime minister': Your guide to Lebanon's first general election in 9 years, **The Associated Press** (May 06, 2018).

The Lebanese Electoral System, Briefing Paper, **IFES** (2009);

The Lebanese Elections and Their Consequences by Rayan El-Amine, **Middle East Research and Information Project** (June 14, 2018).

Is Lebanon's New Electoral System a Path Out of Sectarianism? by Elias Muhanna, **The New Yorker** (June 29, 2017).

Lesotho

Pre-Election Assessment Report for Kingdom of Lesotho, **EISA** (2017).

Lithuania

REPUBLIC OF LITHUANIA, PARLIAMENTARY ELECTIONS 2016, Final Report, **OSCE/ODIHR** (October 9, 2016).

REPUBLIC OF LITHUANIA, PARLIAMENTARY ELECTIONS 2012, Mission Report, **OSCE/ODHIR** (October 14, 2012).

Macedonia

THE FORMER YUGOSLAV REPUBLIC OF MACEDONIA, EARLY PARLIAMENTARY ELECTIONS, Final Report, **OSCE/ODIHR** (February 28, 2017).

Monaco

PRINCIPALITY OF MONACO ELECTIONS OF THE NATIONAL COUNCIL 11 February 2018, Needs Assessment Report, **OSCE/ODIHR** (February 2, 2018).

Moldova

Republic of Moldova—Parliamentary Elections, 30 November 2014, Preliminary Report, **OSCE/ODHIR** (2014).

Mexico

Mexico: Final Report, Observing the 2000 Mexico Elections by Marcela Szymansic, **Carter Center** and **ACE** (2000).

From Politics to Technicalities: Mexican Redistricting in Historical Perspective by Alonso Lujambio and Horacio Vives Segi at page 43 in **Redistricting in Comparative Perspective** by Lisa Handley & Bernard Grofman, eds., Oxford Univ. Press (2008).

Middle East

From Beirut to Baghdad: Elections, Iran and the Future of the Middle East, by Seth J. Frantzman, **The National Interest** (May 4, 2018).

Charting Elections in the Middle East by Mark LeVine, **Middle East Report** (Summer 2018).

Mongolia

MONGOLIA, PARLIAMENTARY ELECTIONS, Election Observation Mission, Final Report, **OSCE/ODIHR** (9 June 2016).

Netherlands

Who can vote and for whom? How the Dutch electoral system works, Dutch Works available at **DutchNews**.nl.

New Zealand

An Independent Commission with Political Input: New Zealand's Electoral Redistribution Practices by Alan McRobie at page 27 in **Redistricting in Comparative Perspective** by Lisa Handley & Bernard Grofman, eds., Oxford Univ. Press (2008).

Norway

NORWAY, PARLIAMENTARY ELECTIONS 14 September 2009, Final Report, **OSCE/ODHIR** (NOVEMBER 2009).

NORWAY, PARLIAMENTARY ELECTIONS 9 September 2013, Election Assessment Mission

Final Report, **OSCE/ODHIR** (December 2013).

NORWAY, PARLIAMENTARY ELECTIONS 11 September 2017, Final Report, **OSCE/ODHIR** (December 2017).

Poland

REPUBLIC OF POLAND, PARLIAMENTARY ELECTIONS 2015, Mission Report, **OSCE/ODHIR** (October 25, 2015).

Russian Federation

Russian Parliamentary Election Report on Duma Elections in 2016, **OSCE/ODIHR** (2016).

Putin and the Russian Electoral System; Reforms to Prevent Regime Change by Darrell Slider and Paul Rodrick Gregory, **Soviet and post-Soviet Review** (2012) and Forbes (March 14, 2016).

The Electoral System of the Russian Federation by Bill BOWRING, DIRECTORATE-GENERAL FOR EXTERNAL POLICIES OF THE UNION OF THE EUROPEAN PARLIAMENT (2011) available at www.europarl.europa.eu.

Legislative Voting Behavior in the Russian Duma: Understanding the Effect of Mandate by Frank C. Thames, Jr., 53 **Europe-Asia Studies** 869-884 (2001).

Slovenia

REPUBLIC OF SLOVENIA, EARLY PARLIAMENTARY ELECTIONS 3 June 2018, Final Report, OSCE/ODHIR (September 12, 2018).

Sweden

SWEDEN, GENERAL ELECTIONS on 9 September 2018, NEEDS ASSESSMENT MISSION REPORT, **ODIHR** (15–17 May 2018).

SWEDEN, GENERAL ELECTIONS on 9 September 2018, Final Report, **ODIHR** (November, 2018).

Turkey

REPUBLIC OF TURKEY. PARLIAMENTARY ELECTIONS, Assessment Report, **OSCE/ODHIR** (November 3, 2002).

REPUBLIC OF TURKEY, EARLY PRESIDENTIAL AND PARLIAMENTARY ELECTIONS 2018, Final Report, **OSCE/ODHIR** (June 2018).

United Kingdom

UNITED KINGDOM OF GREAT BRITAIN AND NORTHERN IRELAND, GENERAL ELECTION, Final Report, **OSCE/ODHIR** (May 7, 2005).

UNITED KINGDOM OF GREAT BRITAIN AND NORTHERN IRELAND, GENERAL ELECTION, Final Report, **OSCE/ODIR** (May 6, 2010).

UNITED KINGDOM OF GREAT BRITAIN AND NORTHERN IRELAND, GENERAL ELECTION, Final Report, **OSCE/ODHIR** (May 7, 2015).

Guide to the 2018 Review of Parliamentary Constituencies, **Boundary Commission of Northern Ireland** (August 2016).

New registration system sees more accurate registers; but further action still needed to encourage electoral registration, **The Electoral Commission of the United Kingdom** (July 14, 2016).

When Is a Gerrymander Not a Gerrymander: Who Benefits and Who Loses from the Changed Rules for Defining Parliamentary Constituencies? by Ron Johnston, David Rossiter, and Charles Pattie, January 2017 **The Political Quarterly** 88 (2017).

Parliamentary Constituency Boundary Reviews and Electoral Bias: How Important Are Variations in Constituency Size? By Galina Borisyuk, Ron Johnston, Colin Rallings, and Michael Thrasher, January 2010 **Parliamentary Affairs** 63 (2010).

National Parliaments: United Kingdom, **Library of Congress** (accessed July, 2018).

Electoral statistics, UK: 2017, **Office for National Statistics** (2017).

Electoral Distortion Despite Redistricting by Independent Commissions: The British Case, 1950-2005 by Ron Johnson, Charles Pattie, and David Rossiter at page 205 in **Redistricting in Comparative Perspective** by Lisa Handley & Bernard Grofman, eds., Oxford Univ. Press (2008).

Uruguay

Uruguay: The Electoral Process, **Library of Congress** (accessed on July 29, 2018).

Uruguay Elections, **Election Passport** (accessed in July 2018).

General—Arranged basically by their usefulness

Seat bias formulas in proportional representation systems by Friedrich Pukelsheim, Karsten Schuster, Mathias Drton, and Norman R. Draper, 22 **Electoral Studies** (2003), also presented at the 4th ECPR General Conference (2007).

Reserved Seats in National Legislatures: A Comparative Approach by Andrew Reynolds at page 115 in **Redistricting in Comparative Perspective** by Lisa Handley & Bernard Grofman, eds., Oxford Univ. Press (2008).

A Comparative Survey of Structures and Criteria for Boundary Delimitation by Lisa Handley at page 265 in **Redistricting in Comparative Perspective** by Lisa Handley & Bernard Grofman, eds., Oxford Univ. Press (2008).

The Role of Courts in the Electoral Boundary Delimitation Process by Lisa Handley in INTERNATIONAL ELECTION REMEDIES (Jack Young, ed., American Bar Association (2017).

Degrees of proportionality of proportional representation formulas by Arend Lijphart in **Electoral Laws and Their Political Consequences,** Agathon series on representation, **Algora' Publishing** (2003).

Seeking to End Gerrymandering's Enduring Legacy by Carl Hulse at page A17, **New York Times** (January 26, 2016).

Considering the Prospects for Establishing a Packing Gerrymander Standard by Robin Boyd, Shawn Donahue, Daniel Magleby, and Michael McDonald, **Election Law Journal** (2016), published online at https://doi.org (September 26, 2017).

Values and Validations: Proper Criteria for Comparing Standards for Packing Gerrymanders by Robin E. Best, Shawn J. Donahue, Jonathan Krasno, Daniel B. Magleby, and Michael D. McDonald, **Election Law Journal** (2017), published online (March 1, 2018) @ https://doi.org/10.1089/elj.2017.0471.

Toward a Talismanic Redistricting Tool: A Computational Method for Identifying Extreme Redistricting Plans by Wendy K. Tam Cho and Yan Y. Liu, **Election Law Journal** (2016), published online (Dec 1, 2016) @ https://doi.org/10.1089/elj.2016.0384

Gerrymandering from the Bench? The Electoral Consequences of Judicial Redistricting by James B. Cottrill and Terri J. Peretti, **Election Law Journal** (2012), published online (Sep 3, 2013) @ https://doi.org.

Delimiting Electoral Boundaries in Post-Conflict Settings by Lisa Handley at page 191 in **Redistricting in Comparative Perspective** by Lisa Handley & Bernard Grofman, eds., Oxford Univ. Press (2008).

Comparative survey of multiwinner election methods by Warren D. Smith (June 18 2006) published online @ https://pdfs.semanticscholar.org.

Seat biases of apportionment methods for proportional representation by Karsten Schuster, Friedrich Pukelsheim, Mathias Drton, and Norman Draper, 4 **Electoral Studies** 22 (2003).

Political Participation of Refugees, ***Institute for Democracy Electoral Assistance*** **(IDEA)** (April 19, 2018).

Making Local Redistricting Less Political: Independent Redistricting Commissions for U.S. Cities by Steve Bickerstaff, 13 **Election Law Journal** 419 (2014).

How Proportional Representation Elections Work, **FairVote** online @ www.FairVote.com.

Electoral systems with a Majority Bonus as Unconventional mixed Systems by Camille Bedock and Nicolas Sauger, **Project: Electoral systems and their consequences** (2014) online @ www.researchgate.net.

Delimitation Consulting in the US and Elsewhere by Lisa Handley, 1 **Zeitschrift für Politikberatung** 400–411 (2008).

Overseas Territories, Dependent Areas, and Disputed Territories, **One World Online** @ www.nationsonline.org and www.worldonline (The Nations Online Project).

Electoral Systems and Political Parties by Jack Bielasiak online @ http://apcentral.collegeboard.com.

How Many Countries Are There in the World in 2018? **Political Geography Now** (January 11, 2018).

Does Bicameralism Matter? by Michael Cutrone and Nolan McCarty (Princeton Univ. 2006) later printed by Oxford University as part of The **Oxford Handbook of Political Economy** (2008).

The ReDistricting Game, **USC Annenberg Center** (2017) online @ www.redistrictinggame.org.

Reapportionment by State Legislatures: A Guide for the 1980s by Steve Bickerstaff, 34 **Southwestern Law Journal** 607 (1980).

Statement of Gay J. McDougall, United Nations Independent Expert on Minority Issues, **Hearing of the U.S. Helsinki Commissio**n available @ www.csce.gov/sites/helsinkicommission. Reports of the U. N. Independent Expert on minority issues based on her observations are available for many different countries.

Index

S. Bickerstaff, *Election Systems and Gerrymandering Worldwide*, Studies in Choice and Welfare, https://doi.org/10.1007/978-3-030-30837-7

R

S

T

The manufacturer's authorised representative in the EU is Springer Nature Customer Service Centre GmbH, Europaplatz 3, 69115 Heidelberg, Germany. If you have any concerns regarding our products, please contact ProductSafety@springernature.com

Printed and bound by CPI Group (UK) Ltd, Croydon, CR0 4YY
30/09/2026
02225648-0006